MENTOR'S GUIDE

Practicing Christian Leadership

Effective Worship Leading:

WORSHIP, WORD, and SACRAMENT

Effective Christian Education:

INCORPORATING, PARENTING, and DISCIPLING

Effective Church Discipline:

EXHORTING, REBUKING, and RESTORING

Effective Counseling:

PREPARING, CARING, and HEALING

This curriculum is the result of thousands of hours of work by The Urban Ministry Institute (TUMI) and should not be reproduced without their express permission. TUMI supports all who wish to use these materials for the advance of God's Kingdom, and affordable licensing to reproduce them is available. Please confirm with your instructor that this book is properly licensed. For more information on TUMI and our licensing program, visit *www.tumi.org* and *www.tumi.org/license*.

Capstone Module 11: Practicing Christian Leadership Mentor's Guide

ISBN: 978-1-62932-031-1

© 2005, 2011, 2013, 2015. The Urban Ministry Institute. All Rights Reserved.
First edition 2005, Second edition 2011, Third edition 2013, Fourth edition 2015.

Copying, redistribution and/or sale of these materials, or any unauthorized transmission, except as may be expressly permitted by the 1976 Copyright Act or in writing from the publisher is prohibited. Requests for permission should be addressed in writing to: The Urban Ministry Institute, 3701 E. 13th Street, Wichita, KS 67208.

The Urban Ministry Institute is a ministry of World Impact, Inc.

All Scripture quotations, unless otherwise noted, are from The Holy Bible, English Standard Version, copyright © 2001 by Crossway Bible, a division of Good News Publishers. Used by permission. All Rights Reserved.

Contents

Course Overview
3   About the Instructor
5   Introduction to the Module
7   Course Requirements

13   **Lesson 1**
Effective Worship Leading: Worship, Word, and Sacrament

47   **Lesson 2**
Effective Christian Education: Incorporating, Parenting, and Discipling

81   **Lesson 3**
Effective Church Discipline: Exhorting, Rebuking, and Restoring

121   **Lesson 4**
Effective Counseling: Preparing, Caring, and Healing

161   Appendices

241   **Mentoring the Capstone Curriculum**

249   Lesson 1 Mentor's Notes

257   Lesson 2 Mentor's Notes

265   Lesson 3 Mentor's Notes

273   Lesson 4 Mentor's Notes

About the Instructor

Rev. Dr. Don L. Davis is the Executive Director of The Urban Ministry Institute and a Senior Vice President of World Impact. He attended Wheaton College and Wheaton Graduate School, and graduated summa cum laude in both his B.A. (1988) and M.A. (1989) degrees, in Biblical Studies and Systematic Theology, respectively. He earned his Ph.D. in Religion (Theology and Ethics) from the University of Iowa School of Religion.

As the Institute's Executive Director and World Impact's Senior Vice President, he oversees the training of urban missionaries, church planters, and city pastors, and facilitates training opportunities for urban Christian workers in evangelism, church growth, and pioneer missions. He also leads the Institute's extensive distance learning programs and facilitates leadership development efforts for organizations and denominations like Prison Fellowship, the Evangelical Free Church of America, and the Church of God in Christ.

A recipient of numerous teaching and academic awards, Dr. Davis has served as professor and faculty at a number of fine academic institutions, having lectured and taught courses in religion, theology, philosophy, and biblical studies at schools such as Wheaton College, St. Ambrose University, the Houston Graduate School of Theology, the University of Iowa School of Religion, the Robert E. Webber Institute of Worship Studies. He has authored a number of books, curricula, and study materials to equip urban leaders, including *The Capstone Curriculum*, TUMI's premiere sixteen-module distance education seminary instruction, *Sacred Roots: A Primer on Retrieving the Great Tradition*, which focuses on how urban churches can be renewed through a rediscovery of the historic orthodox faith, and *Black and Human: Rediscovering King as a Resource for Black Theology and Ethics*. Dr. Davis has participated in academic lectureships such as the Staley Lecture series, renewal conferences like the Promise Keepers rallies, and theological consortiums like the University of Virginia Lived Theology Project Series. He received the Distinguished Alumni Fellow Award from the University of Iowa College of Liberal Arts and Sciences in 2009. Dr. Davis is also a member of the Society of Biblical Literature, and the American Academy of Religion.

Introduction to the Module

Greetings, dearest friends, in the strong name of Jesus Christ!

Welcome to Module 11 in our Capstone Curriculum series, entitled *Practicing Christian Leadership*. We demonstrate our devotion to our Savior by practicing a kind of leadership that both honors and glorifies our Lord and edifies and builds up his people. We will explore these important concepts and practices throughout this important study.

The first lesson, **Effective Worship Leading** considers the idea of representation of the Lord Jesus as fundamental in practicing every dimension of Christian leadership as his agents and servants. Closely connected to this important idea, we will also consider carefully the role of ministering the Word and Sacrament among the people of God. Throughout this lesson we will see how we as Christian leaders may lead God's people to experience his grace and direction through an effective ministry of the Word of God and a faithful practice of the sacraments of the Church.

In our second lesson, **Effective Christian Education**, we will explore the idea of bringing new believers into our churches, dealing specifically with how we welcome and integrate new believers into our community life together. We will also explore the concept of parenting new Christians and discipling them in the Church. We will look carefully together at the meaning of spiritual parenthood, seeking to biblically define and practically outline how we can enable new and growing believers in the Lord to mature in Christ.

Next, lesson three deals with an important aspect of Christian leadership, **Effective Church Discipline**. The practice of Christian leadership involves our thorough knowledge of the principles of biblical exhortation, and here we will explore reasons why this ministry is so necessary for Christian leaders among God's people. In this lesson we will also address the question of the practice of church discipline. We will look at both the biblical definitions and practical guidelines of godly rebuke and restoration in the context of God's community.

Finally, in lesson four we will focus on **Effective Counseling: Preparing, Caring, and Healing**. Here we will define effective biblical counseling, starting with a general explanation of it and its implications for us as urban Christian leaders. Our goal will be to understand both the therapeutic and pastoral implications of counseling and leading God's people. Together we will discover how we can become better care givers for those encountering the dark side of life, trials, tribulations, and distress. As God's servants and under-shepherds of his people, we will discover how we may come to bear the burdens of those who are experiencing trouble or stress, and do all we can in order to edify the flock of God, even as he gives us opportunity.

What an adventure it is to serve the living God by caring for his dear people! My prayer for you is that you become that Christian leader God desires you to be, all for his glory!

- Rev. Dr. Don L. Davis

Course Requirements

Required Books and Materials

- Bible (for the purposes of this course, your Bible should be a translation [ex. NIV, NASB, RSV, KJV, NKJV, etc.], and not a paraphrase [ex. The Living Bible, The Message]).

- Each Capstone module has assigned textbooks which are read and discussed throughout the course. We encourage you to read, reflect upon, and respond to these with your professors, mentors, and fellow learners. Because of the fluid availability of the texts (e.g., books going out of print), we maintain our *official* Capstone Required Textbook list on our website. Please visit *www.tumi.org/books* to obtain the current listing of this module's texts.

- Paper and pen for taking notes and completing in-class assignments.

Suggested Readings

- Sanders, J. Oswald. *Spiritual Leadership*. Chicago: Moody Press, 1994.

- Dodd, Brian J. *Empowered Church Leadership*. Downers Grove: InterVarsity Press, 2003.

- Bennett, David W. *Metaphors of Ministry*. Eugene: Wipf and Stock Publishers, 2004.

- Hyde, Douglas. *Dedication and Leadership*. Notre Dame: University of Notre Dame Press, 2001.

Course Requirements

Summary of Grade Categories and Weights

Attendance & Class Participation	30%	90 pts
Quizzes	10%	30 pts
Memory Verses	15%	45 pts
Exegetical Project	15%	45 pts
Ministry Project.	10%	30 pts
Readings and Homework Assignments.	10%	30 pts
Final Exam	<u>10%</u>	<u>30 pts</u>
Total:	100%	300 pts

Grade Requirements

Attendance and Class Participation

Attendance at each class session is a course requirement. Absences will affect your grade. If an absence cannot be avoided, please let the Mentor know in advance. If you miss a class it is your responsibility to find out the assignments you missed, and to talk with the Mentor about turning in late work. Much of the learning associated with this course takes place through discussion. Therefore, your active involvement will be sought and expected in every class session.

Quizzes

Every class will begin with a short quiz over the basic ideas from the last lesson. The best way to prepare for the quiz is to review the Student Workbook material and class notes taken during the last lesson.

Memory Verses

The memorized Word is a central priority for your life and ministry as a believer and leader in the Church of Jesus Christ. There are relatively few verses, but they are significant in their content. Each class session you will be expected to recite (orally or in writing) the assigned verses to your Mentor.

Exegetical Project

The Scriptures are God's potent instrument to equip the man or woman of God for every work of ministry he calls them to (2 Tim. 3.16-17). In order to complete the requirements for this course you must select a passage and do an inductive Bible study (i.e., an exegetical study) upon it. The study will have to be five pages in length (double-spaced, typed or neatly hand written) and deal with one of the four aspects of the nature of practical Christian leadership highlighted in this course. Our desire and hope is that you will be deeply convinced of Scripture's ability to change and practically affect your life, and the lives of those to whom you minister. As you go through the course, be open to finding an extended passage (roughly 4-9 verses) on a subject you would like to study more intensely. The details of the project are covered on pages 10-11, and will be discussed in the introductory session of this course.

Ministry Project

Our expectation is that all students will apply their learning practically in their lives and in their ministry responsibilities. The student will be responsible for developing a ministry project that combines principles learned with practical ministry. The details of this project are covered on page 12, and will be discussed in the introductory session of the course.

Class and Homework Assignments

Classwork and homework of various types may be given during class by your Mentor or be written in your Student Workbook. If you have any question about what is required by these or when they are due, please ask your Mentor.

Readings

It is important that the student read the assigned readings from the text and from the Scriptures in order to be prepared for class discussion. Please turn in the "Reading Completion Sheet" from your Student Workbook on a weekly basis. There will be an option to receive extra credit for extended readings.

Take-Home Final Exam

At the end of the course, your Mentor will give you a final exam (closed book) to be completed at home. You will be asked a question that helps you reflect on what you have learned in the course and how it affects the way you think about or practice ministry. Your Mentor will give you due dates and other information when the Final Exam is handed out.

Grading

The following grades will be given in this class at the end of the session, and placed on each student's record:

A - Superior work	D - Passing work
B - Excellent work	F - Unsatisfactory work
C - Satisfactory work	I - Incomplete

Letter grades with appropriate pluses and minuses will be given for each final grade, and grade points for your grade will be factored into your overall grade point average. Unexcused late work or failure to turn in assignments will affect your grade, so please plan ahead, and communicate conflicts with your instructor.

Exegetical Project

As a part of your participation in the Capstone *Practicing Christian Leadership* module of study, you will be required to do an exegesis (inductive study) on one of the following passages on the practice of Christian leadership in the Church and community:

- ❐ Matthew 20.20-28
- ❐ John 13.1-17
- ❐ 1 Peter 5.1-4
- ❐ Acts 20.24-28
- ❐ Philippians 2.5-11

The purpose of this exegetical project is to give you an opportunity to do a detailed study of a major passage on the practice of Christian leadership. Using the text as a base and lens, think critically about the ways in which this text makes plain your duty, privilege, and responsibility to lead others according to the structure of Christ's own leadership. As you study one of the above texts (or a text which you and your Mentor agree upon which may not be on the list), our hope is that your analysis of your selected text will make more clear to you the shape and texture of the practice of Christian leadership in the Church. We also desire that the Spirit will give you insight as to how you can relate its meaning directly to your own personal walk of discipleship, as well as to the leadership role God has given to you currently in your church and ministry.

Purpose

This is a Bible study project, and, in order to do *exegesis*, you must be committed to understand the meaning of the passage in its own setting. Once you know what it meant, you can then draw out principles that apply to all of us, and then relate those principles to life. A simple three step process can guide you in your personal study of the Bible passage:

1. What was *God saying to the people in the text's original situation*?

2. What principle(s) does *the text teach that is true for all people everywhere*, including today?

3. What is *the Holy Spirit asking me to do with this principle here, today*, in my life and ministry?

Once you have answered these questions in your personal study, you are then ready to write out your insights for your *paper assignment*.

Here is a *sample outline* for your paper:

1. List out what you believe is *the main theme or idea* of the text you selected.

Outline and Composition

2. *Summarize the meaning* of the passage (you may do this in two or three paragraphs, or, if you prefer, by writing a short verse-by-verse commentary on the passage).

3. *Outline one to three key principles or insights* this text provides on the practice of Christian leadership.

4. Tell how one, some, or all of the principles may relate to *one or more* of the following:

   a. Your personal spirituality and walk with Christ

   b. Your life and ministry in your local church

   c. Situations or challenges in your community and general society

As an aid or guide, please feel free to read the course texts and/or commentaries, and integrate insights from them into your work. Make sure that you give credit to whom credit is due if you borrow or build upon someone else's insights. Use in-the-text references, footnotes, or endnotes. Any way you choose to cite your references will be acceptable, as long as you 1) use only one way consistently throughout your paper, and 2) indicate where you are using someone else's ideas, and are giving them credit for it. (For more information, see *Documenting Your Work: A Guide to Help You Give Credit Where Credit Is Due* in the Appendix.)

Make certain that your exegetical project, when turned in meets the following standards:

- It is legibly written or typed.
- It is a study of one of the passages above.
- It is turned in on time (not late).
- It is 5 pages in length.
- It follows the outline given above, clearly laid out for the reader to follow.
- It shows how the passage relates to life and ministry today.

Do not let these instructions intimidate you; this is a Bible study project! All you need to show in this paper is that you *studied* the passage, *summarized* its meaning, *drew out* a few key principles from it, and *related* them to your own life and ministry.

Grading

The exegetical project is worth 45 points, and represents 15% of your overall grade, so make certain that you make your project an excellent and informative study of the Word.

Ministry Project

Purpose

The Word of God is living and active, and penetrates to the very heart of our lives and innermost thoughts (Heb. 4.12). James the Apostle emphasizes the need to be doers of the Word of God, not hearers only, deceiving ourselves. We are exhorted to apply the Word, to obey it. Neglecting this discipline, he suggests, is analogous to a person viewing our natural face in a mirror and then forgetting who we are, and are meant to be. In every case, the doer of the Word of God will be blessed in what he or she does (James 1.22-25).

Our sincere desire is that you will apply your learning practically, correlating your learning with real experiences and needs in your personal life, and in your ministry in and through your church. Therefore, a key part of completing this module will be for you to design a ministry project to help you share some of the insights you have learned from this course with others.

Planning and Summary

There are many ways that you can fulfill this requirement of your study. You may choose to conduct a brief study of your insights with an individual, or a Sunday School class, youth or adult group or Bible study, or even at some ministry opportunity. What you must do is discuss some of the insights you have learned from class with your audience. (Of course, you may choose to share insights from your Exegetical Project in this module with them.)

Feel free to be flexible in your project. Make it creative and open-ended. At the beginning of the course, you should decide on a context in which you will share your insights, and share that with your instructor. Plan ahead and avoid the last minute rush in selecting and carrying out your project.

After you have carried out your plan, write and turn in to your Mentor a one-page summary or evaluation of your time of sharing. A sample outline of your Ministry Project summary is as follows:

1. Your name
2. The place where you shared, and the audience with whom you shared
3. A brief summary of how your time went, how you felt, and how they responded
4. What you learned from the time

Grading

The Ministry Project is worth 30 points and represents 10% of your overall grade, so make certain to share your insights with confidence and make your summary clear.

LESSON 1

page 249

Effective Worship Leading
Worship, Word, and Sacrament

Lesson Objectives

page 250

Welcome in the strong name of Jesus Christ! After your reading, study, discussion, and application of the materials in this lesson, you will be able to:

- Recite the different ways in which leadership is a form of representation, i.e., representing the Lord, his person, his people, and his purposes in the community.

- Give reasons why in leadership we do not represent our own purposes or interests in our lives and ministries, but the Lord's purposes and interests in all we say and do.

- Outline the importance of the role of worship in bringing glory and honor to God in the midst of his people.

- Detail the importance of liturgy by worshiping God in the spirit, in truth, in order, and in faith.

- List the key reasons behind the role of the Word and Sacrament in practical Christian leadership.

- Give the key principles involved in nourishing the people of God on a full and steady diet of the Word of God and helping them experience genuine body life through a joyous celebration of Baptism and the Lord's Supper.

Devotion

page 253

Learn How to Represent

Read Luke 10.1-16. In order to lead in a Christian way, you must never interpret it in an overly personalized way. To lead is to represent another. This seems odd, but, after first glance, it becomes perfectly clear how this works. If you desire to lead others as a sergeant, you must be willing to follow the orders of the captain. If you reject the captain, you cannot order around privates, if you are a sergeant. The foreman on the factory floor must obey the department head, or he loses the right to lead those under him. The key to leadership is always submission. If you find a person who struggles with or is unwilling to submit to others, they forfeit the right to lead others.

Christian leadership is representation. As our Lord Jesus Christ represented the Father in all that he said and did while on the earth, so we, following his example, represent him in all that we do. Christian leadership is about the authority of Jesus, and the one who is unwilling to follow Jesus loses all right to serve and care for the members of his body in their own leadership. What is interesting about this, is that it works also for *those who respond to* the leader. In other words, if you are truly representing the Lord Jesus, then the one who rejects your word is rejecting him, and according to Christ's own testimony, also rejecting the Father who sent our Lord. The entire vision of Christian leadership is anchored therefore on a simple but profound idea: leadership is representation. No Christian leader can function on the basis of their own authority, power, and position. It is not gifting or resources or education or brilliance that makes a Christian leader legitimate. It is the call of God. If God has called a man or woman to represent him, then they must act as God's ambassador, God's representative, God's diplomat. We speak his words, represent his interests, share his burdens, carry out his commands. The emerging Christian leader who learns this lesson will not only carry out their ministry with dignity and excellence, but they will also open themselves up to be used by the Lord to transform others. In order to be God's leader, learn how to represent.

After reciting and/or singing the Nicene Creed (located in the Appendix), pray the following prayer:

Nicene Creed and Prayer

You sent your Son Jesus Christ, who came not to be served but to serve, and to give his life a ransom for many. We praise you that he calls his faithful servants to lead your holy people in love; to proclaim your Word and to celebrate the sacraments of the new covenant.

~ Presbyterian Church (USA) and Cumberland Presbyterian Church. **Book of Common Worship**. Louisville: Westminister/John Knox Press, 1993. p. 137

No quiz this lesson

Quiz

No Scripture memorization this lesson

Scripture Memorization Review

No assignments due this lesson

Assignments Due

"I Don't Need Your Permission."

During a rather heated discussion among the leaders of a local inner city church, the pastor claimed that he did not need the permission of his deacon board to go forward with his plan to expand the sanctuary. After all, they had called him to be the pastor, the by-laws said that he had the authority to establish and expand ministry in the church, and there were enough resources in the treasury to actually go forward with the building. While some of the deacons wanted further discussion of the wisdom of such a move, the pastor closed down debate. He announced that he believed the Lord wanted the church to proceed forward, and finished with the statement, "I really don't need your permission on this. I am the pastor, and God has called me to lead." What do you think about the style of the pastor's leadership?

"It Just Don't Seem Right."

In an effort to become more "contemporary" in their worship style with the youth service, the youth pastor has begun his new "Hip Hop Hallelujah" service. It is a worship service, but done completely in sync with the hip-hop culture which dominates the minds and hearts of the kids in the neighborhood. Although the service continues to expand and grow, attracting more of the lost kids around the community, some of the leaders are concerned with the flavor of the service. To them, it looks no different than an MTV program; the kids dress the same, they use all kinds of electronic instruments and turn-tables, and essentially is nothing more than worldliness with a little Jesus thrown in. As one of the deacons said about it, "Looking at what our youth pastor is doing, I just feel uneasy. It just don't seem right." What would you say to the deacon if he asked you about the hip-hop hallelujah service–is it right, is it wrong, does it matter what they're doing? How so?

Only the Believing

(This is based on a true story) Recently, in a growing church, the pastor noticed that when he only made the Lord's Supper available to those who believed, that many unbelievers felt judged and isolated during their communion service. After consulting with his other leaders, the pastor decided to open up communion to whoever was present for the service. Remarkably, this opened up the service greatly and, brought much added enthusiasm to the service. The pastor actually testified that there have been some unbelievers who have actually come to faith in Jesus

Christ as a result of participating in the Lord's Supper event! Some are troubled at this trend, believing that Communion should be reserved only for those who have repented and put their trust in Jesus for the salvation of their souls. While all believe that communion is an important service, they genuinely disagree about the pastor's "new direction." How would you counsel the pastor and the church to understand the Lord's Supper in the midst of the people of God?

Effective Worship Leading: Worship, Word, and Sacrament

Segment 1: Representing the People of God in Giving God His Due

Rev. Dr. Don L. Davis

In order to effectively lead the people of God in worship, we must be certain that we represent the Lord in our leadership, i.e., we have been appointed to act on his behalf as his agent before his people for his purposes.

Our objective for this segment, *Effective Worship Leading: Representing the People of God in Giving God His Due*, is to enable you to see that:

- The biblical understanding of representation is the fundamental concept in practical Christian leadership

- The Christian leader is called to represent the Lord and his purposes to his people and within the community

- As those who belong to the Lord, our leadership can never be about ourselves, but rather we must speak and act for God as we strive to represent his purposes and interests in all we say and do.

- The critical role where this representation shows itself is how we lead the people of God into the presence of God, for his glory through Jesus Christ

- Practical Christian leadership begins with the worship of God in Christ, leading the people of God in liturgy by worshiping God in the spirit, in truth, in order, and in faith.

Summary of Segment 1

Video Segment 1 Outline

2 Cor. 5.18-20
All this is from God, who through Christ reconciled us to himself and gave us the ministry of reconciliation; [19] that is, in Christ God was reconciling the world to himself, not counting their trespasses against them, and entrusting to us the message of reconciliation. [20] Therefore, we are ambassadors for Christ, God making his appeal through us. We implore you on behalf of Christ, be reconciled to God.

I. **The Christian Leader as God's Called *Representative* (i.e., His *Ambassador*)**

A. Definition: *a practicing Christian leader is one called by God to represent his purposes and interests in the midst of the people of God.*

1. Called by God: *the Christian leader is a person who has sensed from the Lord a particular call from God.*

   a. The leader has been placed in their position by *God's own choice*, John 15.16.

   b. A leader may be called *directly or through appointment*, but they still represent God in their leadership.

   (1) Direct call from God

   (a) John 20.21

   (b) 2 Tim. 1.11

   (c) Acts 26.17-18

   (2) Appointment through God's representatives

   (a) 1 Tim. 5.22

   (b) Titus 1.5

   (c) 2 Tim. 2.2

   (d) 1 Tim. 1.18

c. This calling is *irrevocable*. (God will not cancel a calling; his calling may be fulfilled or ignored, but he never takes it back.)

   (1) Rom. 11.29

   (2) 1 Tim. 1.11-12

   (3) Rom. 1.5

d. This calling is accompanied by *God's giftings and enablements*.

   (1) 2 Cor. 3.6

   (2) Eph. 3.7

   (3) Col. 1.25

2. To represent his purposes and interests: *this calling is focused on God's intentions and purposes, and not those of the leader.*

   a. The leader is an ambassador. He speaks and acts on behalf of another.

      (1) Eph. 6.20

      (2) 1 Cor. 9.16-17

   b The leader has *no authority to go beyond his or her mandate* from the Lord to build up his people.

      (1) 2 Cor. 13.10

      (2) 2 Cor. 10.8

   c. Promotion and demotion comes from the Lord alone: *God sets up one and puts down another.*

      (1) Ps. 75.6-7

      (2) John 15.16

3. In the midst of the people of God: *the leader exercises authority and provides service to those who belong to God in the midst of Christian community.*

   a. There is no such thing as a leader who exists for themselves, Rom. 15.15-16.

   b. Jesus Christ is the prime example of a leader for others, Phil. 2.5-11.

   c. All of the efforts of the practicing Christian leader are to edify the people of God, to enable them to be what God intends for them to be, and to do what God intends for them to do.

B. Three dimensions of representing God as one called to lead his people

   1. The Leader *is first and foremost a Representative of Jesus Christ.*

      a. Jesus Christ is Lord and Head over all things to the Church, Eph. 1.20-23.

      b. He has selected men and women to represent his interests and will in the Church, John 15.16.

   2. The Leader is also *a Representative of the Christian Community.*

      a. They serve as undershepherds under God's authority.
         (1) 1 Cor. 12.28
         (2) 1 Cor. 12.7
         (3) 1 Pet. 5.1-4

b. They possess no authority to destroy or tear down, only to edify the saints, 2 Cor. 13.10.

c. We as leaders are to see God's people fulfill God's desire that they might represent him with honor in the world as his people and his witnesses, Eph. 2.10.

3. The Leader is finally a *Representative of the Christian faith*.

a. They are to contend for the faith, Jude 1.3.

b. They are to equip others to share their faith, Eph. 4.11-12.

II. Giving God His Due: Leading God's People into Worship

A. Definition: the practicing Christian Leader is one who ushers the people of God into the presence of God by giving God his due in acceptable worship.

1. Ushers the people of God into the presence of God: *the leader, as a worshiper of God, is charged with ushering God's people into his very presence.*

a. Rom. 15.15-19

b. Paul's aim is to so minister among the Gentiles that they might bring glory to God through his ministry, Rom. 1.5.

---

*Bob Webber in his book **Worship is a Verb** highlights eight indispensable principles of participating in worship. They are:*
1) worship celebrates Christ
2) worship tells and acts out the Christ-event
3) in worship, God speaks and acts
4) worship is an act of communication
5) in worship we respond to God and each other
6) return worship to the people
7) all creation joins in worship
8) worship is a way of life

2. By giving God his due: *the goal of all worship, whatever the form, is to offer God the praise and glory due his name.*

   a. We are called to preach the unsearchable riches of Christ to those who do not know him, Eph. 3.7-8.

   b. This worship is linked directly to obedience, not merely our outward acts of religious devotion, Acts 26.20.

3. Through worship that is acceptable to him: *we are not to simply encourage outward religious show, but to lead in such a way that those who respond to our ministries may give to God the kind of service and obedience that bring pleasure and honor to him.* To bring about the obedience of faith was Paul's ministry aim, Rom. 16.26.

B. Implications of this high calling

1. No one can lead others unless they are out in front of them.

2. Only God can empower us to fulfill this high calling.

3. We are free to experiment and find as many ways as possible to bring more and more honor to the name of God through Jesus Christ.

III. Four Dimensions of Effective Worship Leading

A. Worship in the Spirit: being led by the Holy Spirit, John 4.22-24

1. We have access to God through faith in Christ by the Spirit.

    a. We are saved by the purpose of the Father, 2 Tim. 1.8-9.

    b. We are made whole through the blood of Christ, Heb. 10.12-14.

    c. These salvation blessings are made real in our lives by the Holy Spirit, John 16.13-14.

2. Worship is not proper form, but must be accompanied by a faith and lifestyle that makes the forms meaningful to him.

    a. Mere outward signs of devotion are not acceptable to God, Isa. 1.13-14.

    b. Worship must be accompanied by justice and righteousness to be acceptable to God, Isa. 1.16-17.

3. Being saved by grace through faith alone, we are now free in Christ to offer worship to God that corresponds to our own cultural identity, Gal. 5.1.

    a. In our own styles of music, hymns, worship, and celebration

    b. In our own styles of learning and presentation

    c. In our own ways of preaching, teaching, and sharing together

B. Worship in Truth: grounded in the true revelation of God, Phil. 3.3

1. Christ is the end of the law for righteousness: we do not worship God on the basis of liturgy and tradition alone, but by the filling and leading of the Holy Spirit, Rom. 10.3-4.

2. All acceptable worship, whatever the form or liturgy, is done in the name and person of Christ Jesus alone; he is our only access to God, John 14.6.

3. We put no confidence "in the flesh," that is, our own ability to please or draw near to God except through Jesus Christ, 1 Pet. 1.23-25.

C. Worship in Order: approaching God in liturgical order

1. God is a God of order and of peace: the Holy Spirit has given gifts to all members of the church to use, but these must be used wisely for the benefit of all.

    a. 1 Cor. 14.12

    b. 1 Cor. 14.26

    c. 1 Cor. 14.33

2. As God used times of remembrance and celebration in the yearly schedule of Israel to remind them of their history, so we can use the Church calendar and liturgical order to rehearse the great stories of our redemption in Christ.

a. Paul referred to Christ as our Passover, 1 Cor. 5.7.

b. Paul referred to the great stories of deliverance in the history of Israel as signs for us, 1 Cor. 10.1ff.

c. The early Church developed liturgy (the Church calendar and the service order) to help members of the Church recall the important moments in our history of redemption.

3. As leaders of God's people, we employ order in worship not to encourage dead tradition, but to train others to lead in worship.

a. We are to be careful not to be faithful to our tradition and ignore the plain statements of the Word of God, Matt. 15.3.

b. Mark 7.13

c. Col. 2.8

4. We employ liturgy because it can help the family of God recall our salvation history (going through the key events and stories year by year for encouragement and instruction).

D. Worship in faith: avoid empty tradition to celebrate God and his provision.

1. Without faith, it is impossible to please God; regardless of the way in which we lead the people of God in worship, we must always beware of the power of tradition to become stale and meaningless.

> *Worship in the Bible is the due response of rational creatures to the self-revelation of their Creator. It is honoring and glorifying of God by gratefully offering back to him all the good gifts, and all the knowledge of his greatness and graciousness, that he has given. It involves praising him for what he is, thanking him for what he has done, desiring him to get himself more glory by further acts of mercy, judgment, and power, and trusting him with our concern for our own and others' future well-being.*
> ~ J. I. Packer. *Concise Theology: A Guide to Historic Christian Beliefs.* (electronic version). Wheaton, IL: Tyndale House, 1995.

    a. Heb. 11.6

    b. Col. 2.23

2. No one can approach God except through the person and work of our Lord Jesus Christ.

    a. Acts 4.12

    b. 1 John 2.23

3. Use and employ worship methods but do not substitute them for our need to approach and relate to God only through his Son.

    a. 2 John 1.9

    b. 1 Pet. 3.18

    c. Titus 2.14

Conclusion

» The fundamental concept of Christian leadership is representation. As representatives of Jesus, his Church, and the Christian faith, we are called by God to lead God's people to bring glory and honor to God.

» Perhaps the most critical way in which we represent God is to lead his people in worship.

» Worship is not mere form, tradition, and going through the motions of weekly service; true worship involves our obedience to the Spirit, according to the truth of God's Word, in proper liturgical order, grounded in a living faith that celebrates God and his work in the world.

» We lead the people into the presence of God in dependence on the Lord Jesus Christ alone to bring us before the Father.

Please take as much time as you have available to answer these and other questions that the video brought out. This segment outlined one of the critical concepts of practical Christian leadership, which is the representing of God in Christ before his people for his purpose and the advance of his Kingdom, to his glory. Be clear and concise in your answers, and where possible, support with Scripture!

1. What does it mean to say that "a practicing Christian leader is one called by God to represent his purposes and interests in the midst of his people?"

2. As ambassadors of God, how do we as practicing Christian leaders "stay in touch" with headquarters to speak and act on his behalf most accurately?

3. In what ways may a Christian leader be called to represent God's interests in the body?

4. What similarities are there between the role of an ambassador to his appointed nation and the Christian leader in relationship to Christ?

5. What are the three dimensions in which a Christian leader is called to represent God? Is there any authority from the Lord to tear others down or destroy? Explain.

Segue 1

Student Questions and Response

page 255 4

6. Why do you think it might be important for the Christian leader to understand his or her role first as one who ushers the people of God into God's presence?

7. What role does the Holy Spirit play in leading others into the presence of God?

8. Why is it significant that all worship of God in Christ be grounded upon the truth of Scripture? What role does Christ himself play in giving God worship that is acceptable to him?

9. Why is order important in leading others into worship? Can form alone guarantee acceptable worship before the Lord? Why or why not?

10. In what ways can we avoid empty tradition as we lead others into the celebration and worship of God? What role does faith play in leading others to relate to God?

Effective Worship Leading: Worship, Word, and Sacrament

Segment 2: Ministering the Word and Sacrament in the People of God

Rev. Dr. Don L. Davis

Summary of Segment 2

As leaders called to represent God's purposes and interests in the midst of the Church, we must work tirelessly to ensure that each member of the family is properly fed and nourished with a full and steady diet of the Word of God and experiencing genuine body life through a joyous celebration of Baptism and the Lord's Supper.

Our objective for this segment, *Effective Worship Leading: Ministering the Word and Sacrament in the People of God*, is to enable you to see that:

- The practicing Christian leader leads the people of God to experience his grace and direction through an effective ministry of the Word of God and a faithful practice of the sacraments of the Church.

- The ongoing practice of the people of God in word and sacrament is critical to their maturity and development in Christ.

- As leaders called to represent God's purposes and interests in the midst of the Church, we must work tirelessly to ensure that each member of the family is properly fed and nourished with a full and steady diet of the Word of God and experiencing genuine body life through a joyous celebration of Baptism and the Lord's Supper.

- The leader in the family of God uses his or her gifts to nourish believers in Scripture, incorporate new believers into the Church through baptism, and celebrate the Lord's death and coming in the meal of the Lord's Supper.

I. Defining the Leader's Role in Word and Sacrament

Video Segment 2 Outline

A. Definition: the practicing Christian Leader is one who leads the people of God into the presence of God through the Word and the Sacrament.

Augustine defined a sacrament as a visible form of an invisible grace.
~ D. N. Freedman. The Anchor Bible Dictionary. Vol. 6. New York: Doubleday, 1996. p. 983.

1. Leads the people of God into the presence of God: *the leader leads God's people into his presence.*

    a. Paul conceived his entire ministry as an offering to enable the Gentiles to glorify God in worship, praise, and obedience.

        (1) Rom. 15.8-13

        (2) Rom. 15.18

    b. God called Paul to represent his purpose and interests for salvation among the Gentiles, to lead them into a lifestyle of discipleship, accompanied by worship and praise and thanksgiving to God.

        (1) 2 Cor. 5.20

        (2) Gal. 2.7-8

        (3) Eph. 3.1

        (4) 1 Tim. 2.7

c. Paul could therefore lead and exhort the Gentile believers in the worship of God through Jesus Christ.

      (1) Eph. 5.18-21

      (2) Col. 3.17

      (3) 1 Thess. 5.18

2. Through the Word and the Sacrament: *the ministry of the Word of God and the obedience to the sacraments help us receive grace from the Lord in order to glorify him in all we say and do.*

   a. Matt. 28.18-20

   b. 2 Tim. 3.16-17

B. Implications of this high calling

1. We as leaders *represent God before his people*; we are called to help God's people know and do God's holy will, 2 Cor. 5.20.

2. *God's Word* enables God's people to receive from him instruction regarding his salvation, direction regarding his will, and strength for the obedience he demands, John 8.31-32.

3. As the family of God, we are to *live as his people*. We are therefore called to welcome new members through the act of baptism and fellowship together through the Lord's Supper celebration, 1 John 3.2.

II. The Ministry of the Word of God

A. What it is not

1. Asserting that your view is more important than the others members of God's people

2. Making agreement with your ideas the standard of Christian discipleship

3. Assuming that whatever the leader suggests must be taken as the gospel truth

B. What it is: *ensuring that the people of God whom I represent and serve are nourished upon the Word of God*

It is your solemn duty and privilege to ensure that the people of God in your assembly are nourished, enlightened, and equipped through a deep and satisfying knowledge of the Word of God!

1. Enable the people of God *to hear the voice of God.*

    a. 1 Cor. 1.17-18

    b. 2 Cor. 4.2

2. Enable the people of God *to remember the Word of God.*

    a. 2 Tim. 2.2

Acts 6.3-4
Therefore, brothers, pick out from among you seven men of good repute, full of the Spirit and of wisdom, whom we will appoint to this duty. [4] But we will devote ourselves to prayer and to the ministry of the word.

When I listen to the reading of Scripture in worship, I try to remember that it is the record of how God has initiated a relationship with me, sought me out, and brought me to himself.
~ Robert Webber. *Worship is a Verb.* Peabody, MA: Hendrickson Publishers, 1995. p. 73.

b. John 15.7

3. Enable the people of God *to understand the Word of God*, Col. 1.24-27.

4. Enable the people of God *to confess the Word of God*.

   a. Recall the Shema: Deut. 6.4-9

   b. Rom. 10.8-10

   c. 2 Cor. 4.13-14

   d. 1 Tim. 3.16

5. Enable the people of God *to obey the Word of God*.

   a. Matt. 7.24-27

   b. James 1.22-25

6. Enable the people of God *to share the Word of God with others*, 1 Pet. 3.15-16.

C. How to ensure a vibrant ministry of the Word of God in your church context

1. Make the Word of God *the central textbook* of Christian faith and discipleship, 2 Tim. 3.16-17.

2. Don't merely give talks about the text of the Bible; actually *study the Scriptures* themselves, John 8.31-32.

3. Encourage members to check and *double check all teaching they hear by the Scriptures* themselves, Acts 17.10-11.

4. Teach informally, in the homes of the believers you lead, and allow for opportunities for people *to share with one another their insights and questions* on the Word of God, Acts 20.18-21.

5. Teach through *the entire Bible*, not just a favorite portion of it, Acts 20.26-27.

6. As leader, *be ready always to share the Word of God, regardless of the situation and give yourself over to the Scriptures* to show through your own life their power and significance.

    a. 2 Tim. 4.1-2

    b. 1 Tim. 4.15-16

*The **sacraments**, also referred to in some Christian circles as **ordinances** (i.e., those practices commanded for the Church by the Lord), are sometimes referred to as **means of grace**. This expression, while not mentioned in Scripture, is widely used to speak of those practices and rites ordained by God where he conveys to believers his blessing and grace to his people.*

III. The Ministry of the Sacraments

Matt. 28.19-20 - Go therefore and make disciples of all nations, baptizing them in the name of the Father and of the Son and of the Holy Spirit, [20] teaching them to observe all that I have commanded you. And behold, I am with you always, to the end of the age.

A. What the ministry of the sacraments is not

1. Keeping the sacraments as an alternative way to salvation, 1 Cor. 1.14-17

2. Acting as if the sacraments must be practiced and celebrated in one and only one fashion

3. Assuming that only special individuals among God's people may participate or officiate in these services, Matt. 18.20

B. What the ministry of the sacraments is

1. An *expression of our obedience to Jesus* as Lord (he commanded us to practice both baptism and to celebrate the Supper), 1 Cor. 11.23-26

2. As a *way to worship God* in their close affiliation with the work of Jesus Christ on the cross, Rom. 6.3-4

3. A *way to identify* both as individuals and as a group *our unconditional allegiance to Jesus Christ* in his death, his resurrection, and his return, John 6.51-56

C. Principles to remember in ministering the sacrament of Baptism

1. Conceive the ordinance/sacrament of Baptism *as a washing and bath*.

    a. Acts 22.12-16

    b. 1 Pet. 3.21

    c. 1 Cor. 6.11

    d. Heb. 10.22

2. Emphasize the ordinance/sacrament of Baptism as *a living expression of faith and allegiance with Jesus Christ.*

    a. Gal. 3.27

    b. Acts 8.12-13

    c. Acts 10.46-48

3. Employ the ordinance/sacrament of Baptism as *a sign of incorporation* (affiliation with the people of God).

    a. 1 Cor. 12.13

b. Acts 10.46-48

c. Acts 18.8

D. Principles to remember in ministering the ordinance/sacrament of the Lord's Supper

1. Conceive the Lord's Supper as a *Family meal*, Acts 2.46-47.

2. Teach the Lord's Supper as time of community thanksgiving and remembrance, 1 Cor. 11.23-25.

3. Experience the Lord's Supper as *expression of our hope to see Messiah Jesus soon*.

    a. Matt. 26.26-29

    b. 1 Cor. 11.26

E. How to ensure a vibrant ministry of Baptism and the Lord's Supper in your church context

1. Teach the meaning of these practices clearly (provide ongoing biblical instruction and good theological justification for their observance).

2. Respect your tradition's conception of the sacraments, and understand the freedom associated with these acts of identity and celebration.

3. Reflect on the history and meaning of Baptism and the Eucharist in the history of the Church.

4. Make these events central and regular in all your gatherings together as the Family of God.

5. Allow members of the people of God to participate in the sharing of these celebration events, but to do so reverently and soberly, 1 Cor. 11.27-29.

6. Place celebration, reverence, and joy at the very heart of these observances.

Conclusion

» The Christian leader, in representing the Lord, nurtures the body of Christ on the Word of God, and through the sacraments of Baptism and the Lord's Supper.

» As God's representatives, we are called to ensure that the members of the body of Christ are properly fed and nourished with a full and steady diet of the Word of God, as well as celebrate with full understanding the ordinance of Baptism and the Lord's Supper.

The following questions were designed to help you review the material in the second video segment. As a representative of the Lord, the Christian leader is called to feed the Church with the Word of God, and to lead the body in celebration of the sacraments of Baptism and the Lord's Supper. Be clear and concise in your answers, and where possible, support with Scripture!

Segue 2

Student Questions and Response

1. Why is the presence of God such a critical concept for the Christian leader? What is the connection between the call of the Christian leader and the

responsibility to lead people in their worship, praise, and thanksgiving to God?

2. In what ways does God provide the believers in the Church with his grace through an effective ministry of the Word and the sacraments? What are the implications of this for the people of God and the Christian leader?

3. Explain the significance of the following statement: "It is your solemn duty and privilege to ensure that the people of God in your assembly are nourished, enlightened, and equipped through a deep and satisfying knowledge of the Word of God."

4. List four ways in which you as a practicing Christian leader might help those under your teaching to grow in their knowledge of and nourishment upon the Word?

5. Describe the reasons why the practice of the sacraments are significant for the growth and maturity of the body of Christ.

6. What principles should we keep in mind as we seek to understand the role of Baptism in the Church? What principles should inform us as we minister the Lord's Supper?

7. List four ways in which you as a practicing Christian leader might help those under your teaching to grow as they celebrate together the Lord's Supper? Which of these ways is most important for you in your ministry today?

CONNECTION

Summary of Key Concepts

page 255 □ 5

This lesson focuses upon the role of the practicing Christian leader as a representative of the Lord, one who is called to speak and act on behalf of the purposes and interests of the Lord. We demonstrate this representation first and foremost in our ushering people into the presence of God through our leading them in worship, through the nourishment of the Word of God in the lives of believers in the body, and through our ongoing celebration of the sacraments in our services of worship in the Church.

- The biblical understanding of representation is the fundamental concept in practical Christian leadership: the leader does not represent himself or herself but the authority and purpose of the Lord.

- The Christian leader has sensed his or her particular call from the Lord to represent his purposes to his people within the community.

- As those who belong to the Lord, our leadership can never be about ourselves, but rather we must speak and act for God as we strive to represent his purposes and interests in all we say and do.

- The critical role where this representation shows itself is how we lead the people of God into the presence of God, for his glory through Jesus Christ.

- The four dimensions of effective worship leading for the practicing Christian leader is to lead God's people to worship him in the Spirit, to worship him in truth, to worship him with order and peace, and to worship him in faith through Jesus Christ.

- As leaders called to represent God's purposes and interests in the midst of the Church, we must work tirelessly to ensure that each member of the family is properly fed and nourished with a full and steady diet of the Word of God.

- Christian leadership also seeks to help the members of the body experience genuine body life through a joyous celebration of Baptism and the Lord's Supper.

Now is the time for you to discuss with your fellow students your questions about the insights you have gleaned in this lesson regarding our representation of the Lord, and our leading the body into the presence and purpose of God through worship, Word, and sacrament. What particular questions do you have in light of the material you have just studied? Maybe some of the questions below might help you form your own, more specific and critical questions.

Student Application and Implications

page 255 6

* How do we know in fact that we have sensed a call from God to represent him? What role do other Christian leaders and the congregation play in confirming the authenticity of my call to ministry, to represent God in the church?

* Can you lead others into God's presence if you are not dwelling there yourself? Explain your answer.

* Why is it impossible to be a leader for the Lord and be isolated from the life, worship, and ministry of the local body?

* What kinds of attitudes and habits must be cultivated in order to be an effective worship leader in the way described in this lesson? Which of these do you express best, least?

* Why is commitment to the faithful Word of God so critical in all phases of representing God in the midst of the Church?

* What about those traditions which recognize other significant events and practices as sacraments, more than simply Baptism and the Lord's Supper? What role does tradition play in acknowledging these other practices as sacramental?

* Of all the aspects of effective worship leading, which ones do you believe are critical for the emerging Christian leader to master first?

* How do we ensure that members of the body continue to grow in the Word and sacrament even as they are faithful in attendance to our services of worship? How can we instill a sense of celebration and refreshment in our teaching and worship leading that continues to encourage them in their faith?

CASE STUDIES

"The Lord Told Me to Come."

A young person with real personality and apparent spiritual gifts begins to attend your church for a few weeks, but, as time has gone on, you have become concerned about his understanding of God's leading. He has more and more asserted himself as the Lord's prophet in the church, and will state authoritatively to others on some point of conduct or doctrine, "This is what I believe God is saying to you about this." You as pastor have heard more and more concern from members about some of the things this young fellow is saying, but you believe the Lord is upon him. The young fellow's constant word about himself in the church is "The Lord told me to come." How would you lead this young person to maturity in the body, i.e., to help him understand the principle of leadership as representation.

"You're Doing it all Wrong."

With the entrance of new ways of worship; singing, Scripture and responsive reading, and prayer into your services, some of your older members are concerned about the break with their traditional ways of worship. A growing divide is occurring between those who prefer more contemporary styles of worship and those who embrace more traditional forms and liturgies of service. One dear mother in the church, frustrated with the kinds of things going on in service, shared with the pastor recently, "This new kind of worship is not right. You're doing it all wrong. We need to return to how we always did it." How would you counsel the pastor in his leading the church in these new/old style dialogues about services of worship?

"I'm Not Being Fed."

While using the lectionary (i.e., those ordered yearly lists of texts shared by many denominations and assemblies guiding worship), you notice that many in the body are expressing dissatisfaction both in the subject matter and the presentation of the sermons. While many have commented that they are growing much through your teaching, a small but vocal group is expressing deep concern over your teaching. One dear member bluntly said the other week, "I am spiritually hungry. Your sermons and teaching aren't helping me grow. I'm not being fed!" If confronted with these concerns, how would you respond.

"I Don't Believe I Need to Do That."

While teaching the importance of our shared devotional life and ongoing practice of the sacraments together, one member disagreed openly. She believes that only her personal faith in Jesus Christ is necessary for her to mature in Christ. Salvation is through him, and growth is in him. She flatly disagrees with the idea that she must attend weekly services or participate in sacramental observances to grow. She has her faith, her Bible, and her love for Christ, and she is convinced that she needs nothing else. How would you go about seeking to persuade her that she cannot grow without her shared worship in the body, her nourishment of the Word in community, and her participation in the sacraments of the Church? What would you do if she remained firm and unconvinced?

The biblical understanding of representation is the fundamental concept in practical Christian leadership: the leader does not represent him or herself but the authority and purpose of the Lord. As those who belong to the Lord, our leadership can never be about ourselves, but rather we must speak and act for God as we strive to represent his purposes and interests in all we say and do. The four dimensions of

Restatement of the Lesson's Thesis

effective worship leading for the practicing Christian leader is to lead God's people to worship him in the Spirit, to worship him in truth, to worship him with order and peace, and to worship him in faith through Jesus Christ. As we lead God's people into his presence, we must work tirelessly to ensure that each member of the family is properly fed and nourished with a full and steady diet of the Word of God.

Resources and Bibliographies

If you are interested in pursuing some of the ideas of *Effective Worship Leading: Worship, Word, and Sacrament*, you might want to give these books a try:

> Boschman, LaMar. *Future Worship*. Ventura, CA: Gospel Light Publications, 1999.
>
> Webber, Robert E. *Worship is a Verb*. Peabody, MA: Hendrickson Publishers, 1992.
>
> ------. *Blended Worship*. Peabody, MA: Hendrickson Publishers, 1998.
>
> Wiersbe, Warren W. *Real Worship*. Grand Rapids: Baker Books, 2000.

Ministry Connections

Now is the time to try to nail down this high theology to a real practical ministry connection, one which you will think about and pray for throughout this next week. In all that has been covered in this lesson on the nature of practical Christian leadership, what application or idea specifically connects with your experience in your life and ministry today? What in particular is the Holy Spirit suggesting to you regarding your own worship, your own nourishment in the Word of God, and your own celebration of the sacraments in the midst of the body? Are you growing in your sense of God's call on your life, and do you flesh out that call in the context of the local church, under the leadership of godly pastoral authority? What particular situation comes to mind when you think about how you might need to change or adapt something in your life so you could better represent the Lord in your worship, your ministry of the Word, and your practice and celebration of the sacraments?

Counseling and Prayer

Receiving prayer for the areas that the Spirit brings to mind is one of the key means of receiving the needed grace we must have to glorify God in our role as Christian leaders. Do not hesitate to share with your mentor and fellow students your need for prayer, and be careful to offer faithful intercession for them as you lift them up before the Lord. Prayer is not merely a little pause at the beginning and end of a session, it is the life blood of receiving Christ's ongoing aid in times of need. Remember the good advice of Hebrews:

Heb. 4.14-16 - Since then we have a great high priest who has passed through the heavens, Jesus, the Son of God, let us hold fast our confession. [15] For we do not have a high priest who is unable to sympathize with our weaknesses, but one who in every respect has been tempted as we are, yet without sin. [16] Let us then with confidence draw near to the throne of grace, that we may receive mercy and find grace to help in time of need.

ASSIGNMENTS

John 4.21-24

Scripture Memory

To prepare for class, please visit *www.tumi.org/books* to find next week's reading assignment, or ask your mentor.

Reading Assignment

Please be prepared in your next class session to take a quiz on the materials and key concepts covered on the video and outline of this lesson. You will be quizzed on the key principles and ideas covered in the video content of this lesson next week. Make sure that you spend time covering your notes, especially focusing on the main ideas of the lesson. In addition, please read your assignment from the textbooks, and summarize your reading with no more than a paragraph or two for each. Your summary should provide your best understanding of the main point in each of the readings. Do not be overly concerned about giving detail; simply comment briefly on what you consider to be the main point discussed in that section of the book. Please bring these summaries to class next week. (Please see the *Reading Completion Sheet* at the end of this lesson.)

Other Assignments

page 256 7

Looking Forward to the Next Lesson

In lesson one, we considered together the importance of the concept of leadership as representation. As representatives of Jesus, his Church, and the Christian faith, we are called by God to lead God's people to honor him in worship, in the Word of God, and in the celebration of the sacraments. In our next lesson we will look at the idea of welcoming and integrating new believers into the Church, together with the meaning of spiritual parenthood, and explore what is involved in bringing new-born Christians to full maturity in Christ.

Capstone Curriculum

Module 11: Practicing Christian Leadership
Reading Completion Sheet

Name _____

Date _____

For each assigned reading, write a brief summary (one or two paragraphs) of the author's main point. (For additional readings, use the back of this sheet.)

Reading 1

Title and Author: _____ Pages _____

Reading 2

Title and Author: _____ Pages _____

LESSON 2

Effective Christian Education
Incorporating, Parenting, and Discipling

Lesson Objectives

Welcome in the strong name of Jesus Christ! After your reading, study, discussion, and application of the materials in this lesson, you will be able to:

- Identify the critical steps in welcoming and integrating new believers into the Church.

- Define the meaning of incorporation from a biblical point of view, and recite some of its key implications as it relates to practicing Christian leadership.

- Articulate the key elements of incorporation, including bringing new believers into the body of believers, accepting new believers on the basis of their repentance and faith, grounding new believers in the truth of Jesus, guiding them into body life, and finally the importance of introducing them to pastoral care.

- Outline the concept of spiritual parenthood, biblically defining what precisely is the definition of parenting new and growing believers in the Lord.

- Explain the nature of spiritual parenthood in the framework of the Apostle Paul in the New Testament.

- Lay out carefully the elements of spiritual parenthood and relate how these elements relate to the spirituality and growth of new and immature urban disciples of Christ.

Devotion

"Act Your Age!" No Longer a Kid in the Faith

Read Ephesians 4.7-16. Perhaps nothing in all the world is sweeter than seeing a little new born grow from infant, to child, to teenager, to adult. The growth we experience from a toddler to an adult is an amazing and challenging process. Each stage is filled with its own wonder, struggles, and reward, and all of us undergo these phases in our own unique way. It is not unusual, therefore, for the Apostle Paul to use this growth process as one of the central metaphors to explain the nature of the Christian life. The walk of a Christian is likened to a little baby that is born, that continues to grow through the loving care of its parents, that undergoes discipline from wise oversight, and that emerges after such nurture and care into a full grown adult, ready and willing to have her own family.

While it is fully understandable to enjoy the first phases of the life of a person, it would be very sad indeed if a child were stunted in a phase of perpetual childhood. Can you imagine it–staying an infant for 15 years, nursing on your mother's bosom for 20 years, or being untrained to use the toilet independently at 45 years old? What is understandable and acceptable at 2 months is not acceptable at 2 years and would be considered scandalous at 12 years. Most of us have heard from our parents that proverbial adage "Act your age!" when we were caught acting younger than we truly were. The idea is that growth matters; we shouldn't act like a baby when we are a child, and shouldn't act like a teenager when we are an adult. Truly, a healthy person will not remain in the infancy and childhood stages of growth; the developing person will mature, outgrow certain modes and grow into others.

Paul in this text challenges the Ephesians to be no longer children, tossed around by every kind of odd idea and notion, being gullible to any puff of exaggerated teaching or outlandish lie. The goal of the Christian life is maturity, after the measure of the stature of our Lord Jesus himself. God's intent is to fashion us all individually to the maturity of Christ, and this occurs through the proper functioning of the body of Christ. We cannot become mature alone; we grow as every joint and ligament supplies in the body what it must for the upbuilding of the entire body through the love shown, one for the other.

God's call on your life in Christ is always to grow, to mature, to become fully adult, becoming more and more like his Son. Frankly, being a spiritual baby is acceptable and understandable for the first few months, but it is absolutely not appropriate to stay there. God's will is for you to grow "so that we may no longer be children, tossed to and fro by the waves and carried about by every wind of doctrine, by human cunning, by craftiness in deceitful schemes. Rather, speaking the truth in love, we are to grow up in every way into him who is the head, into Christ" (Eph. 4.14-15). "Act your age!" Amen!

After reciting and/or singing the Nicene Creed (located in the Appendix), pray the following prayer:

Nicene Creed and Prayer

Almighty God, by our baptism into the death and resurrection of your son Jesus Christ, you turn us from the old life of sin. Grant that we, being reborn to new life in him, may live in righteousness and holiness all our days; through Jesus Christ our Lord, who lives and reigns with you and the Holy Spirit, one God, now and for ever. Amen.

~ Episcopal Church. **The Book of Common Prayer and Administrations of the Sacraments and Other Rites and Ceremonies of the Church, Together with the Psalter or Psalms of David.** New York: The Church Hymnal Corporation, 1979. p. 254.

Quiz

Put away your notes, gather up your thoughts and reflections, and take the quiz for Lesson 1, *Effective Worship Leading: Worship, Word, and Sacrament*.

Scripture Memorization Review

Review with a partner, write out and/or recite the text for last class session's assigned memory verse: John 4.21-24.

page 259 3

Assignments Due

Turn in your summary of the reading assignment for last week, that is, your brief response and explanation of the main points that the authors were seeking to make in the assigned reading (Reading Completion Sheet).

Hard to Get In

With no advance warning, one of the new members of your church comes to you and says that they will no longer remain in your church. Surprised, you ask why, and they answer. "I have not felt welcomed at all since I came here. You and a few others are warm enough, but I have never been in a church that was harder to get in. The people, it's like they really don't want anybody else to come into their church. I tried, too. I went to the Bible studies, the fellowship times, even helped out in some of the outreach activities. But here it is, after two years, I still don't have a single friend in this church. I give up. I don't think that God wants me here." What would you say to such a new Christian who recently decided to leave your fellowship?

"Only God Is My Father."

In a Bible study group discussion on the nature of spiritual parenthood in the New Testament, one member of the group confesses his uneasiness with all the talk of parenthood. "I know it is in the Bible and therefore is a valid idea, but I think we should be careful talking about spiritual parenthood. I thought that only God was my Father? Didn't Jesus warn us about people taking on this kind of authority over our lives?" With these comments, a heated discussion broke out on whether or not this idea, this metaphor is really valid for us today. While some thought it had great value in describing the Christian life, others felt it was only relevant to the Apostles and their apprentices (i.e., people like Timothy, Titus, and others). What would you have said in the study about the validity of spiritual parenthood, and its meaning for us today?

Discipleship Gone Out of Control

As associate pastor of a growing church, you hear of one of your cell groups that the leader is becoming overly aggressive with the members of his little flock. A Christian who loves the Lord and his people, you know this leader to be a fine person and solid leader in the church, but his oversight of the members of his group has gotten out of control. He is dictating what they read in the Bible, demanding that they check with him before they do certain things, and even has been denying communion to those he suspects of not walking with the Lord. A few of the members of the church have threatened to leave unless the situation in the group changes. How would you handle this situation, both for the sake of the leader as well as for the sake of those in his cell group who are becoming increasingly nervous about his level of control?

Effective Christian Education: Incorporating, Parenting, and Discipling

Segment 1: Incorporating New Believers into the People of God

Rev. Dr. Don L. Davis

As a practicing Christian leader, we are to incorporate new believers into the fellowship of the body, and provide new and growing believers with the requisite care as spiritual parents to ensure their ongoing maturity in Christ.

Our objective for this segment, *Effective Christian Education: Incorporating New Believers into the People of God*, is to enable you to see that:

- As practicing Christian leaders, we must incorporate new believers into the fellowship of Christ, both welcoming and integrating them into our community life and relationship.

- Incorporation is a critical biblical principle of Christian care, involving creating an environment where new members of the body are welcomed into God's family.

- Our ability to welcome new believers warmly and smoothly into our community life will determine the overall success of our Christian leadership in a church.

- No one need change their cultural identity in order to join into the body of Christ.

- New members are to be accepted based upon their repentance and faith in Jesus Christ, and must be grounded immediately into sound Christian doctrine (*catechesis*).

- Incorporation also involves entrance into the life of the community, along with the assignment of loving pastoral oversight.

Video Segment 1 Outline

I. **Meaning of Incorporating New Converts into the People of God**

　　A. Definition: *the practicing Christian Leader is one who welcomes new members of the people of God by incorporating new believers into the family of God.*

　　　　1. Welcomes new members of the people of God: *the practicing Christian leader helps to create an environment where new members of the community are welcomed into God's family.*

　　　　　　a. Peter's acceptance of the Gentiles went against his sensibilities, but he did it because God received them, Acts 10.44-48.

　　　　　　b. We are called to welcome each other in the Lord, Rom. 15.5-7.

　　　　　　c. We all, regardless of our background, are accepted on the basis of our faith in Jesus Christ, and we therefore must receive each other on the basis of our confession, Gal. 3.13-14.

　　　　2. Incorporating new believers into the family of God: *the Christian leader helps to bring these new members into the family of God as smoothly and warmly as possible.*

　　　　　　a. Paul rebuked Peter for his struggle with Gentile acceptance, Gal. 2.11-16.

b. The early Church found this warm welcome to be a challenge for Gentiles in the family of God, Acts 11.17-18.

c. In Christ, all the exterior barriers have been overcome, and we are to welcome people into the family of God on the basis of their faith alone.

(1) Col. 3.11

(2) Rom. 3.29

(3) 1 Cor. 12.13

(4) Gal. 3.28

B. Implications for Christian leadership

1. No one has to change their cultural identity to enter into the family of God; they may come just as they are, Rom. 10.12.

2. The lesson of the early Church in welcoming Gentiles must apply to us today in our welcoming of people whose cultural backgrounds and tastes are different from ours, Eph. 3.6.

3. The Lord is adding to the body as he sees fit, and our responsibility is to ensure their place, Acts 2.46-47.

4. Our ability to incorporate new believers reveals our maturity in Jesus Christ, and even our identity as believers before God, Gal. 3.28-29.

5. Incorporating those who repent and believe in Jesus, regardless of their background or history, is a litmus test of our understanding of the Gospel and its kingdom implications.

a. John 13.34-35

b. Gal. 5.6

c. Gal. 5.13-14

d. 1 John 4.7-8

II. Elements of Incorporating New Members into the People of God

A. Accept new members on the basis of their repentance and faith in Jesus Christ.

Eph. 2.13-19 - But now in Christ Jesus you who once were far off have been brought near by the blood of Christ. [14] For he himself is our peace, who has made us both one and has broken down in his flesh the dividing wall of hostility [15] by abolishing the law of commandments and ordinances, that he might create in himself one new man in place of the two, so making peace, [16] and might reconcile us both to God in one body through the cross, thereby killing the hostility. [17] And he came and preached peace to you who were far off and peace to hose who were near. [18] For through him we both have access in one Spirit to the Father. [19] So then you are no longer strangers and aliens, but you are fellow citizens with the saints and members of the household of God.

1. Celebrate the coming of new believers into the people of God, regardless of the background from which they came, or the acts they did before they repented and believed.

   a. Gal. 3.26-28

   b. Col. 3.11

2. Introduce new members to other members of the family as soon as possible, Philem. 1.8-16.

3. Include all members as full partners, and show no partiality with new believers, James 2.1-4.

B. Ground new believers into the faith by teaching sound doctrine immediately (*catechesis*).

1. Arrange for their instruction for the purpose of baptism (their public confession of Jesus among his disciples).

   a. Mark 16.15-16

   b. Matt. 28.19

2. Follow up new Christians in small group settings, even together as families.

   a. 2 Tim. 2.1-2

   b. 1 Tim. 6.12

   c. Matt. 10.32-33

   d. John 13.34-35

3. Teach them the nature of salvation by grace through faith in Christ Jesus.

   a. Assurance of salvation, 1 John 5.10-13

   b. Repentance from dead works to serve God, Heb. 9.13-14

   c. Adoption of a godly kingdom lifestyle

      (1) 1 John 2.1-3

      (2) 1 John 3.2-5

4. Provide an overview of the Christian worldview immediately, Rom. 12.1-2.

   a. Help them understand the story of the Kingdom of God, and Jesus as the NT fulfillment of the OT promise, Luke 24.44-48.

   b. Explain the warfare motif of our faith: Jesus came to destroy the devil and all effects resulting from the curse, 1 John 4.4.

   c. Teach the Nicene Creed as a summary of the historic Christian faith.

5. Explain the role of the Word, the Sacraments, the Disciplines, and the Holy Spirit in the Church.

C. Guide new believers into the basics of Christian community.

1. Instruct the new believers in the Church's role in Christian discipleship (the importance of the unity of the faith), Phil. 2.1-2.

   a. As the Family of God: the home where those who belong to God's family live, work, and play, 1 John 3.2

   b. As the body of Christ: the person through which God acts in the world, Rom. 12.4-8

   c. As the Temple of the Holy Spirit: the place where God lives and is worshiped in the world, 1 Cor. 6.19-20

2. Introduce them publicly to the believers in the fellowship, Rom. 15.7.

3. Connect them with godly friends who can ground them in the faith.

   a. Gal. 6.2

   b. 1 Pet. 3.8

   c. Phil. 2.3-4

4. Link them to an active member, family, and cell (small group) who can ground them in the faith, 1 Cor. 12.24-27.

D. Assign new believers to pastoral oversight.

1. Teach them the biblical principles surrounding the need for pastors and undershepherds among the people of God.

    a. Heb. 13.17

    b. 1 Thess. 5.12

2. Explain the role of Christian leadership in the development of their faith and growth in the Lord.

    a. To labor among them in the Word of God, 1 Tim. 5.17

    b. To guard them from error and destruction, Acts 20.28-31

3. Encourage them to get to know their leaders and interact with them, Heb. 13.7.

Conclusion

» The process of welcoming and integrating new believers into the Church is called incorporation.

» As practicing Christian leaders, we are called as God's representatives to do all we can to incorporate new believers into our fellowships as smoothly and warmly as possible.

» Incorporation involves accepting new believers on the basis of their repentance and faith, grounding them in the Word of God regarding Jesus, guiding them personally into the dimensions of Church family life, and ensuring that they are given godly pastors who will shepherd them in the body.

Please take as much time as you have available to answer these and other questions that the video brought out. The principle of incorporation could very well be one of the most important responsibilities we face in our urban churches. Certainly, the inability to welcome new believers into our churches, and integrate them into the life of our body ranks as one of the greatest problems we face in conserving the fruit of our evangelism in the city. Be clear and concise in your answers, and where possible, support with Scripture!

1. Why should our understanding of Christian education begin with our welcoming of new believers into our churches? What is at stake if new believers do not feel welcome into our urban churches, once they profess faith in Christ?

2. How does the example of Peter's relationship to the Gentiles inform our need to welcome people into our churches who are radically different from us in culture and background?

3. Why must we strive to incorporate new believers into our fellowship as soon as possible? Why is delay here a deadly practice for both our churches and the new believers coming to us?

4. Does someone have to change their cultural identity in order to join the body of Christ? Why or why not?

5. Why is our ability to incorporate new believers into our fellowship a barometer of our maturity and depth in Christ? What does it say about a church that cannot incorporate new believers into its life and worship?

6. Why is profession of faith in Jesus Christ the most important criteria for incorporation into the body?

7. What role does sound doctrine play in the first steps of bringing a new Christian into contact with the Church? What kinds of subjects should be covered with a brand new believer in the Church? How should we cover them?

8. What is the best way to help new believers form lasting, deep friendships with others in the body of Christ?

9. Describe some ways in which we might want to assign new believers to those who could offer them clear and excellent pastoral oversight. Can this be delegated to others, and if so, to whom?

Segue 1

Student Questions and Response

page 260 4

Effective Christian Education: Incorporating, Parenting, and Discipling

Segment 2: Parenting and Discipling in the Church

Rev. Dr. Don L. Davis

Summary of Segment 2

Spiritual parenthood is the art of nurturing and protecting new and growing believers in the context of the local church.

Our objective for this segment, *Effective Christian Education: Parenting and Discipling in the Church*, is to enable you to see that:

- Practicing Christian leaders are called to build up the Church as they exercise spiritual parenthood of new and immature believers in the body of Christ.

- This parent is neither lording it over new believers nor controlling them, but equipping them through example and teaching to live as mature, fruit-bearing disciples of Christ.

- All efforts toward equipping and parenting are for the purpose of maturing the members of the body of Christ, and not for the purpose of the control by the leader or teacher.

- Paul used the metaphor of spiritual parenthood to describe his relationship both to individuals and churches under the care of his ministry. In same way a parent cares for a child, so Paul nurtured new believers in the faith through his personal correspondence with them, his personal intercession for them, his personal example, his instruction, and the representatives he sent to them.

- In the same way the Apostles raised up spiritual children through faithful care and nurture, so the Lord is calling us to take personal responsibility for the care, feeding, and protection of new and growing believers under our care, using the same insights and practices as the Apostles.

I. **Meaning of Parenting New Believers in the Family of God**

    A. Definition: *the practicing Christian leader is one who equips the people of God by parenting spiritual sons and daughters toward maturity in the family of God.*

        1. Equips the people of God: *by example and teaching, the godly Christian leader equips members of the Church to live as fruit-bearing disciples of Jesus.*

            a. God has given select individuals to the Church to equip his people for the work of the ministry, Eph. 4.11-13.

            b. These individuals are specially called and gifted to build up God's people, 1 Pet. 5.1-3.

        2. Parenting spiritual sons and daughters: *spiritual parenthood involves offering tender, loving care to growing Christians in their lives as disciples,* 1 Cor. 4.14-15.

        3. Toward maturity in the family of God: *all efforts toward equipping and parenting are for the purpose of maturing the members of the body of Christ,* Eph. 4.13-16.

    B. Implications for Christian leadership

        1. God has made provision for the growth and fruitfulness of his people.

        2. The Lord has called and gifted special men and women to equip his people to do the work of the ministry.

Video Segment 2 Outline

[Exposition on 1 Thess. 2.7]: Paul and his companions cared for their converts as a nursing mother gently cares for her little children. This instructive illustration provides a good example for all who are responsible for the care of new believers. If a nursing mother does not feed herself, she cannot feed her baby. If she eats certain foods, her baby will get sick. Similarly the spiritual diet of a parent Christian is vitally important to the health of a newer Christian. The gentleness and unselfishness of Paul as a spiritual parent shines through in this illustration.
~ J. F. Walvoord, *The Bible Knowledge Commentary: An Exposition of the Scriptures.* (electronic ed.) Wheaton, IL: Victor Books: 1983, c1985.

3. These special individuals provide care to believers in the same way that parents provide for their own children.

4. The purpose of the special care is for the upbuilding of Christ's Church, which grows up into the fullness of Christ, to the glory and honor of God: God is building up his house to dwell in.

    a. Eph. 2.19-22

    b. 1 Pet. 2.4-5

5. God wants every leader to participate in this exciting ministry of building up the people of God!

II. Understanding Paul's Apostolic Model of Spiritual Parenthood

By understanding the way Paul ministered as a spiritual parent to growing believers, we can discern new models of discipling believers in Christ Jesus.

A. Personal correspondence

1. Paul composed personal letters to be read to all of the believers, some of which make up the books of our New Testament.

    a. 1 Thess. 5.27

    b. Col. 4.16

2. Paul authenticated the message of these letters by signing with his own hand.

   a. 1 Cor. 16.21

   b. 2 Thess. 3.17

3. The Apostle Paul felt it critical to address the specific questions of the issues of each situation with its own specially-crafted letter (which accounts for the differences in his epistles to different churches).

   a. *The Corinthians*, problems with sexual immorality, 1 Cor. 5.9-11

   b. *The Galatians*, problems with legalism, Gal. 3.1-3

   c. *The Thessalonians*, problems with laziness, 2 Thess. 3.6-8

   d. *The Romans*, problems with pride, Rom. 11.11-14

   e. *The Colossians*, problems with weird philosophies, Col. 2.8-10

4. It is evident that Paul was aware of what each situation required, and answered the particular issues with letters which addressed those specific concerns, cf. 1 Cor. 7.1-2.

5. Paul often wrote the same things to congregations, not to nag them but to "pile-drive" home certain critical truths in the faith, Phil. 3.1-2.

B. Personal intercession

1. Paul prayed without ceasing for the spiritual development and growth of new believers, cf. Rom. 1.9-12.

2. The prayers cover the gamut of topics and themes.

    a. For spiritual illumination, Eph. 1.15-23

    b. For an opportunity to see them and encourage them, Rom. 1.9-12

    c. With thanksgiving as he recalled their faith and love, 1 Thess. 1.3ff.

    d. For their strength and provision in the Father, Eph. 3.14ff.

3. Paul's prayer was neither casual or irregular; his prayer ministry for believers covered their lives in every way.

    a. Rom. 1.8-9

    b. Phil. 1.3-4

    c. Col. 1.3

    d. 2 Thess. 1.3

4. In all of Paul's ministry, nothing took the place of fervent, regular prayer for new believers.

C. Personal presence and example

1. Paul exhorted others to follow his example in Christ as a model for discipleship.

    a. 1 Cor. 4.16

    b. 1 Cor. 10.33

    c. Phil. 3.17

    d. 1 Thess. 1.6

    e. 2 Thess. 3.7-9

    f. 2 Thess. 3.9

    g. Heb. 6.12

2. Paul recalled his own faith journey as he exhorted believers to grow in Christ.

    a. Acts 20.31

b. 1 Thess. 2.9-10

3. Paul's suffering became a badge of honor in his discipling new believers in the faith, 2 Cor. 6.3-10.

4. In exhorting fellow leaders, Paul often referred to his own walk and trials as a model for others to learn from, 2 Tim. 1.8-13.

D. Personal instruction and mentoring as a parent

1. Paul referred to Timothy and others as his "children in the faith."

    a. 2 Tim. 2.1

    b. 1 Tim. 1.2

    c. 1 Tim. 1.18

    d. Titus 1.4

2. Paul admonished believers as a father would admonish his own children.

    a. 1 Cor. 4.14-17

    b. This parental concern included tender loving care, the kind that a mother or father would have for their children, 1 Thess. 2.7-8.

3. Paul's care as a spiritual parent was demonstrated in a mixture of exhortation and encouragement, as well as conduct and lifestyle, 1 Thess. 2.10-12.

4. Paul suffered anguish and concern for new believers as a concerned parent does for their children, Gal. 4.19.

E. Personal representatives

1. Paul sent Timothy and others on particular missions to do various works of good will for the various churches, Phil. 2.19-22.

2. He often sent representatives from congregations back with word of his own situation, Phil. 2.25-26.

3. Paul used messengers to inform him on the status of different congregations under persecution or enduring tribulation, 1 Thess. 3.6.

4. In order to ground new believers in the faith, Paul would send solid representatives to exhort and encourage growing Christians, 1 Thess. 3.2.

III. Applying the Pauline Model of Spiritual Parenthood in our Leading of Urban Congregations

A. Commit to faithful intercessory prayer for their souls: *the importance of supplication*

It seems odd that the man Paul should compare himself to a "nursing mother" in v. 7. (Consider also 1 Cor. 4.14–15 where he states that as a spiritual parent he had "begotten" the Corinthian saints through the Gospel.) In 2.9–13, Paul uses the image of a father, but the main thought here is that of loving care. New Christians need love, food, and tender care, just as a mother would give to her own children. Newborn babes need the milk of the Word (1 Pet. 2.2) and then must "graduate" to the meat (1 Cor. 3.1–4; Heb. 5.11–14), the bread (Matt. 4.4, and see Exod. 16, the manna), and the honey (Ps. 119.103). How a mother feeds her child is almost as important as what she feeds it. How important it is that we who are older Christians feed the younger believers lovingly and patiently. ~ W. W. Wiersbe. Wiersbe's Expository Outlines on the New Testament (1 Thess. 2.1), (electronic ed.). Wheaton, IL: Victor Books 1997 (original print copyright 1992).

1. Make and keep a broad prayer list and be faithful in it, 1 Tim. 2.1-4.

2. Cultivate a spirit of prayer in all that you do on behalf of those whom you lead.

   a. Rom. 12.12

   b. Ps. 62.8

   c. Acts 6.4

   d. Eph. 6.18-19

   e. Phil. 4.6-7

   f. Col. 4.2

B. Share a life in common with and model the Christian life for your spiritual children: *the importance of presence*

   1. Let your own life be a model of what it means to be a follower of Messiah Jesus, 1 Tim. 4.12.

   2. 1 Cor. 11.1

   3. Titus 2.7

4. 1 Pet. 5.3

C. Ensure personal feeding and proper nutrition: *the importance of provisions*

1. The heart of Christian leadership is tending and feeding the sheep of the Lord, John 21.15-17.

2. Feed individual babies; don't use a waterhose approach to feeding! 1 Thess. 2.7-8.

3. Pay careful attention to the flock in every particular, Acts 20.28.

D. Provide personal care and 24/7 protection against harm: *the importance of care*

1. Your role is to *watch over the souls of those whom God has given to you*, Heb. 13.17.

2. *Providing oversight and offering nourishment* are the two dimensions of shepherding we must attend, 1 Pet. 5.2-3.

E. Give ongoing instruction and good discipline: *the importance of nurture*

1. Your role is to labor *in the Word of God in teaching and preaching*, 1 Tim. 5.17.

2. *Put the believers in remembrance* of our hope in Christ, 1 Tim. 4.6.

3. *Be disciplined in your own training* for the sake of your spiritual parenting, 1 Tim. 4.16.

4. Be a solid parent by being *constantly encouraging and challenging your spiritual children* to maturity in Christ, 2 Tim. 4.2.

Conclusion

» The practicing Christian leader is one who equips the people of God by parenting spiritual sons and daughters toward maturity in the family of God.

» We derive much of our understanding of spiritual parenthood from the Apostle Paul, who equipped through his personal correspondence, prayer, example, instruction, and representatives.

» We can employ the same model Paul used to raise up a new generation of churches and leaders who can go on to impact their generation for Jesus Christ.

Segue 2

Student Questions and Response

The following questions were designed to help you review the material in the second video segment. The power of spiritual parenting is waiting to be felt in our urban church experience. We need to discover new practical and creative ways to disciple new and growing believers in the city. Ponder the questions well, and seek to be concise in your answers, and as always, support your analysis with Scripture!

1. In what sense has the Lord gifted select individuals with the responsibility to equip the body of Christ for the work of the ministry? How do we go about discerning who these individuals are in our local church experience?

2. What might some of the traits be that would be important in a good spiritual parent? What kind of person should not be placed in a role to spiritually parent new and/or immature believers?

3. Why is it important to develop disciples in the context of the family of God, that is, the local church setting? Is it possible to equip disciples to live the Christian life apart from the local church? Explain your thoughts.

4. How does the parenting image help us understand the nature of all authentic Christian leadership?

5. How did Paul use personal correspondence to individuals and churches to equip them for the Christian life? How might we adapt his approach for making disciples in our context, e.g., email?

6. What role did personal prayer and intercession play in Paul's ministry to growing disciples and their churches? How might we learn from this intense commitment to personal prayer in our ministries in the church and among the lost?

7. In what ways did Paul exhort others to follow his example in Christ as a pattern for spiritual maturity? In what ways may we do the same with those whom we lead today?

8. How does Paul's example of personal instruction to his "children in the faith" offer us a valid model for understanding our training to others today?

9. Paul sent representatives to the various churches with messages of hope and instruction to growing churches. How might we employ this same strategy today in equipping believers to live the Christian life?

10. Of all the traits mentioned in this lesson on effective Christian education, which do you believe is most important in discipling urban Christians today? Explain your answer.

CONNECTION

Summary of Key Concepts

This lesson focuses upon the kinds of practices that Christian leaders engage in to both incorporate new believers in the Church, as well as equip new and growing believers to live the Christian life. This relates to the concepts we covered in the previous lesson on leading the believers in worship, the Word, and the sacrament. In a real sense, these practices lie at the very heart of what it means to be a nurturing, servant leader to others in the Church. Gaining an understanding and mastery of these concepts is critical if we are to fulfill our responsibility to "feed the sheep" of the Lord Jesus (note John 21.17 He said to him the third time, "Simon, son of John,

page 260  *5*

do you love me?" Peter was grieved because he said to him the third time, "Do you love me?" and he said to him, "Lord, you know everything; you know that I love you." Jesus said to him, "*Feed my sheep*.")

- As practicing Christian leaders, we must incorporate new believers into the fellowship of Christ, creating an environment where they can be both welcomed and quickly integrated within our church community life and relationships.

- Incorporation is a critical biblical principle of Christian care, involving creating an environment where new members of the body are welcomed into God's family.

- Our ability to welcome new believers warmly, quickly, and smoothly into our community life will determine the overall viability of our church and its witness among those different than us in background and culture.

- No one need change their cultural identity in order to join into the body of Christ. We are free in Christ to remain who we are culturally when we first received Christ.

- New members are to be accepted based upon their repentance and faith in Jesus Christ, and must be grounded immediately into sound Christian doctrine (*catechesis*).

- Incorporation also involves making new believers feel at home in the very life of the Christian community, as well as ensuring that each new believer receives godly loving pastoral oversight.

- Practicing Christian leaders are called to build up the Church as they exercise spiritual parenthood of new and immature believers in the body of Christ.

- Godly spiritual parenting neither lords it over nor controls those children under his care, but rather equips them through personal example and teaching, all of which is designed to enable them to live as mature, fruit-bearing disciples of Christ.

- All efforts toward equipping and parenting are for the purpose of maturing the members of the body of Christ, and not for the purpose of the control of the leader or teacher.

- Paul used the metaphor of spiritual parenthood to describe his relationship both to individuals and churches under the care of his ministry. In same way a parent cares for a child, so Paul nurtured new believers in the faith through his personal correspondence with them, his personal intercession for them, his personal example, his instruction, and the representatives he sent to them.

- In the same way the Apostles raised up spiritual children through faithful care and nurture, so the Lord is calling us to take personal responsibility for the care, feeding, and protection of new and growing believers under our care, using the same insights and practices as the Apostles.

Student Application and Implications

Now is the time for you to discuss with your fellow students your questions about the necessity to strongly incorporate new believers into the Church, as well as establish them in the faith through godly discipling through spiritual parenthood. No believer is to remain or to be treated as a spiritual orphan. Each one needs the tender, loving care of godly support and oversight, both from pastors as well as teachers. These concepts undoubtedly have produced for you pointed and key questions that relate to you and your expression of the principles in your personal life. What particular questions do you have in light of the material you have just studied? Maybe some of the questions below might help you form your own, more specific and critical questions.

* When I look back on my own experience, was I quickly welcomed and integrated within the Church after I first repented and believed in Christ? What kind of problems did I encounter with incorporation when I first believed that I should be aware of today when I seek to incorporate others?

* Am I really convinced that you cannot grow as a disciple without the care and nurture of godly leaders in the context of a local body? What do I really believe about this?

* Who discipled me in the faith? Did I "raise myself," spiritually speaking, or who would I count as my spiritual father or mother in the Lord?

* Would my spiritual leaders characterize me as a 1) easy child to raise or 2) a problem child, hard-headed and stubborn? Explain your answer.

* What are the key characteristics and attitudes needed to truly make someone who has been on the outside of the family of God feel immediately at home in the Church?

* What kind of spiritual parent could I be, given where I am right now with the Lord and my place in the church? Do I consider myself ready to care for others spiritually? Explain your answer.

* Of the five ways that Paul nurtured his "children in the faith," which of these areas am I strongest, and in which do I have the greatest lack? How would my leaders describe my fitness to lead others spiritually right now?

* Of all the attitudes and skills needed to be a competent and godly spiritual parent, which one do I believe the Holy Spirit wants me to seek from him most right now in my life?

"I Don't Know the Pastor at All."

A dear sister, urban and poor with children, attends a mega-church which she enjoys, especially the sermons of the pastor which are funny, rich, and challenging. In several years, however, she has never met the pastor, and yet has encountered any number of problems, the latest of which involves her husband abandoning the family and leaving her and the children financially strapped and psychologically stressed. She is in real need of pastoral care and guidance, but in a large church she barely knows anyone. Her small group (admittedly of a different culture than hers) sympathizes, but none of them are accustomed to dealing with someone with such difficulties and complexities in her life. This dear sister comes to you for help, not knowing anyone else, sadly exclaiming, "I like my church, but I don't know the pastor at all." What kind of help and advice would you give to this dear sister, both about her immediate situation as well as her place and role in the church.

"That's Too Dangerous for Me."

A dear brother, being exposed to the teaching of the New Testament on the need for spiritual parenting of new and immature believers, agreed with the principle, but completely rejected the idea as a strategy for pastoral care. "While I see that Paul spoke of himself that way, I don't believe that is for us; after all, I'm not Paul and neither are you! Furthermore, what is to prevent somebody from becoming a mini-pope, ordering people around and acting like they know everything you're supposed to do and be. Jesus is my Lord, and I don't want anybody, including my pastor or Bible study leader, snooping around my life, pretending that they are my spiritual mother or father. If you ask me, that sounds too much like a cult or something. It's simply too dangerous for me." How would you discuss the biblical perspective of spiritual parenthood with someone like this? What is true in their analysis? What is exaggerated? How would you answer his fears and cautions about this as a strategy for discipling new believers?

"Church-ianity Doesn't Work."

Perhaps the most troubling part of a vision that emphasizes spiritual nurture in the context of the local church is the focus on the necessity of the church for spiritual growth. Many people today have a relationship with God through their individual devotional lives and selected teachings and events that they associate with. Many travel from church to church for the "spiritual food" they receive on Sunday morning, but are not a part of any kind of spiritual nurturing environment. Some receive their entire spiritual nurture from a televangelist, or radio preacher, and neither have membership with any local church, although they attend the services of several. What do you make of this kind of anti-local church religion which is so prevalent among so many Bible believers today? What is the root of this issue? Are they correct–is it really not necessary to affiliate with a particular local church, since so much is available over CDs, the radio, television, and different events? Are they correct–is it true that *church-ianity doesn't work*? (Church-ianity to some refers to an unhealthy focus on the necessity of the local church in the growth and fruitfulness of believers).

As practicing Christian leaders, we must do all we can to quickly incorporate new believers into the fellowship of Christ, creating an environment where they can be both welcomed and quickly integrated within our church community life and relationships. We must do this as soon as possible, ensuring their care, protection and oversight in the body. In addition to incorporation, we must as practicing Christian leaders exercise spiritual parenthood of new and immature believers in the body of Christ. Godly spiritual parenting neither lords it over nor controls those children under his care, but rather equips them through personal example and teaching, all of which is designed to enable them to live as mature, fruit-bearing

Restatement of the Lesson's Thesis

disciples of Christ. As Paul's nurtured new believers in the faith through his personal correspondence with them, his personal intercession for them, his personal example, his instruction, and the representatives he sent to them, so we too can follow his model in establishing urban Christians in the context of the Church today.

Resources and Bibliographies

If you are interested in pursuing some of the ideas of *Effective Christian Education: Incorporating, Parenting and Discipling,* you might want to give these books a try:

Eims, Leroy. *The Lost Art of Disciplemaking.* Grand Rapids: Zondervan Books, 1978.

Henrichsen, Walter A. *Disciples are Made, Not Born.* Colorado Springs: ChariotView Publishing, 1988.

Moore, Wayon B. *New Testament Follow-up.* Grand Rapids: Eerdmans, 1963.

Ortiz, Juan Carlos. *Disciple.* Altamonte Springs, FL: Creation House, 1975.

Phillips, Keith. *The Making of A Disciple.* Old Tappan, NJ: Fleming H. Revell Co., 1981.

Ministry Connections

This lesson touches upon one of the critical themes in all of personal ministry, our ability to welcome and accept new believers into the body of Christ, and then to provide them with tender, loving care, the same care that a nursing mother or a protective father would provide their own cherished child. All species of ministry demand this kind of loving, sacrificial care, and now it is time to consider your own life in light of this kind of care and loving service. To connect these principles to your life will demand the highest level of honest evaluation and openness to the Holy Spirit's searching of your own heart motive and personal character. This is your opportunity to go beyond merely the biblical descriptions and make a personal life and/or ministry connection to your own life, a connection that you will continue to ponder and apply throughout this next week. Search your own life and ministry before the Lord. What particular insights is the Holy Spirit suggesting to you in light of the insights in this lesson that relate to your own development and growth as a leader for him? What particular situation comes to your mind when you think about the principles included in this lesson? Is there someone who needs to be welcomed, cared for, included in your own life and ministry? Be open to the Lord's own gentle prodding and leading as you meditate in his presence on these critical issues.

Again, the power of prayer is well established in the body of Christ, and as mentioned in the lesson above, has a wonderful history in the example of the Apostles in both developing future leaders and establishing Christians in the faith. Like them, we all need faithful intercession and supplication for the needs and challenges we face today. Do not be ashamed to share your personal requests with your mentor and instructor, and with your fellow students. Be ready to seek their prayer support as you seek to respond to the Holy Spirit's leading and instruction in this lesson.

Counseling and Prayer

page 261  *7*

ASSIGNMENTS

2 Timothy 2.1-2

Scripture Memory

To prepare for class, please visit *www.tumi.org/books* to find next week's reading assignment, or ask your mentor.

Reading Assignment

Please read carefully the assignments above, and as last week, write a brief summary for them and bring these summaries to class next week (please see the "Reading Completion Sheet" at the end of this lesson). It is also time for you to begin to consider what you will want to do in regard to your particular ministry project, that is, those audiences or places you will want to share your insights about practicing Christian leadership. Also, you should begin to consider which of the given texts you will study for your particular exegetical project. Do not delay in determining either your ministry or exegetical project. The sooner you select, the more time you will have to prepare!

Other Assignments

Looking Forward to the Next Lesson

We began our investigation into the nature of practical Christian leadership with a consideration of our responsibility to represent our Lord and his purposes before his people, in worship, Word, and sacrament. In this lesson we explored our responsibility to quickly incorporate new believers into the Church, and our need to provide care and feeding for them as our own spiritual children.

In our next lesson, we will begin to explore the difficult but necessary topic of Church discipline, how we as leaders are to handle sin in the body, and in what ways we can so exhort and challenge the body as to ensure its ongoing depth and growth in Christ. We will look carefully at the role of biblical exhortation, as well as a key biblical outline for restoring the wayward disciple back to fellowship with the Lord and his people.

This curriculum is the result of thousands of hours of work by The Urban Ministry Institute (TUMI) and should not be reproduced without their express permission. TUMI supports all who wish to use these materials for the advance of God's Kingdom, and affordable licensing to reproduce them is available. Please confirm with your instructor that this book is properly licensed. For more information on TUMI and our licensing program, visit www.tumi.org and www.tumi.org/license.

Capstone Curriculum

Module 11: Practicing Christian Leadership
Reading Completion Sheet

Name _____

Date _____

For each assigned reading, write a brief summary (one or two paragraphs) of the author's main point. (For additional readings, use the back of this sheet.)

Reading 1

Title and Author: _____ Pages _____

Reading 2

Title and Author: _____ Pages _____

LESSON
3

Effective Church Discipline
Exhorting, Rebuking, and Restoring

page 265 1

Lesson Objectives

Welcome in the strong name of Jesus Christ! After your reading, study, discussion, and application of the materials in this lesson, you will be able to:

- Define the concept of biblical exhortation, and explore reasons why this ministry is so necessary for Christian leaders among God's people.

- Distinguish the difference between the standing and the state of a Christian's position and discipleship, and apply that knowledge to the issue of Christian exhortation.

- Connect the practice of exhortation to the challenge of believers remaining faithful to the Lord in their walks with God, each other, and in the world.

- List the basic reasons why it is necessary to exhort one another to remain faithful, including the devil's opposition, the nature of our adoption in Christ, avoiding judgment from God, maintaining our integrity, and being conformed to the model of Christ.

- Understand the basic principles associated with the theology and practice of exhorting others in a God-honoring way.

- Recite the basic biblical definitions of practicing discipline in the Church, and outline the nature of what it means to rebuke and restore members of God's community.

- Exegete Matthew 18 with an eye to discover Jesus' instruction regarding carrying out discipline in the Church.

- Outline the critical cautions associated with carrying out discipline in the Church, including pride, acting on uncorroborated accusations, and a neglect of genuine authority in discipline.

- Detail the benefits of discipline, i.e., a sound faith, a strong community, a safe family, a solid testimony, and a glorified Savior.

Strengthen Your Brothers

Read Luke 22.31-34. "Simon, Simon, behold, Satan demanded to have you, that he might sift you like wheat, [32] but I have prayed for you that your faith may not fail. And when you have turned again, strengthen your brothers." [33] Peter said to him, "Lord, I am ready to go with you both to prison and to death." [34] Jesus said, "I tell you, Peter, the rooster will not crow this day, until you deny three times that you know me."

Can you imagine a situation causing greater shame, angst, and horror than of being told by the Lord that you would betray him before the night was over? Can you further conceive of the kind of pain that Peter must have suffered after his fateful denial of the Lord–the unbelievable guilt and self-loathing, and the terrible despair. Yet, even in the face of this betrayal, our Lord had made provision for the restoration and return of the great Apostle. Jesus, knowing what would happen, even instructed him in what he would have to do after he had been restored from his terrible condition of guilt and condemnation. Jesus assured him not only of his betrayal, but also his return, and exhorted Peter "And when you have turned again, strengthen your brothers." Jesus heaped no coals of condemnation upon Peter, held no recriminations against him, and refused to shame him for his cowardice and deception. Rather, he exhorted him to *strengthen his brothers*. Here Jesus provides a clear and compelling witness to the power and meaningfulness of restoration after a fall.

The overarching point is not to shame or demean, not to insult or condemn. Rather, the purpose of restoration of the fallen brother is that the experience might so strengthen the fallen in order that they may be in a position to strengthen their brothers who are also prone to fall. We should be mindful of the fact the high priest had to be someone who could sympathize with the weaknesses and tribulations of the people, seeing that he was their advocate before the Lord. Just so, the man or woman of God must be a person who understands the power of restoration to restore, and the goodness of grace to be gracious. Here we are not demanding that the Christian leader sin in order to know the wonders of God's mercy. Instead, we are saying that every Christian leader must know in their hearts and lives the same grace and care that Christ has for them in order that they can be vessels through whom he can work for others.

It should never cease to amaze us, this matchless grace of our risen Lord, his willingness to care for us, even when we are undeserving of it, and then, after he has restored us, to give us a way to care for our brothers and sisters with the very same care with which he cared for us. Such is the wonder of the love of God in Jesus Christ. *"And when you have turned again, strengthen your brothers."*

Devotion

page 266 2

Nicene Creed and Prayer

After reciting and/or singing the Nicene Creed (located in the Appendix), pray the following prayer:

> *Suffer me never to think that I have knowledge enough to need no teaching, wisdom enough to need no correction, talents enough to need no grace, goodness enough to need no progress, humility enough to need no repentance, devotion enough to need no quickening, strength sufficient without thy Spirit; lest, standing still, I fall back for evermore.*
>
> ~ Eric Milner-White, 1884-1964.
> Appleton, George, ed. **The Oxford Book of Prayer**.
> Oxford/New York: Oxford University Press, 1988. p. 121.

Quiz

Put away your notes, gather up your thoughts and reflections, and take the quiz for Lesson 2, *Effective Christian Education: Incorporating, Parenting, and Discipling.*

Scripture Memorization Review

Review with a partner, write out and/or recite the text for last class session's assigned memory verse: 2 Timothy 2.1-2.

Assignments Due

Turn in your summary of the reading assignment for last week, that is, your brief response and explanation of the main points that the authors were seeking to make in the assigned reading (Reading Completion Sheet).

"You Haven't Proven You Are Sorry."

We have all experienced situations where, after wrong was done to someone and the wrong acknowledged, there has been serious debate about what constitutes a "repentant attitude." Opinions vary greatly among Bible-believing Christians as to what a restored person must do in order to "prove" that they are sorry for what they have done. This difference of opinions varies from full restoration and restitution of all that was done wrong, to simply the verbal acknowledgment that we are sorry for what we have done. In your judgment, what is the most appropriate expression that a person can give to show that they are in fact sorry for what they have done against the Lord and others, and to restore those who have been hurt through their actions?

"That's Going Too Far!"

In a men's Bible study in church, a group of brothers has genuine concerns about the behavior and conduct of a brother, Larry, who also is a member of the church. The concern focuses on what is perceived by all as to Larry's drinking habits. No one has actually said anything to him about it, but much discussion has gone on behind the scenes. During a study on Christlike character, one of the brothers mentions to Larry (in the presence of the other men of the study group) his concerns about Larry's drinking habits. Although it was said in love and truth, Larry is deeply offended by the entire episode, and before he leaves the room (and the church!) he blurts out, "You guys are such hypocrites! I don't mind you talking to me about my religion and all, but being so nosy to intrude into my private affairs, well, that's going too far!" Was Larry right?

Once Gone, Always Gone

In a Sunday School discussion on the nature of backslidden Christians, a dear sister suggests that once a person turns their back on the Lord, it is not possible to bring them back again. She then turns in her Bible to Hebrews 10 and says, "Look at what the Word says. In Hebrews 10.26-27 it reads that 'For if we go on sinning deliberately after receiving the knowledge of the truth, there no longer remains a sacrifice for sins, [27] but a fearful expectation of judgment, and a fury of fire that will consume the adversaries.' See? I told you! This verse says that if we continue to sin, there no longer remains a sacrifice for sins, only a fearful judgment." Some believe she is interpreting the text correctly, while many suggest that she is not understanding the text appropriately. How do you understand this, i.e., the relationship between restoration and one's eternal salvation?

CONTENT — **Effective Church Discipline: Exhorting, Rebuking, and Restoring**

Segment 1: Exhorting as a Principle of Biblical Discipline

Rev. Dr. Don L. Davis

Summary of Segment 1

The Christian leader is one who challenges the people of God to remain faithful in their discipleship in Jesus Christ by exhorting them for the purpose of edification. Such exhortation should be done with humility, a deep desire for healing and restoration, building on the wisdom of the Spirit, and backed up with personal example.

Our objective for this segment, *Effective Church Discipline: Exhorting as a Principle of Biblical Discipline*, is to enable you to see that:

- The practicing Christian leader is one who challenges the people of God to remain faithful in their discipleship in Jesus Christ by exhorting them for the purpose of edification.

- Godly exhortation is backed up by personal example, given with grace, built on the foundation of Christ and Scripture, and is informed by the wisdom of the Holy Spirit.

- While our position before the Lord (our standing) is secure due to our faith in Christ, our daily walk with him and others (our state) is subject to change with our obedience to God; we must be willing to be taught so our state may line up in our conduct with our high standing in Christ.

- We must avoid the problems associated with poor exhortation, the problems of pride, micro-management, and legalism.

Video Segment 1 Outline

I. Exhorting Believers for Christian Maturity

A. Definition: *the practicing Christian leader is one who challenges the people of God to remain faithful in their discipleship in Jesus Christ by exhorting them for the purpose of edification.*

1. Challenges the people of God to remain faithful in their discipleship in Jesus Christ: *the Christian leader is charged with the responsibility to reprove, rebuke, and exhort believers to remain faithful to the Lord.*

    a. Titus 2.11-15

    b. 1 Tim. 4.12

2. By exhorting them for the purpose of edification: *the Christian leader does not lord it over others, but encourages them to fulfill their responsibility in Jesus Christ.*

    a. 2 Tim. 4.2

    b. 1 Thess. 5.14

B. The implications of biblical exhortation

1. No disciple of Jesus can live in this world without having to fight the three-fold enemy of the saints: the world, the flesh, and the devil.

    a. The world: that *external* system of temptation and deception, 1 John 2.15-17

    b. The flesh: that *internal* nature of sin and rebellion which must be reckoned to have died with Christ, Rom. 6.1-11

The absence of church discipline and high standards of Christian conduct indicates that we don't take holiness too seriously. In our promotion, we try to "sell" the Church to the world by conveying the unbiblical idea that Christianity is "fun" and every pagan ought to join the club and start living on the sunny side of the street.
~ W. W. Wiersbe.
Be Holy. (Electronic ed.) Wheaton, IL: Victor Books, 1996.

c. The devil: that *infernal* enemy who deceives the whole world and seeks to devour any believers who are neither alert nor prepared for his tactics, cf. 1 John 5.19; Rev. 12.10; 1 Pet. 5.8-9

2. The Christian life is not a 100-yard dash sprint, but a marathon: a crown of life is given to those who withstand the trials which will inevitably come to every disciple, James 1.12.

3. God has given leaders to the Church to reprove, rebuke, and exhort believers to stay true to the kingdom promise that he has given them, Titus 2.15.

II. Why Is Exhortation and Spiritual Discipline Necessary: the Reality of Backsliding

A. The devil tempts and deceives believers to turn their backs on the truth and resume their former ways.

1. The devil pursues believers to destroy their faith and testimony before God, 1 Pet. 5.8-9.

2. We can withstand the devil's schemes with God's armor, Eph. 6.11.

3. Believers are to resist the devil's lies and schemes, James 4.7.

B. Discipline confirms your calling as God's child (our identity as God's own people).

1. Christ disciplines all those whom he loves, Rev. 3.19.

2. Discipline shows parental connection, Heb. 12.5-11.

C. Without it, people who turn back suffer horrible consequences.

1. Prov. 14.14

2. Jer. 10.24

3. Gal. 6.7-8

D. It maintains our integrity as the people of God ("inside and outside").

1. Those who belong to the Lord stay with the Lord, 1 John 2.19.

2. The Lord knows those who are truly his, 2 Tim. 2.19.

E. It is possible to restore the one who has turned back from the Lord.

1. Jer. 3.11-12

2. Jer. 3.14

3. Jer. 3.22

F. It allows us to share in the process that Jesus endured.

   1. Heb. 5.7-9

   2. John 15.10

III. Standing Versus State: the Dilemma of Backsliding in the NT

   A. Standing and spiritual position: *the position of the believer in the NT is secure and constant.*

   1. A believer is said to be "in Christ," which is the position of being anchored in the unchangeable, final, and perfect work of Jesus for the believer.

      a. We have been saved from God's wrath, Rom. 5.9-10.

      b. Rom. 8.1

      c. Gal. 3.13

   2. This standing is secured by a believer's *faith in Jesus Christ*.

      a. John 1.12-13

      b. Rom. 5.1-2

c. Rom. 8.16

d. Eph. 1.3

e. Col. 2.9

f. Heb. 10.10, 14

3. For those who authentically belong to Christ, they are secure in their position before him as those who are his.

   a. They have eternal life, John 5.24.

   b. They cannot be lost, if they are in the hand of Jesus, John 10.27-30.

   c. Their salvation is not dependent on what they do, Eph. 2.8-9.

   d. Nothing can separate them from the love of God in Christ Jesus, Rom. 8.38-39.

4. Example: the high standing and *exalted position* of the Corinthians, 1 Cor. 1.2-9

B. State and spiritual condition: *the condition of a Christian may change depending on their availability to God and obedience to him.*

1. If we fail to walk in the light, we will lose communion with the Father through the Son, 1 John 1.6-8.

2. Backsliding involves not only a changed relationship with the Lord but misery and confusion in personal experience.

    a. 1 Cor. 3.18

    b. Gal. 6.3

    c. James 1.26

3. Unchecked and unrepentant sin can also result in God's direct discipline and chastening of the believer.

    a. Heb. 12.6

    b. 1 Cor. 11.31-32

4. Living in unrepentant sin can result in a believer's loss of rewards and fellowship.

    a. 2 Cor. 5.9-10

    b. 1 John 2.28

    c. 1 John 3.19-21

5. In extreme cases, God may elect to cause sickness or even death (in order that the believer not suffer condemnation).

   a. Suffering judgment and illness, 1 Cor. 11.28-32

   b. Suffering premature death

      (1) 1 Cor. 5.5

      (2) 1 John 5.16

6. Example: the changeable standing and *affectable condition* of the Corinthians

   a. 1 Cor. 1.11

   b. 1 Cor. 3.1-4

   c. 1 Cor. 4.18

   d. 1 Cor. 5.2

C. Issues in exhorting those who backslide

1. What are the kinds of things that can cause a person to turn their back on God and his kingdom call?

a. Spiritual apostasy

   (1) 2 Thess. 2.3

   (2) 1 Tim. 4.1

   (3) 2 Tim. 3.1

   (4) 2 Pet. 3.3

   (5) Jude 1.4

b. Moral degradation, 1 Cor. 3.1-3

c. Doctrinal error, Eph. 4.13-14

2. Can you be restored again if you backslide?

   a. Prov. 28.13

   b. 1 John 1.9

3. Is there a kind of backsliding that is complete?

   a. Texts which appear that one's backslidden nature can result in complete loss of salvation

   (1) Heb. 6.4-6

   (2) Heb. 10.26-31

   (3) Heb. 10.38-39

b. The problem with this view

   (1) Such a view seems to contradict the biblical idea that God will forgive us and cleanse us from all unrighteousness if we confess our sin before him, cf. 1 John 1.7-10.

   (2) If it is possible to lose salvation, it doesn't appear from these texts that simple repentance could restore it again.

   (3) It is simply too easy for us to pass judgment on a person's eternal status before God based on how they're doing this week; this is unwise, cf. 2 Cor. 10.12.

IV. The Christian Leader as One Who Exhorts the Backsliden

page 268 *4*

A. Purpose of exhortation: edification

   1. To build up the people of God in Jesus Christ: *maturity*, Eph. 4.15-16

   2. To see the people of God bear fruit in good works and evangelism: *fruitfulness*, Eph. 2.10; Matt. 5.14-16; Phil. 2.12-13

B. Principles of exhortation

   1. Backed up by *personal example*, 1 Cor. 11.1

   2. Done with grace and sensitivity to *build up, not tear down*, 2 Cor. 13.8

   3. Built on the *foundation of Christ and the Word of God*, 2 Tim. 3.15-17

4. Based upon *spiritual wisdom and insight from the Holy Spirit*, Gal. 5.16; Eph. 5.18

C. Problems with unbiblical exhortation

1. Exhorting with a *personal pride of place and position*

    a. 1 Cor. 3.5

    b. 2 Cor. 4.5

    c. 2 Cor. 6.4

    d. 1 Cor. 3.7

2. Exhorting as a form of *micro-managing the lives of believers*, Matt. 23.2-4

3. Exhorting as a form of *legalistic meddling in other's affairs (lording it over others)*

    a. 2 Cor. 1.24

    b. 1 Pet. 5.2-3

D. Practicing Christian exhortation

1. Listen to the Holy Spirit; offer counsel and response based on the clear standards of Scripture and not your own ideas or intuitions, Gal. 5.16-24.

2. Don't speculate on the salvation status of the offender, let God determine who belongs to him (not us).

    a. 2 Tim. 2.19

    b. Ps. 1.6

    c. 1 Cor. 8.3

    d. Rom. 8.28

3. Get and keep your facts straight when exhorting about particular situations, 2 Cor. 13.1.

4. Let your words be few and "seasoned with salt" (carefully chosen and spoken), Eph. 4.29-30.

5. Be aware of the purpose of your exhortation: encouragement and challenge for edification, James 5.19-20.

6. Challenge backslidden believers to prove to themselves by their works that they actually belong to the Lord, not merely in profession but in expression.

   a. 2 Cor. 13.5

   b. Gal. 6.4

   c. 2 Pet. 1.10-11

7. Do everything in a spirit of meekness and fear, considering yourself and your own weakness.

   a. Gal. 6.1-3

   b. Matt. 7.1-5

8. Bathe all exhortation in prayer, seeking God's wisdom at every step of seeking to challenge the individual with God's Word, James 5.16-18.

Conclusion

» Scripture teaches us that we must all be open and subject to biblical exhortation for the sake of our edification in Christ.

» Because we live in a world filled with worldly temptation, fleshly pressure, and demonic deception, all believers will be tempted to return to their former worldly ways.

» God has provided his people with Spirit-filled leadership in order to guard and watch over his people, and exhort them to be faithful to his call.

Please take as much time as you have available to answer these and other questions that the video brought out. The concept of exhortation and spiritual discipline requires the most careful distinctions and understandings, all of which must be tested against Scripture for their accuracy and truth value. Dealing with the rough edges of the Christian life is a serious and valuable gift for the urban Christian leader. Therefore, as you discuss your reaction to the teaching, be careful that you make your answers both clear and concise. As ususal, you should do all you can to include support for your claims and interpretations from the Scriptures, God's authoritative source for this and all other concepts related to the Christian's maturity.

Segue 1

Student Questions and Response

page 269 5

1. What is the definition of exhortation? What is the relationship between the Christian leader's responsibility to exhort believers and their need to be built up in Christ? Explain.

2. Why is it not valid to associate exhorting with lording it over others, and getting overly involved in their personal affairs? Why does our understanding of the world, our sin nature, and the devil make biblical exhortation a desirable and important part of Christian leadership?

3. List three reasons why exhortation and spiritual discipline are necessary for the well-being of growing Christians. Which of these do you find most convincing?

4. What is the definition of a Christian's "standing before God?" What is the definition of a Christian's "state in the world?" How are we to understand the relationship between the two?

5. Why it is so important to not allow sin to go unchecked in our lives, and in the lives of those whom we are called to protect and serve? What are the consequences of letting immorality and sin remain unconfronted and not dealt with?

6. What kinds of things will tempt the Christian to turn their back on God and his Kingdom? Can a Christian be restored again if they backslide? Explain your answer.

7. Is it possible to so turn one's back on the Lord as a professing Christian that they would actually lose the salvation in Christ that they once had? Explain your answer.

8. What is the purpose of exhortation, and what are the key principles associated with it? What are the problems associated with exhorting others in an unbiblical way?

9. What insights should we use as we seek to exhort others to remain faithful to Christ, and attain to the maturity that he desires and demands of us as his disciples?

Effective Church Discipline: Exhorting, Rebuking, and Restoring

Segment 2: Practicing Discipline in the Church: Rebuking and Restoring

Rev. Dr. Don L. Davis

Summary of Segment 2

The practicing Christian leader is charged with guiding the process to discipline a backslidden or estranged member of God's people for the purpose of restoring him or her to full fellowship in the body. All spiritual discipline is a family affair, done with a corrective purpose in mind, to restore the fallen back into full membership within the body of Christ.

Our objective for this second segment of *Effective Church Discipline: Exhorting, Rebuking, and Restoring* is to enable you to see that:

- The Christian leader is charged with guiding the process to discipline a backslidden or estranged member of God's people for the purpose of restoring them to full fellowship.

- Discipline is God's way to protect his people and restore the fallen to full fellowship, and should never be done to shame, condemn, or impose guilt on others.

- Condemnation has no connection to discipline; discipline has to do with restoring a Christian to the Lord and the Church whose *condition* or *state* has momentarily fallen into sin.

- Discipline is given to the Church to prevent sin from occurring, to correct a problem that already exists, to vindicate openly a person accused wrongly of an act, and to instruct the Church in God's standard of holiness.

- Matthew 18 provides a clear outline of the procedure that believers ought to take when confronted with a situation that requires attention (i.e., where sound doctrine must be defended, where Christian holiness must be upheld, and the integrity of Christ demonstrated).

- In exercising spiritual discipline, we must be ever vigilant against our own pride and judgmentalism, the need to verify all accusations in the mouths of two or three witnesses, and the need to exercise pastoral authority in severe cases.

I. **Practicing Discipline in the Church: Rebuking and Restoring the Estranged among the People of God**

Video Segment 2 Outline

A. Definition: *the practicing Christian Leader is charged with guiding the process to discipline a backsliden or estranged member of God's people for the purpose of restoring them to full membership.*

1. Charged with guiding the process to discipline a backsliden or estranged member of God's people: *the Christian leader has been charged with the role to reprove, rebuke, and exhort with all authority to ensure a sound faith and a strong healthy church.*

    a. Titus 2.11-15

    b. 2 Tim. 4.2

    c. Heb. 3.13

2. For the purpose of restoring them to full membership: *all exercise of authority for discipline is done only for the purpose of edifying and restoring (no authority exists to tear down another member of God's family).*

   a. 2 Cor. 13.8-10

   b. 2 Cor. 10.8

B. Implications for the Christian Leader

   1. God is holy and demands a lifestyle of holiness from those who dwell among his people, 1 Pet. 1.14-17.

   2. Discipline is God's way to protect the people of God as well as restore those who desire to return to obedience to Christ's lordship after backsliding from him, Heb. 12.6.

   3. Leaders should oversee the process of biblical discipline as a part of their responsibility to shepherd the flock.

II. The Nature of Biblical Discipline in the Church

A. Discipline is a Family Affair

   1. Definition of discipline: (*paideuo*) = Greek, "to instruct, train, or correct"

The question of forgiveness and discipline is squarely within the domain of the Church: "But as it is now our purpose to discourse of the visible Church, let us learn, from her single title of Mother, how useful, nay, how necessary the knowledge of her is, since there is no other means of entering into life unless she conceive us in the womb and give us birth, unless she nourish us at her breasts, and, in short, keep us under her charge and government, until, divested of mortal flesh, we become like the angels (Matt. 22.30). For our weakness does not permit us to leave the school until we have spent our whole lives as scholars. Moreover, beyond the pale of the Church no forgiveness of sins, no salvation, can be hoped for, as Isaiah and Joel testify (Isa. 37.32; Joel 2.32)."
~ John Calvin. *Institutes of the Christian Religion*. Translation of *Institutio Christianae Religionis*. Originally published: Edinburgh: Calvin Translation Society, 1845-1846. (IV, I, 4). Oak Harbor, WA: Logos Research Systems, Inc., 1997.

2. Discipline has to do with one's *condition* (state) before God as a child of God, and not with one's *position* (standing) as a believer.

3. The Heavenly Father disciplines those who belong to him, 1 Cor. 11.31-32.

4. This discipline or correction is directed towards those who are God's very own offspring and children, Heb. 12.6.

5. Condemnation has no connection to discipline; it is to correct the erring believer not to *condemn* them.

   a. There is no condemnation for those in Christ Jesus, Rom. 8.1.

   b. Those who believe in Christ are not judged in the sense of condemnation, John 3.16-18.

B. Discipline has a corrective purpose.

1. It is given to *prevent* a problem from happening: God moves in the life of the disciple to prevent moral or spiritual error (as in the case of Paul's thorn in the flesh), cf. 2 Cor. 12.7-9.

2. It is given to *correct* a problem that already exists: Heb. 12.6; Rev. 3.19.

   a. By dealing with *moral impurity*: by engaging in moral evils with no sign of repentance or openness to change

b. By coming to grips with *doctrinal error*: by believing and teaching things contrary to the doctrine of Jesus Christ

c. By confronting *spiritual rebellion*: by living in disobedience and lifestyles that transgress the clear command of God

d. By addressing *division in relationships*: by causing and living in division and discord with other members of the body

3. It may occur to *vindicate* God's person (Satan's accusation against God in the case of Job), Job 1.

4. It is given to *instruct* us in God's holiness, Heb. 12.11.

5. Discipline in the Old Testament informs these different understandings of how God uses discipline in our lives.

    a. The Wilderness wanderings were harsh and painful, but in the midst of it God provided for his people, seeking to teach them the centrality of his Word, Deut. 2.7; Deut. 8.4.

    b. God's judgment was meant to cause his people to "circumcise their heart and not stiffen their neck any more," Deut. 10.12-22.

    c. The Captivity of Israel by Assyria was the judgment of God to demonstrate his holiness; while it would not lead to final destruction, discipline was critical for God's revelation to his people of who he was, Hos. 12.2.

III. A Biblical Procedure for Discipline in the Church

A. What makes discipline necessary

1. The need to protect and maintain sound doctrine regarding Christ and his Kingdom

   a. 1 Tim. 1.3

   b. Titus 1.13

2. Protecting the integrity of the Lord's Supper, 1 Cor. 11.34

3. Rebuking those who persist in sin in the company of believers

   a. 1 Tim. 5.20

   b. 2 Tim. 4.2

4. Removing those whose lifestyles and actions blaspheme the name of Jesus Christ

   a. 1 Cor. 5.3-5

   b. 1 Cor. 5.13

   c. 1 Tim. 1.20

We should keep in mind that the whole context of this passage on Church discipline is mercy and forgiveness; forgiveness qualifies (but does not annul) the force of this passage on disciplining unrepentant offenders in the Christian community. The contextual emphasis is the hope of bringing back the erring, not confirming them irreparably in their guilt.
~ Charles S. Keener. 1993. *The IVP Bible Background Commentary.* (Comment on New Testament, Matt. 18.15). (Electronic ed.) Downers Grove, IL: InterVarsity Press, 1993.

B. Matthew 18: biblical procedure for exercising discipline in the Church

Matt. 18.15-20 - If your brother sins against you, go and tell him his fault, between you and him alone. If he listens to you, you have gained your brother. [16] But if he does not listen, take one or two others along with you, that every charge may be established by the evidence of two or three witnesses. [17] If he refused to listen to them, tell it to the church. And if he refused to listen even to the Church, let him be to you as a Gentile and a tax collector. [18] Truly, I say to you, whatever you bind on earth shall be bound in heaven, and whatever you loose on earth shall be loosed in heaven. [19] Again I say to you, if two of you agree on earth about anything they ask, it will be done for them by my Father in heaven. [20] For where two or three are gathered in my name, there am I among them.

1. Sin ought to be resolved privately and confidentially wherever possible, Matt. 18.15.

2. If the offender does not respond to private pleas, we are called to take one or two others that the charge may be established in the mouth of two or three witnesses, Matt. 18.16.

    a. Num. 35.30

    b. Deut. 17.6

    c. Deut. 19.15

    d. John 8.17

    e. 2 Cor. 13.1

    f. 1 Tim. 5.19

3. If the offender will not listen to two or three witnesses, they are to be brought to the church, and if they refuse to listen to the church, they are to be treated as an outsider (as a Gentile and a tax collector).

   a. The entire process is based on the *ability or inability of the offender to respond to the truth*, Matt. 18.17.

   b. The decision of the church is a final decision in this regard until it is formally rescinded by the church's determination, Matt. 18.18.

4. Leaders ought to establish and superintend this process on behalf of the church.

   a. Biblical support for leadership involvement in discipline

      (1) Heb. 13.17

      (2) Matt. 16.19

      (3) 1 Tim. 5.19

   b. Leaders should *strive to resolve and address all issues pertinent to the situation* which made the discipline necessary.

   c. Leaders *must represent God's scriptural standards* by reaffirming the biblical truth regarding the offense.

   d. Leaders must *guide the process to restore the offender publicly and formally* back into the family of God.

5. Restoration is possible if the offender repents and turns from their transgression of the Lord's will.

    a. Gal. 6.1-2

    b. James 5.19-20

C. Example of biblical discipline: the Corinthian sexual problem

    1. The offense: *sexual immorality* 1 Cor. 5.1-5

    2. The restoration: *Paul's plea for restoration of the repentant offender*, 2 Cor. 2.6-11

    3. The purpose of the discipline: *godly sorrow leading to restoration*, 2 Cor. 7.10

IV. Cautions and Precautions in Discipline in the Church

A. Beware of pride and judgmentalism, Gal. 6.1-4.

    1. This is a process for those who are spiritual and prepared.

    2. No hint of cruelty, mean-spiritedness, or pride should enter into the process.

The Church cannot be the Church without exercising its responsibility to lovingly yet firmly discipline its members, including the prospect of even excluding from its fellowship those who are unrepentant because of immorality (1 Cor. 5.1–13) or embracing false doctrine (2 Thess. 3.14; 2 John 10). All discipline at all levels must be done in a spirit of meekness and fear, and always for the purpose of restoring the offender to full fellowship, (Gal. 6.1-2).

3. In all discipline, all parties should *become more aware* of their own ability to fail and fall; no sense of a "holier-than-thou" spirit should be tolerated.

B. Confirm all judgments and accusations in the mouth of two or three witnesses, 1 Tim. 5.19; 2 Cor. 13.1.

1. No judgment should be done on the basis of rumor or appearance, John 7.24.

2. Unjust and unrighteous judgments are an abomination to the Lord; get the facts straight *before you dare entertain* any judgments against others, Prov. 17.15.

3. Any kind of partiality violates God's holy standard of kingdom righteousness.

    a. James 2.1

    b. James 2.9

C. Exercise pastoral authority throughout the process of discipline, Heb. 13.17.

1. Do not hesitate to represent the Lord and his Word strongly and clearly in matters where what is true has been proven and made plain, 2 Tim. 4.2.

2. Be careful in all handling of matters, but be clear and firm and fair, 1 Tim. 5.19-21.

Can we really exclude believers from our fellowship?
"The notion of exclusion from the believing community (excommunication or Church discipline) is captured in a host of terms. In one key passage alone, 1 Corinthians 5, it is expressed in five different ways, using the verbs 'to remove', 'to drive out', '(not) to eat with', 'to deliver (to Satan)' and 'to purge away'. However, the topic raises questions about the motivations for such drastic action which are not communicated simply by the appearance of such words. The fact that people are to be disciplined is less instructive than the reasons for the judgment. In the Bible serious offenders are excluded from the community because of the solidarity of the community, in order to maintain the holiness of the group, due to a breach of covenant, in the hope of restoration and because of the prospect of salvation."
~ T. D. Alexander. *New Dictionary of Biblical Theology* (Electronic ed.). Downers Grove: InterVarsity Press, 2001.

3. Never lose sight of the *purpose* of all discipline: soundness in the faith and maturity in Jesus Christ.

    a. Col. 1.28

    b. Titus 1.13

    c. Titus 2.15

D. The blessings of discipline and restoration

    1. A sound faith: *discipline will ensure that heresy and error will not be tolerated among the people of God.*

    2. A strong community: *discipline will strengthen the resolve of the body members to stand for what glorifies and honors God according to his Word.*

    3. A safe family: *discipline will protect members of the body from "wolves in sheep's clothing" who seek to prey on the members of the community.*

    4. A solid testimony: *discipline will build a sense of reputation that suggests that the community has integrity (they believe certain things and are willing to live by their beliefs).*

    5. A Savior who is glorified and pleased: *discipline will handle delicate and difficult issues with grace and mercy when godly spiritual leaders guide the process with sensitivity and openness to God the Holy Spirit and the truth.*

Conclusion

» As Christian leaders, we must recognize that God has charged us as his representatives to help guide his people through a fair and just process that will seek to restore an offender back to full participation in our body.

» The practice of biblical discipline will result in a sound faith and strong Christian community, bringing honor to our Lord.

Segue 2

Student Questions and Response

page 270 6

The following questions were designed to help you review the material in the second video segment. In today's environment, many churches and their leaders avoid questions and issues of Church discipline altogether, until, unfortunately, they are forced by division, lawsuits, and scandal to address them. No Christian leader can be effective if they do not concentrate their energies and attention on learning Christ's commands on this subject, and then carefully and lovingly applying those principles to the situations that they confront in the Church. As this is especially necessary in urban church contexts, we must master these principles and the supporting Scripture well. As you discuss these questions together, do not hesitate to view them through the lens of the situations that you are facing in your church and community.

1. What is the Christian leader's responsibility to the backsliden or estranged member of the body of Christ? Why is all exercise of authority for discipline's sake only done for the purpose of building up others, and not tearing them down?

2. In what way can we say that discipline is "God's way to protect the people of God as well as restore those who desire to return to obedience to Christ's lordship after backsliding?" In what way are all members of the body of Christ called to participate in restoration and discipline? Explain your answer.

3. What is the relationship of spiritual discipline to one's standing as a child of God? Can one actually be a son or daughter of God and never be chastised or disciplined?

4. List the different ways that the biblical exercise of discipline has a corrective purpose. In what way do these ways touch upon the urban community and the urban church?

5. According to Scripture, why is discipline both a necessary and important dimension in the Christian walk? What role does one's attitude play in being open to learning from others regarding our own life and the need to grow in our Christian lives?

6. In what way does Matthew 18 suggest that sin in the church be dealt with privately and confidentially? Why is this so important when seeking that all things be done for edification?

7. What is the significance of rejecting every charge which cannot be supported by two or three witnesses? How was this principle applied in the Old Testament?

8. If an offender refuses to listen after being entreated by two or three witnesses, what is to be the response of the church? Why is it important that leaders become involved in the process, once it reaches the level of the entire church treating the offender as an "unbeliever?" Explain.

9. What principles can we learn about discipline from the Apostle Paul and his exhortation of the Corinthian church? What are the cautions we must be aware of whenever we enter into a phase of discipline with others in the body?

10. What are some of the primary benefits of exercising godly spiritual discipline in the body? What are the implications of failing to exercise discipline in the Church?

CONNECTION

Summary of Key Concepts

This lesson focuses upon the Christian leader recognizing his or her responsibility to guide his people through acts of restoration and discipline that lead both to the restoration of the offender, and the edification of his people. The practice of Christian exhortation, while commanded to everyone in the body of Christ, is especially important for the Christian leader (cf. Titus 2.15 - Declare these things; exhort and rebuke with all authority. Let no one disregard you.) The challenge to "exhort and rebuke with all authority" is not a license to cruel control of the body, but loving and wise care of the people of God, who themselves need the benefit that wise and godly counsel and input can provide. Listed below are some of the critical insights in this lesson on the subject of Christian exhortation and discipline.

- The practicing Christian leader is one who challenges the people of God to remain faithful in their discipleship in Jesus Christ by exhorting them for the purpose of edification.

- Godly exhortation is backed up by personal example, given with grace, built on the foundation of Christ and Scripture, and is informed by the wisdom of the Holy Spirit.

- While our position before the Lord (our standing) is secure due to our faith in Christ, our daily walk with him and others (our state) is subject to change and our obedience to God; we must be willing to be taught so our state may line up in our conduct with our high standing in Christ.

- We must avoid the problems associated with poor exhortation, the problems of pride, micro-management, and legalism.

- The Christian leader is charged with guiding the process to discipline a backslidden or estranged member of God's people for the purpose of restoring them to full fellowship.

- Discipline is God's way to protect his people and restore the fallen to full fellowship, and should never be done to shame, condemn, or impose guilt on others.

- Condemnation has no connection to discipline; discipline has to do with restoring a Christian to the Lord and the Church whose *condition* or *state* has momentarily fallen into sin.

- Discipline is given to the Church to prevent sin from occurring, to correct a problem that already exists, to vindicate openly a person accused wrongly of an act, and to instruct the Church in God's standard of holiness.

- Matt. 18 provides a clear outline of the procedure that believers ought to take when confronted with a situation that requires attention (i.e., where sound doctrine must be defended, where Christian holiness must be upheld, and the integrity of Christ demonstrated).

- In exercising spiritual discipline, we must be ever vigilant against our own pride and judgmentalism, the need to verify all accusations in the mouths of two or three witnesses, and the need to exercise pastoral authority in severe cases.

Student Application and Implications

Now is the time for you to discuss with your fellow students your questions about the practice of Christian exhortation. The need to charge and exhort others to follow through on the commands and promises of our Lord ties into and builds upon all the insights of the previous lesson. Every dimension of Christian leadership, including the role of representative before God; one who leads God's people in worship, Word, and sacrament; and incorporates and spiritually parents new members in the body; requires a leader who is unafraid both in word and example to challenge God's people to attain to God's standard.

You must be open, therefore, to consider carefully your call and availability to exhort others to fulfill Christ's high purpose for their lives. We begin, as always, with ourselves and our own lives. In light of these insights, then, what are the particular questions you have considering your call to exhort and exercise authority in the body of Christ? Perhaps some of the questions below may enable you to understand your own calling and role in Christian leadership better.

* Do I understand the truths associated with godly exhortation, and do I today see the importance it has for my own leadership in the home and the church?

* Am I secure enough in my walk with the Lord that I do not take counsel and advice personally? Am I able to distinguish between *my standing before the Lord* and *my state or condition* in my ongoing walk with the Lord and others?

* What is my greatest problem in receiving the good discipline of the Lord and exhortation from others? Am I proud, judgmental, unsubmissive?

* If I asked my spiritual leaders to complete the following sentence, what do I think they would say. "When it comes to receiving instruction and discipline from others, I think that I would have to say that you are _____."

* Have I ever participated in the obedience of a Matthew 18 kind of situation in my life? How did I handle it, in other words, was I obedient to the Lord's instruction here? How did it turn out?

* Do I seek to condemn others or restore and build them up whenever I am involved in teaching, counseling ministry?

* Am I willing to persevere in learning the lessons of godly exhortation, even if it is difficult to master and apply the principles correctly? Explain your answer.

CASE STUDIES

"Only the Pastor Is Able to Handle These Kinds of Things."

In a church where the pastor exercises broad and very godly authority, a major disagreement between two believers in the church has erupted. The nature of the disagreement is severe enough between them to cause major division throughout the church, especially so since both of the members are well-known and exercise key roles in the church. While one of the two want to simply handle the matter privately and confidentially, the other insists that "something of this magnitude" needs to be handled by the pastor. After discussing it several times, they do not seem to be able to resolve their disagreement. The pastor, both a godly man and dear brother, knows nothing of the situation. What would be your counsel to the one in the conflict who desires to go to the pastor right away?

page 270 7

When Bending Over Backwards Goes Too Far

In a lively debate at the women's retreat, a sister who is known in church for her commitment to a holy life, shared her recent frustration with the teaching in church. She said, "In an effort to communicate the love and grace of Christ to the lost, I fear that our church has lost its commitment to live as a holy people of the Lord. I believe that we are called to holiness, and the person who chronically and consistently says that they are absolutely unwilling to obey Christ is not a believer. What about First John? What about Hebrews? What about what our Lord says in the Sermon on the Mount? Are we not making it possible to actually claim to belong to Christ while at the same time refusing to do his will, even on the smallest matters? If we continue this kind of teaching, I believe many people will be deceived into thinking that they belong to the Lord, when in fact, they do not." If you had heard her comments, what would you have said in response to her heartfelt desire for holiness before Christ?

The Lord's Hand of Discipline Is on Her

A dear sister of our congregation over the last ten months fell into immorality with an unchristian man. Hard and unbroken, this dear sister resisted any counsel in trying to be restored from her behavior. Here in the last few weeks, however, she has experienced a number of difficult situations. She was recently laid off from her job, her car was stolen (and returned), and she has not been able to find another job. Her relationship with her unbelieving boyfriend hit the rocks and disintegrated, and her health has been deteriorating (tension migraines). While many are saying that these occurrences can be directly linked to the discipline of the Lord, others feel that such a vision makes God out to be too much of a cruel judge rather than the loving Father he is to us. Which group is right? How would we know whether a number of occurrences are actually the ongoing discipline of the Lord or simply mere coincidence? Should we even try to figure things like this out?

Restatement of the Lesson's Thesis

The practicing Christian leader is one who challenges the people of God to remain faithful in their discipleship in Jesus Christ by exhorting them for the purpose of edification. In her own godly personal example, she exhorts believers with grace, focusing on the person of Christ, anchoring exhortation on the Word of God, informed by the wisdom of the Holy Spirit. While our position before the Lord (our standing) is secure due to our faith in Christ, our daily walk with him and others (our state) is subject to change with our obedience to God. In light of our challenge to live for the Lord, we must be willing to learn from others in order that our state may line up in our conduct with our high standing in Christ. In exercising spiritual discipline, we must be ever vigilant against our own pride and judgmentalism, with the need to verify all accusations in the mouths of two or three witnesses, and the need to exercise pastoral authority in severe cases. The Christian leader is charged with guiding the process to discipline a backsliden or estranged member of God's people for the purpose of restoring them to full fellowship. Discipline is given to the Church to prevent sin from occurring, to correct a problem that already exists, to vindicate openly a person accused wrongly of an act, and to instruct the Church in God's standard of holiness. Our Lord has outlined in Matt. 18 a clear procedure that we must obey when confronted with offense and conflict in the Church.

Resources and Bibliographies

If you are interested in pursuing some of the ideas of *Effective Church Discipline: Exhorting, Rebuking, and Restoring* you might want to give these books a try:

Adams, Jay E. *Sibling Rivalry in the Household of God*. Denver: Accent Books, 1988.

------. *Handbook on Church Discipline*. Grand Rapids: Zondervan, 1986.

Sande, Ken. *The Peacemaker: A Biblical Guide to Resolving Personal Conflict*. Grand Rapids: Baker Books, 2004.

Welch, Ed. *Addictions: A Banquet in the Grave*. Phillipsburg, NJ: P & R Publishing, 2002.

White, John and Ken Blue. *Healing the Wounded*. Downers Grove, IL: InterVarsity Press, 1985.

Ministry Connections

God's intent in your studies is not merely the orderly arrangement of truths in a logical way; God wants our lives to be transformed into the likeness of his Son, our Lord Jesus Christ. The goal of this teaching on godly exhortation is that you might learn to responsibly and lovingly care for those little ones under your charge, as well as those who are growing to maturity in the context of your own Christian community. No leader's toolkit is complete who does not understand and apply the Scripture's teaching on the significance of discipline and restoration. You must constantly be open to the Holy Spirit's prompting and leading as you seek to relate these truths to your own ministry through your church represents the core of this teaching. How God might want you to change or alter your ministry approach based on these truths is largely dependent on your ability to hear what the Holy Spirit is saying to you about where you are, where your pastoral leadership is, where the members of your church are, and what specifically God is calling you to do right now, if anything, about these truths. Plan to spend good time this week meditating on your own fitness to exhort others, both in terms of your own character, as well as your ability to restore others in a godly, pastoral way that builds up all parties involved. Ponder, too, how your ministry and that of your church reflects the holiness of Christ as you seek to pastor those under your care. As you consider your ministry project for this module, you can possibly use it to connect to these truths in a practical way. Seek the face of God for insight, and come back next week ready to share your insights with the other learners in your class.

Counseling and Prayer

God has given promises that guarantee his working in all the areas of our lives as we pray. Prayer is the most essential and direct way to receive grace from our Father, not only in our ability to learn to exhort and encourage others to live the Christian life, but also our sensitivity to the Holy Spirit who will guide us into all truth, including the truth regarding godly spiritual discipline. Perhaps in your discussions and meditations you have been illumined by the Lord to discover areas in your life or others, issues that you must deal with, or just concerns that require the Lord's attention. Do not hesitate to find a partner in prayer who can share the burden and lift up your requests to God. Of course, your instructor is extremely open to walking with you on this, and your church leaders, especially your pastor, may be specially equipped to help you answer any difficult questions arising from your reflection on this study. Be open to God and allow him to lead you as he determines. Ask the Lord for the wisdom and grace you need to become the kind of peacemaker he wants you to be in the midst of his people.

Scripture Memory

Hebrews 12.5-8

Reading Assignment

To prepare for class, please visit *www.tumi.org/books* to find next week's reading assignment, or ask your mentor.

Other Assignments

page 271 📖 *8*

As usual you ought to come with your reading assignment sheet containing your summary of the reading material for the week. Also, you must have selected the text for your exegetical project, and turn in your proposal for your ministry project.

Looking Forward to the Next Lesson

In this last lesson we explored the concept of biblical exhortation. In a world filled with fractured relationships, immoral visions, and ungodly practices, the Church of Jesus Christ is called to be a holy people, and as we edify one another in exhortation, God is glorified. God has given his Spirit-filled leaders the high charge to build up and watch over his people, and exhort them to be faithful to his call. In our next lesson, we will deal with our final dimension of practical Christian leadership in this module, that is, the role of the Christian leader as an effective biblical counselor. We will view the Christian counselor as God's Physician. In the same way a compassionate physician cares for the body of a patient, so a spiritual counselor seeks to care for the soul and life of the person he cares for. We will also explore how we can learn to become better care givers for those encountering the dark side of life, trials, tribulations, and distress.

Capstone Curriculum

Module 11: Practicing Christian Leadership
Reading Completion Sheet

Name _____

Date _____

For each assigned reading, write a brief summary (one or two paragraphs) of the author's main point. (For additional readings, use the back of this sheet.)

Reading 1

Title and Author: _____ Pages _____

Reading 2

Title and Author: _____ Pages _____

Lesson 4

Effective Counseling
Preparing, Caring, and Healing

Lesson Objectives

Welcome in the strong name of Jesus Christ! After your reading, study, discussion, and application of the materials in this lesson, you will be able to:

- Understand the practicing Christian leader as one who provides counsel to the people of God by providing effective spiritual direction through a careful, relevant application of the Word of God.

- Define the connection between Christian leadership and godly counseling.

- Correlate the concept of Christian leadership to that of God's physician of the soul and spirit, i.e., a Christian counselor is God's Physician, that is, in the same way a compassionate physician cares for the body of a patient, so a spiritual counselor seeks to care for the soul and life of the person he cares for.

- Trace the importance biblically of the relationship of the Holy Spirit to that of the godly counselor who uses the Word of God to meet the deepest needs of his people.

- Argue how the Word of God can outfit us for the task of biblical counseling, along with the Holy Spirit and good advice from others.

- Envision the Christian leader as shepherd, as one who provides care for and seeks healing for the flock of God during their times of trial and distress to reestablish them on their faith journey with the Lord and his people.

- Recite the ways in which the Word of God sees tribulation as an inevitable reality for all God's people, and the unique role that pastoral care plays in interceding for them, protecting them, and caring for their specific needs in a responsive way.

- Outline some of the special problems associated with offering care to souls in distress, i.e., the problem of evil, of care giving, of anger against God, and of vengeance and forgiveness.

Becoming a Good Shepherd Devotion

Read John 10.7-18. The Christian leader is one who models his or her ministry based on the life and work of our Lord Jesus Christ. Perhaps one of the most familiar images of Christ's leadership over his people is the analogy of a shepherd and his sheep. In the same way that a shepherd protects, feeds, leads, and cares for the needs of his flock, so our Lord Jesus cares for the lives of his people. The image of God as a shepherd over and for his people is a common testimony in the Scriptures (note: all verses are taken from the English Standard Version):

page 273 2

> Ps. 23.1 - The Lord is my shepherd; I shall not want.

> Ps. 80.1 - Give ear, O Shepherd of Israel, you who lead Joseph like a flock! You who are enthroned upon the cherubim, shine forth.

> Isa. 40.11 - He will tend his flock like a shepherd; he will gather the lambs in his arms; he will carry them in his bosom, and gently lead those that are with young.

> Ezek. 34.12 - As a shepherd seeks out his flock when he is among his sheep that have been scattered, so will I seek out my sheep, and I will rescue them from all places where they have been scattered on a day of clouds and thick darkness.

> Micah 5.4 - And he shall stand and shepherd his flock in the strength of the Lord, in the majesty of the name of the Lord his God. And they shall dwell secure, for now he shall be great to the ends of the earth.

What these and other texts bring out is the intimacy, affection, and courage that a good shepherd has as the one who stands watch over his sheep. This is true of our Lord, only in an infinite manner. In the same way that a good shepherd stands and fights every enemy which would threaten the well-being of the flock, so our Lord fights for us, protects us, sacrificing his own life for us on Calvary. No one has ever shown such a valiant, complete, and satisfying love for his own like our Lord for his people.

Now, what is truly amazing is that this image of our Lord protecting and feeding his flock is the very same image that God gives of a Christian leader in their disposition toward those whom they care for. What a remarkable vision and picture God provides us of Christian leadership–a shepherd who knows each of his sheep, cares for each one with genuine care, who sacrifices and gives and suffers for them. This is the picture of our Lord Jesus, and now, it must become the picture of our lives as we willingly lay down our lives for the sheep. "I am the good shepherd. The good shepherd lays down his life for the sheep." May God give us grace as his leaders to become good shepherds of his sheep.

| Nicene Creed and Prayer | After reciting and/or singing the Nicene Creed (located in the Appendix), pray the following prayer:

> Lord, comfort the sick, the hungry, the lonely and those who are hurt and shut in on themselves, by your presence in their hearts; use us to help them in a practical way. Show us how to set about this and give us strength, tact and compassion. Teach us how to be alongside them, and how to share in their distress deeply in our prayer. Make us open to them and give us courage to suffer with them, and that in so doing we share with you in the suffering of the world for we are your body on earth and you work through us.

~ Michael Hollings and Etta Gullick
Appleton, George, ed. **The Oxford Book of Prayer**.
Oxford; New York: Oxford University Press, 1988. p. 121.

| Quiz | Put away your notes, gather up your thoughts and reflections, and take the quiz for Lesson 3, *Effective Church Discipline: Exhorting, Rebuking, and Restoring*.

| Scripture Memorization Review | Review with a partner, write out and/or recite the text for last class session's assigned memory verse: Hebrews 12.5-8.

| Assignments Due | Turn in your summary of the reading assignment for last week, that is, your brief response and explanation of the main points that the authors were seeking to make in the assigned reading (Reading Completion Sheet).

Family First Is More than a Motto

In an urban church filled with dear saints and great need, the elder board was overrun with the specific problems of many of its members. The elders, all good saints and servant leaders, were willing to do whatever was required to meet the needs of the believers. One elder, though, was concerned about his love for his own family first. A fine brother, he was very concerned about how the needier members of the body sapped the energy of everyone else with their problems. He was of the philosophy that his own family was to come first, and was committed to making them first in every way–time, effort, schedule. Although quite noble in motive, this dear brother had no problem in making other elders shift their schedule if it interfered with his date night with his wife, or family night with the children. It became so difficult to work around his schedule that he attended meetings only infrequently, and finally resigned, without even letting the other elders know of his decision. What was right or wrong in the judgment of this dear brother?

Nothing Me and God Can't Handle

In a time where it is quite fashionable to consult psychologists and psychiatrists as the true physicians of the soul, there are many Christians who reject any kind of therapeutic strategies as limited and ineffective. Many Christians today discredit the over-medicated approaches and responses that many therapists have to much of the depression of our time. Others, having been helped by the counsel and chemical treatment they have received from the psychiatric community, believe that there is nothing wrong with strategies where the truth is told, and real physical problems are addressed and dealt with. What is your opinion about the usefulness and validity of much of the psychiatric therapies today? Is it possible for growing disciples to be helped through difficult times with trained therapists, or should we learn to use in a more effective way the resources available to us in the Church?

Theodicy Questions Loom Large

In the wake of the terrible tragedy that recently hit New Orleans, flooding the city and battering the entire Gulf Coast, theologians, ethicists, and religious scholars are seeking to make sense of it all in light of the notion of a good and loving God. On a recent broadcast, a distinguished panel of priests, professors, and rabbis discussed the origin of the hurricane and its destructive power. One rabbi stated boldly without equivocation that God did not and would not cause this hurricane, that it had nothing to do with him in any way. He said that the hurricane should be understood purely in the sense of the warm gulf waters and the environmental conditions which made such a storm possible. The rabbi gave no sense of any kind that God might have had any part in the hurricane and its force. What is right, wrong, or neutral in the rabbi's interpretation of the destructive force of Hurricane Katrina? How do we distinguish what events can be legitimately called "acts of God" from those which, as the rabbi said, have nothing to do with the sovereign will of Almighty God?

CONTENT **Effective Counseling: Preparing, Caring, and Healing**

Segment 1: Effective Biblical Counseling: The Christian Leader as God's Physician

Rev. Dr. Don L. Davis

Summary of Segment 1

The practicing Christian leader is one who provides counsel to the people of God by providing effective spiritual direction through a careful, relevant application of the Word of God. As the Lord's physician of the spirit, the Christian leader uses the Word of God to diagnose, address, and care for the issues of the hurting and helpless, all in the name of the Lord and for the upbuilding of the body.

Our objective for this segment, *Effective Biblical Counseling: The Christian Leader as God's Physician*, is to enable you to see that:

- The Christian leader provides counsel to the people of God by providing effective spiritual direction through a careful, relevant application of the Word of God.

- A Christian counselor is God's physician, that is, in the same way a compassionate physician cares for the body of a patient, so a spiritual counselor seeks to care for the soul and life of the person he cares for.

- As God's physician of the spirit, the Christian leader applies the Word of God with skill and loving-kindness to the issues and concerns of God's people for their upbuilding and growth.

- The Holy Spirit is needed in every phase of effective Christian and biblical counseling.

- Godly counsel from other experienced and wise leaders is an invaluable asset in leading and caring for others encountering difficulties in their lives.

- Ongoing care and contact in the body of believers is integral to the continued healing and care of those who have undergone difficulties and trials.

- Ultimately, the Christian leader must surrender the people under his or her care to the Lord, who alone is able to sustain the kind of transforming grace needed to ensure their ongoing health and blessing.

I. Defining Effective Biblical Counseling

A. Definition: *the practicing Christian leader is one who provides counsel to the people of God by providing effective spiritual direction through a careful, relevant application of the Word of God.*

1. Provides counsel to the people of God: *the Christian leader is charged with giving biblical counsel and wisdom to the people of God, James 1.5.*

2. Providing effective spiritual direction: *the Christian leader strives to give direction that demonstrates care and provides healing to those needing help.*

3. Through a careful, relevant application of the Word of God: *the Christian leader anchors their helping strategies and methods on the teaching and promises of the Scriptures.*

B. Implications for urban Christian leadership

1. Christian leadership is synonymous with being a godly counselor.

2. God desires his leaders to guide his people into the understanding and execution of his will, which is good, acceptable, and perfect, Rom. 12.1-2.

3. The Word of God offers the best, richest, and clearest understanding of the human condition and the way to freedom, wholeness, and justice in the person of Jesus Christ, 1 Pet. 1.23-35.

Video Segment 1 Outline

The Christian leader as counselor touches upon all of the formal offices of leadership mentioned in the New Testament. The Apostles referred to overseers and deacons, who were appointed from among the saints (cf. Phil. 1.1). The designation for "elders" and "bishops" are used interchangeably (see Titus 1.5, 7), and it was they who pastored the people of God (cf. Acts 20.17, 28). The "deacons" (or "servants") cared more for the materials needs of the saints and were supportive of the elders (see Acts 6).

II. A Model for Effective Counseling: the Christian Leader as God's Physician of the Spirit

A. The "medicine" of the Soul: the Living Word of God

A biblical model of effective counseling

Deut. 8.2-3 - And you shall remember the whole way that the Lord your God has led you these forty years in the wilderness, that he might humble you, testing you to know what was in your heart, whether you would keep his commandments or not. [3] And he humbled you and let you hunger and fed you with manna, which you did not know, nor did your fathers know, that he might make you know that man does not live by bread alone, but man lives by every word that comes from the mouth of the Lord.

2 Tim. 3.15-17 - . . . and how from childhood you have been acquainted with the sacred writings, which are able to make you wise for salvation through faith in Christ Jesus. [16] All Scripture is breathed out by God and profitable for teaching, for reproof, for correction, and for training in righteousness, [17] that the man of God may be competent, equipped for every good work.

1. Humankind does not live by meeting its physical needs alone; *full human life only comes from living by every word* that comes from the mouth of the Lord.

2. The Scriptures are able to handle our fundamental malady: to *make us wise for salvation through faith in Messiah Jesus.*

3. All Scripture is *breathed out by God*: divinely inspired wisdom from God the Holy Spirit.

4. The Scriptures are the medicine of God for spiritual sickness: *uniquely profitable* in outfitting God's person for spiritual counseling.

a. Profitable for *teaching*: laying out for us God's good, acceptable, and perfect will, Rom. 12.1

b. Profitable for *reproof*: helping us know in what way our actions have deviated from God's will

c. Profitable for *correction*: instructing us how to remedy our deviations and transgressions from his will

d. Profitable for *training in righteousness*: building us up so we will respond righteously and obediently in future trials and tests

B. The Christian leader as God's physician is aware of the pain of others: *the need for genuine compassion of the hurting*

1. Love is the greatest commandment, that which fulfills all the will of God, and serves as the foundation of all genuine people helping, Matt. 22.36-40.

2. A leader who lacks compassion for others will not be moved to care properly for them, 1 Cor. 13.1-3.

3. All love that we show others is based on the love that we ourselves have received from the Lord, 1 John 4.7-10.

4. Our application: *take inventory on your own heart*, Ps. 139.23-24.

C. The Christian leader as God's physician seeks to understand the underlying root issues that led to the problem: *the need for the mind of the Holy Spirit*.

1. The Holy Spirit searches the deep things of God, even the very thoughts of God Godself, 1 Cor. 2.10-11.

2. God the Spirit can discern the deepest causes of our behavior and actions, penetrating into the very heart of the issues beyond the surface symptoms.

    a. Rom. 11.33-36

    b. Rom. 8.26-27

3. The Holy Spirit filled our Lord Jesus, and led him in all his doings.

    a. John 3.33-34

    b. Luke 4.1

    c. Mark 1.12

4. The Spirit of God filled the Apostles as they spoke and ministered in Christ's name.

    a. On the day of Pentecost, Acts 2.4

    b. After persecution, Acts 4.31

    c. Stephen, Acts 7.55

    d. Peter before addressing the Sanhedrin, Acts 4.8

5. We can be controlled and filled by the Holy Spirit, John 1.16.

    a. He indwells us.

        (1) John 7.37-39

        (2) Rom. 8.14-18

    b. He has sealed us.

        (1) Eph. 1.13

        (2) 2 Cor. 1.21-22

    c. We can walk under his control and influence, John 16.13.

6. The Holy Spirit supplied early believers with specific guidance depending on the situation and circumstance in which they found themselves.

    a. In sharing the Good News with the lost, Acts 8.29

    b. In leading believers in ministry, Acts 11.11-12

c. In selecting among leaders for mission, Acts 13.2,4

d. In settling issues of dispute in the Church, Acts 15.28

e. In leading all those who are true children of God, Rom. 8.14

7. Our application: ask God for wisdom and discernment, and seek the filling of the Holy Spirit.

   a. Eph. 5.18

   b. Gal. 5.16

D. The Christian leader as God's physician seeks the advice of other godly counselors in order to identify the best approach in treating the dis-ease: *the need for biblical discernment*.

   1. The Scriptures universally declare the importance of counsel in proceeding in all matters and projects.

      a. Prov. 11.14

      b. Prov. 12.15

      c. Prov. 13.10

      d. Prov. 15.22

e. Prov. 19.20

f. Prov. 20.18

g. Eccles. 4.13

2. Analyzing the symptoms of behavior and conduct, while helpful, may ignore the weightier matters which arise from deeper, root causes.

   a. External things do not bring defilement to a person, Mark 7.14-15.

   b. Why defilement comes from within, Mark 7.17-23

   c. Titus 1.15

   d. Heb. 12.15

3. No one is competent on their own to be ministers of the new covenant; only through God's supply and provision are we able to fulfill our ministries, 2 Cor. 3.4-6.

4. Problems we deal with as counselors may have physical or physiological roots which lie at the root of some behavior.

5. No counselor's diagnosis is so fool proof that it deserves to be exempt from being double checked or tested for its accuracy.

a. 1 Thess. 5.21

b. Matt. 7.15-20

c. Acts 17.11

d. Rom. 12.2

e. 1 Cor. 2.14-15

f. Eph. 5.10

6. The wisdom that is from above, from the Lord, is different from the wisdom which is earthly, James 3.13-18.

7. Our application

a. Consult with those experienced in treating others spiritually.

b. Give specific suggestion to apply God's wisdom to the specific condition, James 1.5.

E. The Christian leader as God's physician provides for ongoing care after illness has been treated: *the need for continued contact*.

1. Physicians give ongoing counsel as how to continue in good health ("training in righteousness"), 2 Tim. 3.17.

2. Addressing today's symptoms may bring some relief, but long term solutions bring healing and transformation, 2 Cor. 5.17.

3. God comes not merely to change a situation but to transform a person's entire life (the old man is to be put off and the new man put on).

    a. Rom. 12.2

    b. Eph. 4.22-24

    c. Col. 3.8-10

4. Sound biblical counseling, therefore, wants to address both the immediate problem as well as *the situation which caused the problem in the first place.*

    a. Rom. 13.14

    b. Rom. 8.12-14

    c. Gal. 5.25

    d. Gal. 6.8

5. Our application: instruct not merely for the resolution of a symptom but a sowing to the Spirit, Jude 1.19-21.

F. The Christian leader as God's physician ultimately turns over to the person the privilege and responsibility of their own care: *the need for surrender*.

1. Regardless of how much you care for others, you cannot live their lives for them; everyone will receive in their lives what they have done.

    a. 2 Cor. 5.10

    b. Gal. 6.7-8

    c. Eph. 6.8

    d. Col. 3.24-25

2. Granting others the right to their own decisions corresponds to God's gift of limited freedom to us (e.g., the father in the story of the Prodigal son), Luke 15.11-32.

3. If we do not recognize our limits we can become micro-managers and manipulators of what others do.

    a. We are not the final judges of anyone; only the Lord commends or condemns, 1 Cor. 4.5.

    b. All will receive in this life and the age to the come the fruit of their own decisions, Rom. 2.5-10.

4. Every person must bear their own load, and ultimately reap their own crop for what they decide and do.

   a. Gal. 6.2-5

   b. The Lord alone searches the heart and tests the motives of others to give them what is appropriate, Jer. 17.10.

5. Our application: recognize your limits as a care giver and counselor.

III. Benefits for Providing Others with Counseling in the Church

A. The Word of God does not return void, Isa. 55.8-11.

B. Dramatically less expensive, freely received, freely give, Matt. 10.8

C. The strength of a shared Christian worldview, 1 Cor. 6.4-8

D. A real functioning of the body of Christ, 1 Cor. 12.24-27

Conclusion

» The practicing Christian leader is one who provides counsel to the people of God by providing effective spiritual direction through a careful, relevant application of the Word of God.

» A Christian leader is also a counselor of the Word of God, God's own physician who offers compassionate understanding and instruction aimed at helping the person being cared for find God's loving and good will for their lives.

Segue 1

Student Questions and Response

page 275 📖 3

Please take as much time as you have available to answer these and other questions that the video brought out. In these turbulent times, many Christians and non-Christians alike are prone to ignore any spiritual roots of their problems. The Christian leader, however, is called to a kind of vision that gives rise to a host of therapies that are rooted in the wisdom of the Spirit, based on the Word of God, and designed to help believers get at the root of their problems and issues, from a God-kind of perspective. Understanding this responsibility is critical for your own development as a Christian leader, which this lesson equates (to some degree) with some form of Christian counseling. Take the time to review the concepts of this segment together, seeking to get the heart of the biblical concept of the Christian leader as minister of the Word of God among the people of God.

1. Why is it so important to define Christian counseling in the context of our application of the Word of God to our lives? Is it possible to call a form of counseling "Christian" which does not give central place and authority to the Word of God in its therapeutic strategies? Explain your answer.

2. Discuss the truth value of the claim that "Christian leadership is synonymous with being a godly counselor." In what sense is Christian leadership leading his people into his will, which God describes as good, acceptable, and perfect?

3. In what ways does the model of Christian leader as physician of the spirit resonate with the New Testament's understanding of the leader as counselor?

4. What should the role of the Scriptures be in the therapeutic situation when helping believers come to grips with the roots and shoots of their personal concerns and problems?

5. Why is it absolutely necessary for Christian leaders to be filled with the Holy Spirit if they are going to both represent God's will to his people, as well as walk with others through the situations they are bound to face in a world that produces tribulation and trouble?

6. How should Christian leaders view the counsel and influence of others as they strive to care for the needs of others? How should a Christian leader handle issues of confidentiality and privacy when seeking the counsel of others on an issue, problem, or concern?

7. How important is a believer's place and participation in a local church to their ongoing healing and care, even if the first stages of a problem or issue

are identified and dealt with? What role is the Christian community to play in the ongoing health of the person who is experiencing difficulty and hurt in their lives?

8. What benefits occur to the Christian leader who carefully and lovingly engages in a ministry of counseling in the body of Christ? Why do we always need to find, equip, and release godly counselors into the Church?

Effective Counseling: Preparing, Caring, and Healing

Segment 2: The Practice of Biblical Counseling: The Christian Leader as Shepherd

Rev. Dr. Don L. Davis

The practicing Christian leader is one who provides care for and seeks the healing of his flock during their times of trial and distress to reestablish them on their faith journey with the Lord and his people. As one providing pastoral (shepherding) care for others in the body, the Christian leader models their care for the people of God on the care the Lord gives to his people.

Our objective for this segment, *The Practice of Biblical Counseling: the Christian Leader as Shepherd*, is to enable you to see that:

- The Christian leader is one who provides care for and seeks the healing of his flock during their times of trial and distress to reestablish them on their faith journey with the Lord and his people.

- All believers will inevitably encounter situations, concerns, and problems which represent the dark side of life–trials, tribulations, and distress.

- The Christian leader functions, whether formally or informally, as a shepherd, i.e., one who provides care for and seeks the ongoing protection, feeding, and guidance of the members of the flock.

- Christian shepherding involves four distinct dimensions of spiritual development in the body of Christ: guarding and watching the flock, feeding and nourishing the flock, tending and caring for the flock, and guiding and leading the flock.

Summary of Segment 2

page 275 4

- Spiritual shepherds engage in a host of activities to fulfill these roles, including interceding in prayer for them, remaining constant in times of danger, caring for the specific needs of each one, responding in the Holy Spirit, caring for each concern with wisdom and discernment.

- We must seek God's mind as we minister to those who are encountering special problems, dealing with the problem of evil, the problem of limited resources, the problem of anger towards God, and the problem of wanting vengeance over against forgiveness.

Video Segment 2 Outline

I. **Providing Care for and Seeking the Healing of Souls**

"Pastors" were literally "shepherds" (used for overseers in the Old Testament, e.g., Jer. 23.2–4), elsewhere in the New Testament identified as overseers of local congregations (Acts 20.17, 28; 1 Pet 5.1–2); they were called to shepherd God's people by declaring his message accurately (Jer 23.18–22). "Teachers" were expounders of the Scriptures and of the Jesus tradition; if they functioned like Jewish teachers, they probably offered biblical instruction to the congregation and trained others to expound the Scriptures as well.
~ C. S. Keener. The IVP Bible Background Commentary. (commentary on NT, Eph. 4.11). (electronic ed.). Downers Grove: InterVarsity Press, 1993.

A. Definition: *the practicing Christian leader is one who provides care for and seeks healing of his flock during their times of trial and distress to reestablish them on their faith journey with the Lord and his people.*

1. Provides care for and seeks healing on behalf of his flock: *the Christian leader is charged with the responsibility to pastor (to care for and tend) those for whom he is responsible*, Acts 20.28.

    a. Pay careful attention to their well being.

    b. Tend and guard the flock which the Holy Spirit made you "overseers" (tenders).

    c. The purpose of this delegated oversight is "to care for the Church of God."

    d. This Church belongs to Christ (who purchased it with his own blood).

2. During their times of trial and distress: *the Christian leader is present during the times of trial of those to whom he ministers*, (a hireling, according to Christ, runs at the first sign of trouble, cf. John 10.11-13.

    a. Their times of trial and tribulation

    b. Their times of bereavement and loss

    c. Their times of distress and anxiety

3. To reestablish them on their faith journey with the Lord and his people: *the Christian leader seeks to restore strength to the wounded so they can rejoin our faith journey as citizens of the Kingdom of God*, Phil. 3.20-21.

B. The need for providing care and seeking healing: *the certainty of tribulation in the life of disciples*

1. Tribulation and trials are prophesied and inevitable; they cannot be avoided in this sphere.

    a. John 16.33

    b. Acts 14.22

    c. Rom. 8.36

    d. 2 Tim. 3.12

        e. 1 Thess. 3.4

    2. Their presence is associated with our identification with Jesus and with disciples all over the world.

        a. John 15.19-21

        b. 1 Pet. 4.13-14

        c. 1 Pet. 5.9

    3. Their presence is a means of grace (of receiving God's approval and ministering to others the grace of God).

        a. James 1.2-4

        b. James 1.12

        c. Heb. 10.34

        d. Col. 1.24

        e. 2 Cor. 12.9-10

C. The unique role of Christian Leadership: the Pastoral Role

1. To guard and to watch, Heb. 13.17

2. To feed and to nourish, John 21.15-17

3. To tend and to care for, Acts 20.28

4. To guide and to lead, 1 Pet. 5.2-3

II. Critical Principles in Providing the Care for Souls in Distress

    A. Shepherds intercede for their flocks: the importance of *prayer*.

        1. Bathe all that you do and say in fervent, believing prayer to the Lord, James 5.13-16.

        2. Prayer had great impact in the ministry of the Apostles, effecting healing and deliverance in a variety of situations.

            a. Acts 9.40

            b. Acts 28.8

        3. Jesus promised that those who pray in faith will accomplish great things on behalf of others.

            a. Matt. 7.7

Ours is not the first generation to have non-caring pastors. There still remain bishops and rectors of parishes; and I wish that they would contend for the maintenance of their office. I would willingly grant that they have a pious and excellent office if they would discharge it; but when they desert the churches committed to them, and throwing the care upon others, would still be considered pastors, they just act as if the office of pastor were to do nothing. . . . But it is repugnant to common sense to regard him as a shepherd who has never seen a sheep of his flock.
~ John Calvin. *Institutes of the Christian Religion*. Translation of *Institutio Christianae Religionis*. Originally published: Edinburgh: Calvin Translation Society, 1845-1846. (IV, v, 11). (electronic ed.) Oak Harbor, WA: Logos Research Systems, Inc., 1997.

b. Mark 11.22-24

c. Mark 16.17-18

d. John 14.13

e. John 15.7

4. Paul sought prayer on his behalf and others, and believed this prayer would grant blessing to many, 2 Cor. 1.11.

5. The Apostles prayed constantly for the well-being and growth of the believers under their care, cf. Eph. 1.15-16; cf. Rom. 1.8-9; Phil. 1.3-4; Col. 1.3; 2 Thess. 1.3, etc.

B. Shepherds do not run away from the flock or abandon them in the face of danger: the importance of *presence*.

1. Understand the importance of presence (being present with the one suffering during their situation), John 10.11-15.

2. Learn the art of being an empathic listener ("that skill of placing oneself in another's situation").

    a. Rom. 12.15

    b. 2 Cor. 11.28-29

c. Gal. 6.2

d. Heb. 13.3

e. 1 Pet. 3.8

3. Minister to the real needs of the hurting in their situation, covering those "details" that their stress and fatigue may cause them to ignore or overlook.

   a. Matt. 25.36

   b. 2 Tim. 1.16-18

   c. Phil. 4.14-19

   d. Heb. 13.2-3

   e. Col. 4.18

C. Shepherds care for the specific needs of their flock: the importance of *empathy*.

1. Our greatest challenge in pastoral care is empathy, feeling with them the very pain that they are going through, and bearing them with them.

a. Gal. 6.2

b. 1 Pet. 2.24

2. We are to care for others in the same way that we care for ourselves, Gal. 5.13-14.

3. Shepherding sheep is inconvenient! Whatever the burden that others are carrying, we who are strong are to bear them, and bear with their failings, and not please ourselves.

   a. Rom. 15.1

   b. 1 Cor. 9.22

   c. 1 Cor. 12.22-24

   d. 1 Thess. 5.14

4. We must train our people to know that Jesus Christ feels their pain, and understands their needs, since he shares in our human struggle.

   a. Heb. 2.17-18

   b. Heb. 4.15-5.2

5. We are to endure with them, to feel with them, to be willing to suffer alongside them and bear affliction for their sake.

   a. 2 Tim. 2.10-13

   b. Eph. 3.13

   c. Col. 1.24

D. Shepherds respond sensitively to each situation: the importance of being *Spirit-controlled*.

   1. Do not resist the ministry of the Holy Spirit in your pastoral care; be open to the Spirit's leading and prompting as you share the truth, Eph. 5.18; Acts 7.51.

   2. Being controlled by the Spirit will allow us to approach issues with those who need care in a loving and sympathetic manner, Gal. 5.22-24.

   3. The Spirit may provide you with prophetic utterance or a new word as you care for and counsel others; be ready to speak what the Spirit gives you in that hour.

      a. 1 Tim. 4.14

      b. 2 Tim. 1.6

      c. 1 Thess. 5.19-21

d. Eph. 4.30

4. We are to provide the appropriate input based on a spiritual discernment of the situation, 1 Thess. 5.14.

E. Shepherds care for their flock with wisdom and discernment: the importance of *obedient discernment*.

1. God has promised wisdom to those who seek his mind, to those who ask it from him, James 1.5.

2. We must provide assurance that nothing can separate us from the love of God, Rom. 8.35-37.

3. We may not understand all of God's ways in the midst of a situation, but we know God himself, and know him to be good and righteous in all he does.

4. In some way beyond our understanding, we suffer with Christ in order that we might be glorified with him.

    a. Rom. 8.17-18

    b. Matt. 16.24

    c. John 12.25-26

5. We know that nothing that we face will be beyond the grace and love that our Father provides for us in the midst of that struggle.

   a. 2 Cor. 4.8-12

   b. Rom. 8.35-39

6. Above all, we ought to act on what God reveals, even if it appears to be out of sync with our own judgment or what others think.

   a. God's Word provides light and insight into what we must do in every situation, and we must equip people in the Word of God.

      (1) Ps. 119.130

      (2) Prov. 6.23

      (3) 2 Pet. 1.19

   b. The blessing comes to those who do the Word of God, James 1.22-25

      (1) Ps. 111.10

      (2) Ps. 119.105

   c. Those who hear the teachings of Jesus must act on them to endure trial and tribulation, Matt. 7.24-27.

7. We are neither the Holy Spirit nor the person whom we care for; leave the final decision with the person, who alone can determine what they will reap, Gal. 6.7-10.

a. Each individual reaps what they personally sow.

b. They may sow to the flesh or the Spirit, with respective results.

c. We are not to grow weary in doing good, for the reaping does apply to us, if we do not give up.

III. Special Problems with Providing Care and Seeking Healing for Souls in Distress

A. *The problem of evil*: how do you explain God's will when horrible things happen to good people?

1. In this world we are bound to have tribulation, John 16.33.

2. The devil is defeated, but still roams with evil intent to destroy, 1 Pet. 5.8.

3. As Christ's servants, we are not greater than our Lord; if the world treated him with such disdain and wrong, we can expect the same treatment.

a. John 13.16

b. Matt. 10.24

c. John 15.20

4. Nothing can separate us from God's enduring love and cherishing, Rom. 8.35-37.

B. *The problem of care giving*: what are our limits in actually offering help to others–what can we do to help people during times of distress and trial?

1. Outside of being available, giving time, and placing ourselves and our resources at another's disposal we can do nothing for them.

2. Every person must bear their own load, Gal. 6.4.

3. We are to be found faithful over those things that we can and ought to do, the rest is up to the person and the Lord, 1 Cor. 4.1-2.

4. Recognize the importance of time passing in the healing process.

C. *The problem of anger against God*: what ought to be our reaction toward the Lord in the midst of personal trial and struggle? Anger? Vengeance on those who hurt us? Impatience? Outright blame?

1. Trusting in his provision, Prov. 3.5-6

2. Understanding that he knows, Job 23.8-10

3. Assurance that all things will work together to our best, cf. Rom. 8.28; Rom. 5.3-4

4. Confidence that this trial is momentary and preparing us for the true glory to come

   a. 2 Cor. 4.15-17

   b. 1 Pet. 1.7

D. *The problem of vengeance and forgiveness*: ought we encourage sufferers to seek justice and/or vengeance against those who have done evil against them?

   1. We are to counsel others never to pay evil for evil, for vengeance belongs to the Lord alone, Rom. 12.17-21.

   2. Blessing accompanies those who do not answer or respond in kind.

      a. 1 Pet. 3.9

      b. Luke 6.27-30

   3. In all things, the upside-down ethic of the Kingdom of Jesus Christ must govern all we do, for our citizenship is not here, but in heaven, with Christ.

      a. Phil. 3.20-21

      b. Col. 3.1-3

      c. Luke 12.32-34

Conclusion

» The practicing Christian leader is one who provides care for and seeks healing of his flock during their times of trial and distress to reestablish them on their faith journey with the Lord and his people.

» Although every disciple will experience trials, God has called godly shepherds and undershepherds to guard, tend, feed, and protect his people, and help them grow during times of struggle and stress.

The following questions were designed to help you review the material in the second video segment. Informed by the example given to us by Jesus Christ in his love for his people, the Christian leader is called to guard, tend, feed, and protect the people of God in the body of Christ. Perhaps there is no greater honor in all of life than to serve the Lord in tending and feeding his own dear people, whom he has bought with him Blood. To learn the art of caring for the flock of God must be one of the critical priorities of servant leaders in every level of responsibility and work in the Church of God. From the senior pastor to the lowliest Sunday School teacher, if you are in Christian leadership you share in some dimension in this high calling to care for, feed, and protect God's little lambs. Carefully rehearse the critical concepts in this lesson, and seek to understand these principles in the light of God's call for us to care for and feed his sheep.

Segue 2

Student Questions and Response

1. Is it the responsibility of the senior pastor only to tend and care for sheep in God's flock, or does every Christian leader share in this high honor and duty?

2. Why is shepherding such an important spiritual responsibility for Christians living in urban communities plagued by violence and broken families? Why do communities like this call for the most dedicated shepherds to care for God's people in them?

3. Jesus' comment about the hireling fleeing in the face of danger says something fundamental about those who are valid shepherds. What is the significance of shepherds being willing to face and confront those things which threaten the well-being and livelihood of the sheep?

4. What does Scripture teach about the inevitability of tribulations and trials in the lives of God's people? In what sense has God designed it so no believer has to face those trials alone?

5. Define the four dimensions in which the pastoral role is fulfilled by Christian shepherds. In what sense are all pastors serving as *undershepherds* under the authority and Chief Shepherd oversight of our Lord Jesus himself?

6. Why is consistent prayer so important in a viable and growing shepherding ministry?

7. Is it possible to shepherd sheep in the way God demands and not care for them? Explain your answer.

8. What is the role of the Holy Spirit in the life and ministry of the one called to be a shepherd of the Lord? Why do we need the Spirit's discernment as we seek to care for the people of God? Why must we yield our love up to the Lord for the final outcome in our shepherding activities?

9. How do we help others make sense of the evil in the world, especially when so many terrible things are happening to believers while many unbelievers seem to live immune from similar troubles?

10. Is it okay to be angry at God for some occurrence of evil or difficulty that we face in our lives? Explain your answer.

11. Should we encourage those who have suffered grievous wrong at the hands of others to seek justice and/or vengeance against those who have done evil toward them? At what times should we seek justice for wrongdoing against us?

CONNECTION

Summary of Key Concepts

This lesson builds on the previous lessons in every way, culminating with our responsibility to become the same kind of leaders that our Lord was and is to us as our Chief Shepherd. As men and women called by the Lord to represent his interests and purposes among his people, we are charged with the high honor to provide care for and seek the well-being and healing of the members of God's flock, and to do so especially during times of trial and distress. As this will ultimately be the true test of your love for the Lord (i.e., see his interaction with Peter in John 21), it behooves you to take up the task of Christian leadership with the greatest seriousness and sobriety you can give. Review carefully these principles, and seek to understand their implication in every way for the specific calling the Lord has given you in your life and ministry.

- The Christian leader provides counsel to the people of God by providing effective spiritual direction through a careful, relevant application of the Word of God.

- A Christian counselor is God's physician, that is, in the same way a compassionate physician cares for the body of a patient, so a spiritual counselor seeks to care for the soul and life of the person he cares for.

- As God's physician of the spirit, the Christian leader applies the Word of God with skill and loving-kindness to the issues and concerns of God's people for their upbuilding and growth.

- The Holy Spirit is needed in every phase of effective Christian and biblical counseling, especially in seeking his discernment and wisdom as we lead others into God's will.

- Godly counsel from other experienced and wise leaders is an invaluable asset in leading and caring for those encountering difficulties in their lives.

- Ongoing care and contact in the body of believers is integral to the continued healing and care of those who have undergone difficult and trial.

- Ultimately, the Christian leader must surrender the people under his or her care to the Lord, who alone is able to sustain the kind of transforming grace needed to ensure their ongoing health and blessing.

- The Christian leader is also one charged with the responsibility to provide care for and to seek the healing of God's flock during their times of trial and distress to reestablish them on their faith journey with the Lord and his people.

- All believers will inevitably encounter situations, concerns, and problems which represent the dark side of life–trials, tribulations, and distress.

- The Christian leader functions, whether formally or informally, as a shepherd, i.e., one who provides care for and seeks the ongoing protection, feeding, and guidance of the members of the flock.

- Christian shepherding involves four distinct dimensions of spiritual development in the body of Christ: guarding and watching the flock, feeding and nourishing the flock, tending and caring for the flock, and guiding and leading the flock.

- Spiritual shepherds engage in a host of activities to fulfill these roles, including interceding in prayer for them, remaining constant in times of danger, caring for the specific needs of each one, responding in the Holy Spirit, caring for each concern with wisdom and discernment.

- We must seek God's mind as we minister to those who are encountering special problems, dealing with the problem of evil, the problem of limited resources, the problem of anger towards God, and the problem of wanting vengeance over against forgiveness.

Student Application and Implications

Now is the time for you to discuss with your fellow students your questions about your own fitness and readiness to shepherd (i.e., watch, care for, feed, and protect) the lambs of God. Whether God calls you to become a pastor of a church, or you serve the body in some other way, it is absolutely necessary for you wrestle with the implications of the shepherding ministry for your own ministry. It can be truly said that although God has not called everyone to become the pastor, he has in fact called all of us to be *pastoral* to our brothers and sisters in the flock. As you ponder the implications of this for your life, perhaps some of the questions below might help you form your own, more specific and critical questions.

* Has God called me to become a pastor, to be formally recognized as a undershepherd in the local church? If I am serving in that capacity now, how do I understand the nature of my responsibility to shepherd God's people?

* Would I describe myself as a person of courage, i.e., someone willing to place myself and my own welfare in a position to defend and protect others to whom God has called me?

* Have others ever described me as a pastoral person, that is, as someone who seems to fit the characteristics and dispositions of someone called to shepherd others?

* Scan the list of characteristics of elders and bishops in 1 Timothy 3, Titus 2, and 1 Peter 5. How does my own life stack up with Paul's list of traits that

he associates with those called to provide oversight and leadership in the Church?

* Of all the different qualities of shepherding covered in this lesson, which one most resonates with the kind of person I have become so far in my Christian walk? What trait appears to be furthest from my own experience when I consider how I relate to others in ministry?

* Do I currently have the desire, maturity, and opportunity to pursue the pastoral role in a church in a formal way? What would I need to do to confirm this kind of call in my life, i.e., do my leaders see me as the kind of person who could care for others in this role?

* If God has not called me to become the *pastor* of a church, in what way does he want me to serve other believers in a *pastoral way*? Be specific in your answer.

* Have I settled in my mind the difficulties associated with wresting with the tough questions as they relate to evil, being angry at God for difficulties in my life, or wanting to take vengeance on those who have done me grievous harm? Explain your answer.

No Answers Yet

In a Christian support group, a number of parents who suffered the loss of their children have gathered for many months to help one another cope with their loss, and give support and comfort to one another. Some of the families in the group have only recently lost their little ones, while others are still struggling with the after effects of losing their children many years ago. A surprising number of the Christian parents use language such as "I'm still mad at God for what happened" or "God owes me an explanation for this whole thing." How would you help such dear saints struggling with the idea of such loss cope with their lack of answers regarding the purpose and reasons for their children's deaths?

The Over-committed Pastor

All of us have heard of the pastor who overextends himself in his ministry, and explains it in terms of his love for the Lord. While his family never sees him, or eats with him, or really rests alone with him, he quotes texts on the sacrifice of Christ on behalf of the Church, and sincerely calls himself to the same level of heartfelt servanthood as the Lord who called him. Many ministers are on the brink of divorce and broken homes because they have not been able to truly get a handle on the relationship of the priorities of the Kingdom, the Church, and the home. How would help an "over-committed pastor" get his own house in order, i.e., managing his time and life in sync with the priorities of Scripture?

Called to Be the Pastor, but Not to Pastor

In a developing church that is growing and evangelical, the senior pastor is seeking to redefine the role of the shepherd. While he believes that God has in fact called him to be the senior pastor of the church, he does not feel the obligation to shepherd individual families or persons. He has gathered around himself a dramatically gifted staff of associates to whom he delegates the primary responsibility for shepherding–visiting the sick, counseling others, answering questions, dealing with marriages and funerals, etc. This trend, now commonplace among the growing mega-church movement, seems to be the method-of-choice in churches that isolate their senior pastor as a teacher or public figure, and all shepherding duties are given to others. Is this trend of the Lord or not?

Restatement of the Lesson's Thesis

The Christian leader provides counsel to the people of God by providing effective spiritual direction through a careful, relevant application of the Word of God. A Christian counselor is God's physician, that is, in the same way a compassionate physician cares for the body of a patient, so a spiritual counselor seeks to care for the soul and life of the person he cares for. As God's physician of the spirit, the Christian leader applies the Word of God with skill and loving-kindness to the issues and concerns of God's people for their upbuilding and growth. The Christian leader is also one charged with the responsibility to provide care for and to seek the healing of God's flock during their times of trial and distress to reestablish them on their faith journey with the Lord and his people. All believers will inevitably encounter situations, concerns, and problems which represent the dark side of life - trials, tribulations, and distress. The Christian leader functions, whether formally or informally, as a shepherd, i.e., one who provides care and seeks the ongoing protection, feeding, and guidance for the members of the flock, Christ: guarding and watching the flock, feeding and nourishing the flock, tending and caring for the flock, and guiding and leading the flock. We must seek God's mind as we minister to those who are encountering special problems, dealing with the problem of evil, the problem of limited resources, the problem of anger towards God, and the problem of wanting vengeance over against forgiveness.

Resources and Bibliographies

If you are interested in pursuing some of the ideas of *Effective Counseling: Preparing, Caring, and Healing,* you might want to give these books a try:

> Bonhoeffer, Dietrich. *Life Together*. New York: Harper & Row, 1954.
>
> Fisher, David. *The 21st Century Pastor*. Grand Rapids: Zondervan Publishing House, 1996.
>
> Mitchell, Henry H. *The Recovery of Preaching*. New York: Harper and Row, 1977.
>
> Stott, John R. W. *Between Two Worlds*. Grand Rapids: William B. Eerdmans Publishing Company, 1982.
>
> Wagner, Peter. *Your Spiritual Gifts Can Help Your Church Grow*. Ventura, CA: Regal, 1979.

Ministry Connections

One of the most important elements in our Capstone modules is the ministry project, an opportunity for you to apply the insights of your module in a practicum that you and your mentor agree to. The ramifications of your ability to use what you have learned are enormous. God's desire is for us through the application of the Word of God in our lives to actually grow as Christians and leader. Practice is critical to this process; we are called to grow in grace and in the knowledge of our Lord Jesus Christ (2 Pet. 3.18). The ramifications for your own ministry in this are numerous and rich: think of all the ways that this teaching can influence your devotional life, your prayers, your response to your church, your attitude at work, and on and on and on.

What is critical now is that you review these insights from the module and begin to seriously correlate this teaching with your life, work, and ministry. The ministry project is designed for this, and in the next days you will have the opportunity to share these insights in real-life, actual ministry environments. Pray that God will give you insight into his ways as you share your insights in your projects.

Counseling and Prayer

Our own discussion of the role of the Christian leader as counselor and shepherd makes plain the privilege and responsibility associated with our calling. Hopefully, as you have read the texts, thought about the video teaching, and discussed with your colleagues these important and challenging topics, the Holy Spirit has spoken to your heart. In thinking about your work now, what are the specific issues, persons, situations, or opportunities that you need to lift up to the Lord in prayer? What are you looking for God to do for and in your as a result of your studies in this lesson? What particular issues or people has God laid upon your heart that require focused supplication and prayer for in this lesson? Take the time to ponder this, and receive the necessary support in counsel and prayer for what the Spirit has shown you.

Scripture Memory

No assignment due.

Reading Assignment

No assignment due.

Other Assignments

page 276 📖 5

Your ministry project and your exegetical project should now be outlined, determined, and accepted by your instructor. Make sure that you plan ahead, so you will not be late in turning in your assignments.

Final Exam Notice

The final will be a take home exam, and will include questions taken from the first three quizzes, new questions on material drawn from this lesson, and essay questions which will ask for your short answer responses to key integrating questions. Also, you should plan on reciting or writing out the verses memorized for the course on the exam. When you have completed your exam, please notify your mentor and make certain that they get your copy.

Please note: Your module grade cannot be determined if you do not take the final exam and turn in all outstanding assignments to your mentor (ministry project, exegetical project, and final exam).

According to the grace and love of our God and Savior, he has given us the high privilege to represent his purposes and interests in the midst of his people. We who are called are part of an unbroken chain of servants who have sacrificed, labored, and given their best to glorify the Lord Jesus Christ, our Source and Life. As Christian leaders called to reflect the beauty and character of Christ among his people, we have been called to ministry. This ministry has many facets, including leading the people of God in worship, word, and sacrament, and incorporating and parenting new believers into God's family. As his representatives, we are called to exhort and encourage his people for their edification, and oversee responsible spiritual discipline and restoration of the estranged. In this lesson we learned, too, that the practicing Christian leader is also one who provides counsel to the people of God by providing effective spiritual direction through a careful, relevant application of the Word of God, as well as one who cares for and seeks the well-being and healing of the members of Christ's flock during their times of trial and distress. Among others, these lie at the heart of all credible Christian leadership which is based both on the model of Christ and the example of the Apostles.

What is immediately obvious from this list is the reality that no one in their own strength and effort can attain to such a high status or practice. Only in the power of the One who alone fills us with the presence of Christ can this be done. The Father has sent to us the Holy Spirit in order that we might be filled with his fullness, and thus be able to represent our Lord with honor and excellence. Our sincere desire is that the Holy Spirit will fill you with his presence and a mind to understand the Word of God in order that you might be counted worthy to represent our Lord among his dear people.

May our Savior give you grace and direction as you strive to live out your call to leadership with excellence and honor, all to the glory of God in Christ. Amen!

The Last Word about this Module

Appendices

163	Appendix 1: **The Nicene Creed** *(with Scripture memory passages)*
164	Appendix 2: **We Believe: Confession of the Nicene Creed (8.7.8.7. meter)**
165	Appendix 3: **The Story of God: Our Sacred Roots**
166	Appendix 4: **The Theology of Christus Victor**
167	Appendix 5: **Christus Victor: An Integrated Vision for the Christian Life**
168	Appendix 6: **Old Testament Witness to Christ and His Kingdom**
169	Appendix 7: **Summary Outline of the Scriptures**
171	Appendix 8: **From Before to Beyond Time**
173	Appendix 9: **There Is a River**
174	Appendix 10: **A Schematic for a Theology of the Kingdom and the Church**
175	Appendix 11: **Living in the Already and the Not Yet Kingdom**
176	Appendix 12: **Jesus of Nazareth: The Presence of the Future**
177	Appendix 13: **Traditions**
185	Appendix 14: **33 Blessings in Christ**
189	Appendix 15: **Paul's Partnership Theology**
190	Appendix 16: **Six Kinds of New Testament Ministry for Community**
191	Appendix 17: **Spiritual Gifts Specifically Mentioned in the New Testament**
193	Appendix 18: **Paul's Team Members**
195	Appendix 19: **Nurturing Authentic Christian Leadership**
196	Appendix 20: **The Role of Women in Ministry**
200	Appendix 21: **Discerning the Call: The Profile of a Godly Christian Leader**
201	Appendix 22: **Suffering: The Cost of Discipleship and Servant-Leadership**
202	Appendix 23: **Our Declaration of Dependence: Freedom in Christ**

204	Appendix 24: **You Got to Serve Somebody!**
205	Appendix 25: **Spiritual Service Checklist**
206	Appendix 26: **Lording Over versus Serving Among**
207	Appendix 27: **From Deep Ignorance to Credible Witness**
208	Appendix 28: **Ethics of the New Testament: Living in the Upside-Down Kingdom of God**
209	Appendix 29: **Substitute Centers to a Christ-Centered Vision**
210	Appendix 30: **Dealing with Old Ways**
211	Appendix 31: **Three Contexts of Urban Christian Leadership Development**
212	Appendix 32: **Four Contexts of Urban Christian Leadership Development**
213	Appendix 33: **Investment, Empowerment, and Assessment**
214	Appendix 34: **Representin': Jesus as God's Chosen Representative**
215	Appendix 35: **Delegation and Authority in Christian Leadership**
216	Appendix 36: **Re-presenting Messiah**
217	Appendix 37: **You Can Pay Me Now, or You Can Pay Me Later**
218	Appendix 38: **Hindrances to Christlike Servanthood**
219	Appendix 39: **The Ministry of Praise and Worship**
231	Appendix 40: **The Church Year**
233	Appendix 41: **A Guide to Determining Your Worship Profile**
235	Appendix 42: **Understanding Leadership as Representation**
236	Appendix 43: **Fit to Represent**
237	Appendix 44: **Documenting Your Work**

APPENDIX 1
The Nicene Creed

Memory Verses ⇩

Rev. 4.11 (ESV) *Worthy are you, our Lord and God, to receive glory and honor and power, for you created all things, and by your will they existed and were created.*

John 1.1 (ESV) *In the beginning was the Word, and the Word was with God, and the Word was God.*

1 Cor.15.3-5 (ESV) *For what I received I passed on to you as of first importance: that Christ died for our sins according to the Scriptures, that he was buried, that he was raised on the third day according to the Scriptures, and that he appeared to Peter, and then to the Twelve.*

Rom. 8.11 (ESV) *If the Spirit of him who raised Jesus from the dead dwells in you, he who raised Christ Jesus from the dead will also give life to your mortal bodies through his Spirit who dwells in you.*

1 Pet. 2.9 (ESV) *But you are a chosen race, a royal priesthood, a holy nation, a people for his own possession, that you may proclaim the excellencies of him who called you out of darkness into his marvelous light.*

1 Thess. 4.16-17 (ESV) *For the Lord himself will descend from heaven with a cry of command, with the voice of an archangel, and with the sound of the trumpet of God. And the dead in Christ will rise first. Then we who are alive, who are left, will be caught up together with them in the clouds to meet the Lord in the air, and so we will always be with the Lord.*

We believe in one God,   *(Deut. 6.4-5; Mark 12.29; 1 Cor. 8.6)*
    the Father Almighty,   *(Gen. 17.1; Dan. 4.35; Matt. 6.9; Eph. 4.6; Rev. 1.8)*
    Maker of heaven and earth   *(Gen 1.1; Isa. 40.28; Rev. 10.6)*
    and of all things visible and invisible.   *(Ps. 148; Rom. 11.36; Rev. 4.11)*

We believe in one Lord Jesus Christ, the only Begotten Son of God,
    begotten of the Father before all ages,
    God from God, Light from Light, True God from True God,
    begotten not created,
    of the same essence as the Father,   *(John 1.1-2; 3.18; 8.58; 14.9-10; 20.28; Col. 1.15, 17; Heb. 1.3-6)*
    through whom all things were made.   *(John 1.3; Col. 1.16)*

Who for us men and for our salvation came down from heaven
    and was incarnate by the Holy Spirit and the virgin Mary
    and became human.   *(Matt. 1.20-23; John 1.14; 6.38; Luke 19.10)*
    Who for us too, was crucified under Pontius Pilate,
    suffered, and was buried.   *(Matt. 27.1-2; Mark 15.24-39, 43-47; Acts 13.29; Rom. 5.8; Heb. 2.10; 13.12)*
    The third day he rose again
    according to the Scriptures,   *(Mark 16.5-7; Luke 24.6-8; Acts 1.3; Rom. 6.9; 10.9; 2 Tim. 2.8)*
    ascended into heaven,
    and is seated at the right hand of the Father.   *(Mark 16.19; Eph. 1.19-20)*
    He will come again in glory
    to judge the living and the dead,
    and his Kingdom will have no end.
      (Isa. 9.7; Matt. 24.30; John 5.22; Acts 1.11; 17.31; Rom. 14.9; 2 Cor. 5.10; 2 Tim. 4.1)

We believe in the Holy Spirit, the Lord and life-giver,
    (Gen. 1.1-2; Job 33.4; Ps. 104.30; 139.7-8; Luke 4.18-19; John 3.5-6; Acts 1.1-2; 1 Cor. 2.11; Rev. 3.22)
    who proceeds from the Father and the Son,   *(John 14.16-18, 26; 15.26; 20.22)*
    who together with the Father and Son
    is worshiped and glorified,   *(Isa. 6.3; Matt. 28.19; 2 Cor. 13.14; Rev. 4.8)*
    who spoke by the prophets.   *(Num. 11.29; Mic. 3.8; Acts 2.17-18; 2 Pet. 1.21)*

We believe in one holy, catholic, and apostolic Church.
    (Matt. 16.18; Eph. 5.25-28; 1 Cor. 1.2, 10.17; 1 Tim. 3.15, Rev. 7.9)

We acknowledge one baptism for the forgiveness of sin,   *(Acts 22.16; 1 Pet. 3.21; Eph. 4.4-5)*
    And we look for the resurrection of the dead
    And the life of the age to come.   *(Isa. 11.6-10; Mic. 4.1-7; Luke 18.29-30; Rev. 21.1-5; 21.22-22.5)*

Amen.

APPENDIX 2

We Believe: Confession of the Nicene Creed (8.7.8.7. meter*)

Rev. Dr. Don L. Davis, 2007. All Rights Reserved.

* This song is adapted from the Nicene Creed, and set to 8.7.8.7. meter, meaning it can be sung to tunes of the same meter, such as: *Joyful, Joyful, We Adore Thee; I Will Sing of My Redeemer; What a Friend We Have in Jesus; Come, Thou Long Expected Jesus*

Father God Almighty rules, the Maker of both earth and heav'n.
All things seen and those unseen, by him were made, by him were giv'n!
We believe in Jesus Christ, the Lord, God's one and only Son,
Begotten, not created, too, he and our Father God are one!

Begotten from the Father, same, in essence, as both God and Light;
Through him by God all things were made, in him all things were giv'n life.
Who for us all, for our salvation, did come down from heav'n to earth,
Incarnate by the Spirit's pow'r, and through the Virgin Mary's birth.

Who for us too, was crucified, by Pontius Pilate's rule and hand,
Suffered, and was buried, yet on the third day, he rose again.
According to the Sacred Scriptures all that happ'ned was meant to be.
Ascended high to God's right hand, in heav'n he sits in glory.

Christ will come again in glory to judge all those alive and dead.
His Kingdom rule shall never end, for he will rule and reign as Head.
We worship God, the Holy Spirit, Lord and the Life-giver known;
With Fath'r and Son is glorified, Who by the prophets ever spoke.

And we believe in one true Church, God's holy people for all time,
Cath'lic in its scope and broadness, built on the Apostles' line!
Acknowledging that one baptism, for forgiv'ness of our sin,
And we look for Resurrection, for the dead shall live again.

Looking for unending days, the life of the bright Age to come,
When Christ's Reign shall come to earth, the will of God shall then be done!
Praise to God, and to Christ Jesus, to the Spirit–triune Lord!
We confess the ancient teachings, clinging to God's holy Word!

APPENDIX 3
The Story of God: Our Sacred Roots
Rev. Dr. Don L. Davis

The Alpha and the Omega	Christus Victor	Come, Holy Spirit	Your Word Is Truth	The Great Confession	His Life in Us	Living in the Way	Reborn to Serve
The LORD God is the source, sustainer, and end of all things in the heavens and earth. All things were formed and exist by his will and for his eternal glory, the triune God, Father, Son, and Holy Spirit. Rom. 11.36.							
The Triune God's Unfolding Drama — God's Self-Revelation in Creation, Israel, and Christ				**The Church's Participation in God's Unfolding Drama** — Fidelity to the Apostolic Witness to Christ and His Kingdom			
The Objective Foundation: The Sovereign Love of God — God's Narration of His Saving Work in Christ				**The Subjective Practice: Salvation by Grace through Faith** — The Redeemed's Joyous Response to God's Saving Work in Christ			
The Author of the Story	*The Champion of the Story*	*The Interpreter of the Story*	*The Testimony of the Story*	*The People of the Story*	*Re-enactment of the Story*	*Embodiment of the Story*	*Continuation of the Story*
The Father as Director	Jesus as Lead Actor	The Spirit as Narrator	Scripture as Script	As Saints, Confessors	As Worshipers, Ministers	As Followers, Sojourners	As Servants, Ambassadors
Christian Worldview	Communal Identity	Spiritual Experience	Biblical Authority	Orthodox Theology	Priestly Worship	Congregational Discipleship	Kingdom Witness
Theistic and Trinitarian Vision	Christ-centered Foundation	Spirit-Indwelt and -Filled Community	Canonical and Apostolic Witness	Ancient Creedal Affirmation of Faith	Weekly Gathering in Christian Assembly	Corporate, Ongoing Spiritual Formation	Active Agents of the Reign of God
Sovereign Willing	Messianic Representing	Divine Comforting	Inspired Testifying	Truthful Retelling	Joyful Excelling	Faithful Indwelling	Hopeful Compelling
Creator — True Maker of the Cosmos	Recapitulation — Typos and Fulfillment of the Covenant	Life-Giver — Regeneration and Adoption	Divine Inspiration — God-breathed Word	The Confession of Faith — Union with Christ	Song and Celebration — Historical Recitation	Pastoral Oversight — Shepherding the Flock	Explicit Unity — Love for the Saints
Owner — Sovereign Disposer of Creation	Revealer — Incarnation of the Word	Teacher — Illuminator of the Truth	Sacred History — Historical Record	Baptism into Christ — Communion of Saints	Homilies and Teachings — Prophetic Proclamation	Shared Spirituality — Common Journey through the Spiritual Disciplines	Radical Hospitality — Evidence of God's Kingdom Reign
Ruler — Blessed Controller of All Things	Redeemer — Reconciler of All Things	Helper — Endowment and the Power	Biblical Theology — Divine Commentary	The Rule of Faith — Apostles' Creed and Nicene Creed	The Lord's Supper — Dramatic Re-enactment	Embodiment — Anamnesis and Prolepsis through the Church Year	Extravagant Generosity — Good Works
Covenant Keeper — Faithful Promisor	Restorer — Christ, the Victor over the powers of evil	Guide — Divine Presence and Shekinah	Spiritual Food — Sustenance for the Journey	The Vincentian Canon — Ubiquity, antiquity, universality	Eschatological Foreshadowing — The Already/Not Yet	Effective Discipling — Spiritual Formation in the Believing Assembly	Evangelical Witness — Making Disciples of All People Groups

APPENDIX 4

The Theology of Christus Victor
A Christ-Centered Biblical Motif for Integrating and Renewing the Urban Church

Rev. Dr. Don L. Davis

	The Promised Messiah	The Word Made Flesh	The Son of Man	The Suffering Servant	The Lamb of God	The Victorious Conqueror	The Reigning Lord in Heaven	The Bridegroom and Coming King
Biblical Framework	Israel's hope of Yahweh's anointed who would redeem his people	In the person of Jesus of Nazareth, the Lord has come to the world	As the promised king and divine Son of Man, Jesus reveals the Father's glory and salvation to the world	As Inaugurator of the Kingdom of God, Jesus demonstrates God's reign present through his words, wonders, and works	As both High Priest and Paschal Lamb, Jesus offers himself to God on our behalf as a sacrifice for sin	In his resurrection from the dead and ascension to God's right hand, Jesus is proclaimed as Victor over the power of sin and death	Now reigning at God's right hand till his enemies are made his footstool, Jesus pours out his benefits on his body	Soon the risen and ascended Lord will return to gather his Bride, the Church, and consummate his work
Scripture References	Isa. 9.6-7 Jer. 23.5-6 Isa. 11.1-10	John 1.14-18 Matt. 1.20-23 Phil. 2.6-8	Matt. 2.1-11 Num. 24.17 Luke 1.78-79	Mark 1.14-15 Matt. 12.25-30 Luke 17.20-21	2 Cor. 5.18-21 Isa. 52-53 John 1.29	Eph. 1.16-23 Phil. 2.5-11 Col. 1.15-20	1 Cor. 15.25 Eph. 4.15-16 Acts. 2.32-36	Rom. 14.7-9 Rev. 5.9-13 1 Thess. 4.13-18
Jesus' History	The pre-incarnate, only begotten Son of God in glory	His conception by the Spirit, and birth to Mary	His manifestation to the Magi and to the world	His teaching, exorcisms, miracles, and mighty works among the people	His suffering, crucifixion, death, and burial	His resurrection, with appearances to his witnesses, and his ascension to the Father	The sending of the Holy Spirit and his gifts, and Christ's session in heaven at the Father's right hand	His soon return from heaven to earth as Lord and Christ: the Second Coming
Description	The biblical promise for the seed of Abraham, the prophet like Moses, the son of David	In the Incarnation, God has come to us; Jesus reveals to humankind the Father's glory in fullness	In Jesus, God has shown his salvation to the entire world, including the Gentiles	In Jesus, the promised Kingdom of God has come visibly to earth, demonstrating his binding of Satan and rescinding the Curse	As God's perfect Lamb, Jesus offers himself up to God as a sin offering on behalf of the entire world	In his resurrection and ascension, Jesus destroyed death, disarmed Satan, and rescinded the Curse	Jesus is installed at the Father's right hand as Head of the Church, Firstborn from the dead, and supreme Lord in heaven	As we labor in his harvest field in the world, so we await Christ's return, the fulfillment of his promise
Church Year	Advent	Christmas	Season after Epiphany Baptism and Transfiguration	Lent	Holy Week Passion	Eastertide Easter, Ascension Day, Pentecost	Season after Pentecost Trinity Sunday	Season after Pentecost All Saints Day, Reign of Christ the King
	The Coming of Christ	*The Birth of Christ*	*The Manifestation of Christ*	*The Ministry of Christ*	*The Suffering and Death of Christ*	*The Resurrection and Ascension of Christ*	*The Heavenly Session of Christ*	*The Reign of Christ*
Spiritual Formation	As we await his Coming, let us proclaim and affirm the hope of Christ	O Word made flesh, let us every heart prepare him room to dwell	Divine Son of Man, show the nations your salvation and glory	In the person of Christ, the power of the reign of God has come to earth and to the Church	May those who share the Lord's death be resurrected with him	Let us participate by faith in the victory of Christ over the power of sin, Satan, and death	Come, indwell us, Holy Spirit, and empower us to advance Christ's Kingdom in the world	We live and work in expectation of his soon return, seeking to please him in all things

APPENDIX 5
Christus Victor
An Integrated Vision for the Christian Life
Rev. Dr. Don L. Davis

For the Church
- The Church is the primary extension of Jesus in the world
- Ransomed treasure of the victorious, risen Christ
- *Laos:* The people of God
- God's new creation: presence of the future
- Locus and agent of the Already/Not Yet Kingdom

For Theology and Doctrine
- The authoritative Word of Christ's victory: the Apostolic Tradition: the Holy Scriptures
- Theology as commentary on the grand narrative of God
- *Christus Victor* as core theological framework for meaning in the world
- The Nicene Creed: the Story of God's triumphant grace

For Spirituality
- The Holy Spirit's presence and power in the midst of God's people
- Sharing in the disciplines of the Spirit
- Gatherings, lectionary, liturgy, and our observances in the Church Year
- Living the life of the risen Christ in the rhythm of our ordinary lives

For Gifts
- God's gracious endowments and benefits from *Christus Victor*
- Pastoral offices to the Church
- The Holy Spirit's sovereign dispensing of the gifts
- Stewardship: divine, diverse gifts for the common good

Christus Victor
Destroyer of Evil and Death
Restorer of Creation
Victor o'er Hades and Sin
Crusher of Satan

For Worship
- People of the Resurrection: unending celebration of the people of God
- Remembering, participating in the Christ event in our worship
- Listen and respond to the Word
- Transformed at the Table, the Lord's Supper
- The presence of the Father through the Son in the Spirit

For Evangelism and Mission
- Evangelism as unashamed declaration and demonstration of *Christus Victor* to the world
- The Gospel as Good News of kingdom pledge
- We proclaim God's Kingdom come in the person of Jesus of Nazareth
- The Great Commission: go to all people groups making disciples of Christ and his Kingdom
- Proclaiming Christ as Lord and Messiah

For Justice and Compassion
- The gracious and generous expressions of Jesus through the Church
- The Church displays the very life of the Kingdom
- The Church demonstrates the very life of the Kingdom of heaven right here and now
- Having freely received, we freely give (no sense of merit or pride)
- Justice as tangible evidence of the Kingdom come

APPENDIX 6
Old Testament Witness to Christ and His Kingdom
Rev. Dr. Don L. Davis

Christ Is Seen in the OT's:	Covenant Promise and Fulfillment	Moral Law	Christophanies	Typology	Tabernacle, Festival, and Levitical Priesthood	Messianic Prophecy	Salvation Promises
Passage	Gen. 12.1-3	Matt. 5.17-18	John 1.18	1 Cor. 15.45	Heb. 8.1-6	Mic. 5.2	Isa. 9.6-7
Example	The Promised Seed of the Abrahamic covenant	The Law given on Mount Sinai	Commander of the Lord's army	Jonah and the great fish	Melchizedek, as both High Priest and King	The Lord's Suffering Servant	Righteous Branch of David
Christ As	Seed of the woman	The Prophet of God	God's present Revelation	Antitype of God's drama	Our eternal High Priest	The coming Son of Man	Israel's Redeemer and King
Where Illustrated	Galatians	Matthew	John	Matthew	Hebrews	Luke and Acts	John and Revelation
Exegetical Goal	To see Christ as heart of God's sacred drama	To see Christ as fulfillment of the Law	To see Christ as God's revealer	To see Christ as antitype of divine typos	To see Christ in the Temple *cultus*	To see Christ as true Messiah	To see Christ as coming King
How Seen in the NT	As fulfillment of God's sacred oath	As *telos* of the Law	As full, final, and superior revelation	As substance behind the historical shadows	As reality behind the rules and roles	As the Kingdom made present	As the One who will rule on David's throne
Our Response in Worship	God's veracity and faithfulness	God's perfect righteousness	God's presence among us	God's inspired Scripture	God's ontology: his realm as primary and determinative	God's anointed servant and mediator	God's resolve to restore his kingdom authority
How God Is Vindicated	God does not lie; he's true to his word	Jesus fulfills all righteousness	God's fulness is revealed to us in Jesus of Nazareth	The Spirit spoke by the prophets	The Lord has provided a mediator for humankind	Every jot and tittle written of him will occur	Evil will be put down, creation restored, under his reign

APPENDIX 7
Summary Outline of the Scriptures
Rev. Dr. Don L. Davis

1. GENESIS - Beginnings
   a. Adam
   b. Noah
   c. Abraham
   d. Isaac
   e. Jacob
   f. Joseph

2. EXODUS - Redemption, (out of)
   a. Slavery
   b. Deliverance
   c. Law
   d. Tabernacle

3. LEVITICUS - Worship and Fellowship
   a. Offerings, sacrifices
   b. Priests
   c. Feasts, festivals

4. NUMBERS - Service and Walk
   a. Organized
   b. Wanderings

5. DEUTERONOMY - Obedience
   a. Moses reviews history and law
   b. Civil and social laws
   c. Palestinian Covenant
   d. Moses' blessing and death

6. JOSHUA - Redemption (into)
   a. Conquer the land
   b. Divide up the land
   c. Joshua's farewell

7. JUDGES - God's Deliverance
   a. Disobedience and judgment
   b. Israel's twelve judges
   c. Lawless conditions

8. RUTH - Love
   a. Ruth chooses
   b. Ruth works
   c. Ruth waits
   d. Ruth rewarded

9. 1 SAMUEL - Kings, Priestly Perspective
   a. Eli
   b. Samuel
   c. Saul
   d. David

10. 2 SAMUEL - David
    a. King of Judah
       (9 years - Hebron)
    b. King of all Israel
       (33 years - Jerusalem)

11. 1 KINGS - Solomon's Glory, Kingdom's Decline
    a. Solomon's glory
    b. Kingdom's decline
    c. Elijah the prophet

12. 2 KINGS - Divided Kingdom
    a. Elisha
    b. Israel (N. Kingdom falls)
    c. Judah (S. Kingdom falls)

13. 1 CHRONICLES - David's Temple Arrangements
    a. Genealogies
    b. End of Saul's reign
    c. Reign of David
    d. Temple preparations

14. 2 CHRONICLES - Temple and Worship Abandoned
    a. Solomon
    b. Kings of Judah

15. EZRA - The Minority (Remnant)
    a. First return from exile - Zerubbabel
    b. Second return from exile - Ezra (priest)

16. NEHEMIAH - Rebuilding by Faith
    a. Rebuild walls
    b. Revival
    c. Religious reform

17. ESTHER - Female Savior
    a. Esther
    b. Haman
    c. Mordecai
    d. Deliverance: Feast of Purim

18. JOB - Why the Righteous Suffer
    a. Godly Job
    b. Satan's attack
    c. Four philosophical friends
    d. God lives

19. PSALMS - Prayer and Praise
    a. Prayers of David
    b. Godly suffer; deliverance
    c. God deals with Israel
    d. Suffering of God's people - end with the Lord's reign
    e. The Word of God (Messiah's suffering and glorious return)

20. PROVERBS - Wisdom
    a. Wisdom versus folly
    b. Solomon
    c. Solomon - Hezekiah
    d. Agur
    e. Lemuel

21. ECCLESIASTES - Vanity
    a. Experimentation
    b. Observation
    c. Consideration

22. SONG OF SOLOMON - Love Story

23. ISAIAH - The Justice (Judgment) and Grace (Comfort) of God
    a. Prophecies of punishment
    b. History
    c. Prophecies of blessing

24. JEREMIAH - Judah's Sin Leads to Babylonian Captivity
    a. Jeremiah's call; empowered
    b. Judah condemned; predicted Babylonian captivity
    c. Restoration promised
    d. Prophesied judgment inflicted
    e. Prophesies against Gentiles
    f. Summary of Judah's captivity

25. LAMENTATIONS - Lament over Jerusalem
    a. Affliction of Jerusalem
    b. Destroyed because of sin
    c. The prophet's suffering
    d. Present desolation versus past splendor
    e. Appeal to God for mercy

26. EZEKIEL - Israel's Captivity and Restoration
    a. Judgment on Judah and Jerusalem
    b. Judgment on Gentile nations
    c. Israel restored; Jerusalem's future glory

27. DANIEL - The Time of the Gentiles
    a. History; Nebuchadnezzar, Belshazzar, Daniel
    b. Prophecy

28. HOSEA - Unfaithfulness
    a. Unfaithfulness
    b. Punishment
    c. Restoration

29. JOEL - The Day of the Lord
    a. Locust plague
    b. Events of the future day of the Lord
    c. Order of the future day of the Lord

30. AMOS - God Judges Sin
    a. Neighbors judged
    b. Israel judged
    c. Visions of future judgment
    d. Israel's past judgment blessings

31. OBADIAH - Edom's Destruction
    a. Destruction prophesied
    b. Reasons for destruction
    c. Israel's future blessing

32. JONAH - Gentile Salvation
    a. Jonah disobeys
    b. Other suffer
    c. Jonah punished
    d. Jonah obeys; thousands saved
    e. Jonah displeased, no love for souls

33. MICAH - Israel's Sins, Judgment, and Restoration
    a. Sin and judgment
    b. Grace and future restoration
    c. Appeal and petition

34. NAHUM - Nineveh Condemned
    a. God hates sin
    b. Nineveh's doom prophesied
    c. Reasons for doom

35. HABAKKUK - The Just Shall Live by Faith
    a. Complaint of Judah's unjudged sin
    b. Chaldeans will punish
    c. Complaint of Chaldeans' wickedness
    d. Punishment promised
    e. Prayer for revival; faith in God

36. ZEPHANIAH - Babylonian Invasion Prefigures the Day of the Lord
    a. Judgment on Judah foreshadows the Great Day of the Lord
    b. Judgment on Jerusalem and neighbors foreshadows final judgment of all nations
    c. Israel restored after judgments

37. HAGGAI - Rebuild the Temple
    a. Negligence
    b. Courage
    c. Separation
    d. Judgment

38. ZECHARIAH - Two Comings of Christ
    a. Zechariah's vision
    b. Bethel's question; Jehovah's answer
    c. Nation's downfall and salvation

39. MALACHI - Neglect
    a. The priest's sins
    b. The people's sins
    c. The faithful few

Summary Outline of the Scriptures (continued)

1. MATTHEW - Jesus the King
   a. The Person of the King
   b. The Preparation of the King
   c. The Propaganda of the King
   d. The Program of the King
   e. The Passion of the King
   f. The Power of the King

2. MARK - Jesus the Servant
   a. John introduces the Servant
   b. God the Father identifies the Servant
   c. The temptation initiates the Servant
   d. Work and word of the Servant
   e. Death, burial, resurrection

3. LUKE - Jesus Christ the Perfect Man
   a. Birth and family of the Perfect Man
   b. Testing of the Perfect Man; hometown
   c. Ministry of the Perfect Man
   d. Betrayal, trial, and death of the Perfect Man
   e. Resurrection of the Perfect Man

4. JOHN - Jesus Christ is God
   a. Prologue - the Incarnation
   b. Introduction
   c. Witness of Jesus to his Apostles
   d. Passion - witness to the world
   e. Epilogue

5. ACTS - The Holy Spirit Working in the Church
   a. The Lord Jesus at work by the Holy Spirit through the Apostles at Jerusalem
   b. In Judea and Samaria
   c. To the uttermost parts of the Earth

6. ROMANS - The Righteousness of God
   a. Salutation
   b. Sin and salvation
   c. Sanctification
   d. Struggle
   e. Spirit-filled living
   f. Security of salvation
   g. Segregation
   h. Sacrifice and service
   i. Separation and salutation

7. 1 CORINTHIANS - The Lordship of Christ
   a. Salutation and thanksgiving
   b. Conditions in the Corinthian body
   c. Concerning the Gospel
   d. Concerning collections

8. 2 CORINTHIANS - The Ministry in the Church
   a. The comfort of God
   b. Collection for the poor
   c. Calling of the Apostle Paul

9. GALATIANS - Justification by Faith
   a. Introduction
   b. Personal - Authority of the Apostle and glory of the Gospel
   c. Doctrinal - Justification by faith
   d. Practical - Sanctification by the Holy Spirit
   e. Autographed conclusion and exhortation

10. EPHESIANS - The Church of Jesus Christ
    a. Doctrinal - the heavenly calling of the Church
       A Body
       A Temple
       A Mystery
    b. Practical - The earthly conduct of the Church
       A New Man
       A Bride
       An Army

11. PHILIPPIANS - Joy in the Christian Life
    a. Philosophy for Christian living
    b. Pattern for Christian living
    c. Prize for Christian living
    d. Power for Christian living

12. COLOSSIANS - Christ the Fullness of God
    a. Doctrinal - In Christ believers are made full
    b. Practical - Christ's life poured out in believers, and through them

13. 1 THESSALONIANS - The Second Coming of Christ:
    a. Is an inspiring hope
    b. Is a working hope
    c. Is a purifying hope
    d. Is a comforting hope
    e. Is a rousing, stimulating hope

14. 2 THESSALONIANS - The Second Coming of Christ
    a. Persecution of believers now; judgment of unbelievers hereafter (at coming of Christ)
    b. Program of the world in connection with the coming of Christ
    c. Practical issues associated with the coming of Christ

15. 1 TIMOTHY - Government and Order in the Local Church
    a. The faith of the Church
    b. Public prayer and women's place in the Church
    c. Officers in the Church
    d. Apostasy in the Church
    e. Duties of the officer of the Church

16. 2 TIMOTHY - Loyalty in the Days of Apostasy
    a. Afflictions of the Gospel
    b. Active in service
    c. Apostasy coming; authority of the Scriptures
    d. Allegiance to the Lord

17. TITUS - The Ideal New Testament Church
    a. The Church is an organization
    b. The Church is to teach and preach the Word of God
    c. The Church is to perform good works

18. PHILEMON - Reveal Christ's Love and Teach Brotherly Love
    a. Genial greeting to Philemon and family
    b. Good reputation of Philemon
    c. Gracious plea for Onesimus
    d. Guiltless illustration of Imputation
    e. General and personal requests

19. HEBREWS - The Superiority of Christ
    a. Doctrinal - Christ is better than the Old Testament economy
    b. Practical - Christ brings better benefits and duties

20. JAMES - Ethics of Christianity
    a. Faith tested
    b. Difficulty of controlling the tongue
    c. Warning against worldliness
    d. Admonitions in view of the Lord's coming

21. 1 PETER - Christian Hope in the Time of Persecution and Trial
    a. Suffering and security of believers
    b. Suffering and the Scriptures
    c. Suffering and the sufferings of Christ
    d. Suffering and the Second Coming of Christ

22. 2 PETER - Warning Against False Teachers
    a. Addition of Christian graces gives assurance
    b. Authority of the Scriptures
    c. Apostasy brought in by false testimony
    d. Attitude toward Return of Christ: test for apostasy
    e. Agenda of God in the world
    f. Admonition to believers

23. 1 JOHN - The Family of God
    a. God is Light
    b. God is Love
    c. God is Life

24. 2 JOHN - Warning against Receiving Deceivers
    a. Walk in truth
    b. Love one another
    c. Receive not deceivers
    d. Find joy in fellowship

25. 3 JOHN - Admonition to Receive True Believers
    a. Gaius, brother in the Church
    b. Diotrephes
    c. Demetrius

26. JUDE - Contending for the Faith
    a. Occasion of the epistle
    b. Occurrences of apostasy
    c. Occupation of believers in the days of apostasy

27. REVELATION - The Unveiling of Christ Glorified
    a. The person of Christ in glory
    b. The possession of Jesus Christ - the Church in the World
    c. The program of Jesus Christ - the scene in Heaven
    d. The seven seals
    e. The seven trumpets
    f. Important persons in the last days
    g. The seven vials
    h. The fall of Babylon
    i. The eternal state

APPENDIX 8

From Before to Beyond Time:
The Plan of God and Human History

Adapted from: Suzanne de Dietrich. **God's Unfolding Purpose.** *Philadelphia: Westminster Press, 1976.*

I. Before Time (Eternity Past) 1 Cor. 2.7
  A. The Eternal Triune God
  B. God's Eternal Purpose
  C. The Mystery of Iniquity
  D. The Principalities and Powers

II. Beginning of Time (Creation and Fall) Gen. 1.1
  A. Creative Word
  B. Humanity
  C. Fall
  D. Reign of Death and First Signs of Grace

III. Unfolding of Time (God's Plan Revealed Through Israel) Gal. 3.8
  A. Promise (Patriarchs)
  B. Exodus and Covenant at Sinai
  C. Promised Land
  D. The City, the Temple, and the Throne (Prophet, Priest, and King)
  E. Exile
  F. Remnant

IV. Fullness of Time (Incarnation of the Messiah) Gal. 4.4-5
  A. The King Comes to His Kingdom
  B. The Present Reality of His Reign
  C. The Secret of the Kingdom: the Already and the Not Yet
  D. The Crucified King
  E. The Risen Lord

V. The Last Times (The Descent of the Holy Spirit) Acts 2.16-18
  A. Between the Times: the Church as Foretaste of the Kingdom
  B. The Church as Agent of the Kingdom
  C. The Conflict Between the Kingdoms of Darkness and Light

VI. The Fulfillment of Time (The Second Coming) Matt. 13.40-43
  A. The Return of Christ
  B. Judgment
  C. The Consummation of His Kingdom

VII. Beyond Time (Eternity Future) 1 Cor. 15.24-28
  A. Kingdom Handed Over to God the Father
  B. God as All in All

From Before to Beyond Time
Scriptures for Major Outline Points

I. Before Time (Eternity Past)

1 Cor. 2.7 (ESV) - But we impart a secret and hidden wisdom of God, *which God decreed before the ages* for our glory (cf. Titus 1.2).

II. Beginning of Time (Creation and Fall)

Gen. 1.1 (ESV) - *In the beginning*, God created the heavens and the earth.

III. Unfolding of Time (God's Plan Revealed Through Israel)

Gal. 3.8 (ESV) - And the Scripture, foreseeing that God would justify the Gentiles by faith, *preached the Gospel beforehand to Abraham*, saying, "In you shall all the nations be blessed" (cf. Rom. 9.4-5).

IV. Fullness of Time (The Incarnation of the Messiah)

Gal. 4.4-5 (ESV) - *But when the fullness of time had come*, God sent forth his Son, born of woman, born under the law, to redeem those who were under the law, so that we might receive adoption as sons.

V. The Last Times (The Descent of the Holy Spirit)

Acts 2.16-18 (ESV) - But this is what was uttered through the prophet Joel: "'*And in the last days it shall be*,' God declares, 'that I will pour out my Spirit on all flesh, and your sons and your daughters shall prophesy, and your young men shall see visions, and your old men shall dream dreams; even on my male servants and female servants in those days I will pour out my Spirit, and they shall prophesy.'"

VI. The Fulfillment of Time (The Second Coming)

Matt. 13.40-43 (ESV) - Just as the weeds are gathered and burned with fire, *so will it be at the close of the age*. The Son of Man will send his angels, and they will gather out of his kingdom all causes of sin and all lawbreakers, and throw them into the fiery furnace. In that place there will be weeping and gnashing of teeth. Then the righteous will shine like the sun in the Kingdom of their Father. He who has ears, let him hear.

VII. Beyond Time (Eternity Future)

1 Cor. 15.24-28 (ESV) - Then comes the end, when he delivers the Kingdom to God the Father after destroying every rule and every authority and power. For he must reign until he has put all his enemies under his feet. The last enemy to be destroyed is death. For "God has put all things in subjection under his feet." But when it says, "all things are put in subjection," it is plain that he is excepted who put all things in subjection under him. When all things are subjected to him, then the Son himself will also be subjected to him who put all things in subjection under him, that God may be all in all.

APPENDIX 9
"There Is a River"

Identifying the Streams of a Revitalized Authentic Christian Community in the City[1]

Rev. Dr. Don L. Davis • Psalm 46.4 (ESV) - There is a river whose streams make glad the city of God, the holy habitation of the Most High.

Tributaries of Authentic Historic Biblical Faith			
Recognized Biblical Identity	*Revived Urban Spirituality*	*Reaffirmed Historical Connectivity*	*Refocused Kingdom Authority*
The Church Is **One**	The Church Is **Holy**	The Church Is **Catholic**	The Church Is **Apostolic**
A Call to Biblical Fidelity Recognizing the Scriptures as the anchor and foundation of the Christian faith and practice	A Call to the Freedom, Power, and Fullness of the Holy Spirit Walking in the holiness, power, gifting, and liberty of the Holy Spirit in the body of Christ	A Call to Historic Roots and Continuity Confessing the common historical identity and continuity of authentic Christian faith	A Call to the Apostolic Faith Affirming the apostolic tradition as the authoritative ground of the Christian hope
A Call to Messianic Kingdom Identity Rediscovering the story of the promised Messiah and his Kingdom in Jesus of Nazareth	A Call to Live as Sojourners and Aliens as the People of God Defining authentic Christian discipleship as faithful membership among God's people	A Call to Affirm and Express the Global Communion of Saints Expressing cooperation and collaboration with all other believers, both local and global	A Call to Representative Authority Submitting joyfully to God's gifted servants in the Church as undershepherds of true faith
A Call to Creedal Affinity Embracing the Nicene Creed as the shared rule of faith of historic orthodoxy	A Call to Liturgical, Sacramental, and Catechetical Vitality Experiencing God's presence in the context of the Word, sacrament, and instruction	A Call to Radical Hospitality and Good Works Expressing kingdom love to all, and especially to those of the household of faith	A Call to Prophetic and Holistic Witness Proclaiming Christ and his Kingdom in word and deed to our neighbors and all peoples

---

[1] *This schema is an adaptation and is based on the insights of the **Chicago Call** statement of May 1977, where various leading evangelical scholars and practitioners met to discuss the relationship of modern evangelicalism to the historic Christian faith.*

APPENDIX 10

A Schematic for a Theology of the Kingdom and the Church

The Urban Ministry Institute

The Reign of the One, True, Sovereign, and Triune God, the LORD God, Yahweh, God the Father, Son, and Holy Spirit			
The Father Love - 1 John 4.8 Maker of heaven and earth and of all things visible and invisible	**The Son** Faith - Heb. 12.2 Prophet, Priest, and King		**The Spirit** Hope - Rom. 15.13 Lord of the Church
Creation All that exists through the creative action of God.	**Kingdom** The Reign of God expressed in the rule of his Son Jesus the Messiah.		**Church** The one, holy, apostolic community which functions as a witness to (Acts 28.31) and a foretaste of (Col. 1.12; James 1.18; 1 Pet. 2.9; Rev. 1.6) the Kingdom of God.
The eternal God, sovereign in power, infinite in wisdom, perfect in holiness, and steadfast in love, is the source and goal of all things.	**Rom. 8.18-21 →**	**Freedom** (Slavery) Jesus answered them, "Truly, truly, I say to you, everyone who commits sin is a slave to sin. The slave does not remain in the house forever; the son remains forever. So if the Son sets you free, you will be free indeed." John 8.34-36 (ESV)	*The Church is an Apostolic Community Where the Word is Rightly Preached, Therefore it is a Community of:* **Calling** - For freedom Christ has set us free; stand firm therefore, and do not submit again to a yoke of slavery. - Gal. 5.1 (ESV) (cf. Rom. 8.28-30; 1 Cor. 1.26-31; Eph. 1.18; 2 Thess. 2.13-14; Jude 1.1) **Faith** - "... for unless you believe that I am he you will die in your sins". ... So Jesus said to the Jews who had believed in him, "If you abide in my word, you are truly my disciples, and you will know the truth, and the truth will set you free." - John 8.24b, 31-32 (ESV) (cf. Ps. 119.45; Rom. 1.17; 5.1-2; Eph. 2.8-9; 2 Tim. 1.13-14; Heb. 2.14-15; James 1.25) **Witness** - The Spirit of the Lord is upon me, because he has anointed me to proclaim good news to the poor. He has sent me to proclaim liberty to the captives and recovering of sight to the blind, to set at liberty those who are oppressed, to proclaim the year of the Lord's favor. - Luke 4.18-19 (ESV) (cf. Lev. 25.10; Prov. 31.8; Matt. 4.17; 28.18-20; Mark 13.10; Acts 1.8; 8.4, 12; 13.1-3; 25.20; 28.30-31)
O, the depth of the riches and wisdom and knowledge of God! How unsearchable are his judgments, and how inscrutable his ways! For who has known the mind of the Lord, or who has been his counselor? Or who has ever given a gift to him, that he might be repaid?" For from him and through him and to him are all things. To him be glory forever! Amen! - Rom. 11.33-36 (ESV) (cf. 1 Cor. 15.23-28; Rev.)	**Rev. 21.1-5 →**	**Wholeness** (Sickness) But he was wounded for our transgressions; he was crushed for our iniquities; upon him was the chastisement that brought us peace, and with his stripes we are healed. - Isa. 53.5 (ESV)	*The Church is One Community Where the Sacraments are Rightly Administered, Therefore it is a Community of:* **Worship** - You shall serve the Lord your God, and he will bless your bread and your water, and I will take sickness away from among you. - Exod. 23.25 (ESV) (cf. Ps. 147.1-3; Heb. 12.28; Col. 3.16; Rev. 15.3-4; 19.5) **Covenant** - And the Holy Spirit also bears witness to us; for after the saying, "This is the covenant that I will make with them after those days, declares the Lord: I will put my laws on their hearts, and write them on their minds," then he adds, "I will remember their sins and their lawless deeds no more." - Heb. 10.15-17 (ESV) (cf. Isa. 54.10-17; Ezek. 34.25-31; 37.26-27; Mal. 2.4-5; Luke 22.20; 2 Cor. 3.6; Col. 3.15; Heb. 8.7-13; 12.22-24; 13.20-21) **Presence** - In him you also are being built together into a dwelling place for God by his Spirit. - Eph. 2.22 (ESV) (cf. Exod. 40.34-38; Ezek. 48.35; Matt. 18.18-20)
	Isa. 11.6-9 →	**Justice** (Selfishness) Behold, my servant whom I have chosen, my beloved with whom my soul is well pleased. I will put my Spirit upon him, and he will proclaim justice to the Gentiles. He will not quarrel or cry aloud, nor will anyone hear his voice in the streets; a bruised reed he will not break, and a smoldering wick he will not quench, until he brings justice to victory. - Matt. 12.18-20 (ESV)	*The Church is a Holy Community Where Discipline is Rightly Ordered, Therefore it is a Community of:* **Reconciliation** - For he himself is our peace, who has made us both one and has broken down in his flesh the dividing wall of hostility by abolishing the law of commandments and ordinances, that he might create in himself one new man in place of the two, so making peace, and might reconcile us both to God in one body through the cross, thereby killing the hostility. And he came and preached peace to you who were far off and peace to those who were near. For through him we both have access in one Spirit to the Father. - Eph. 2.14-18 (ESV) (cf. Exod. 23.4-9; Lev. 19.34; Deut. 10.18-19, Ezek. 22.29; Mic. 6.8; 2 Cor. 5.16-21) **Suffering** - Since therefore Christ suffered in the flesh, arm yourselves with the same way of thinking, for whoever has suffered in the flesh has ceased from sin, so as to live for the rest of the time in the flesh no longer for human passions but for the will of God. - 1 Pet. 4.1-2 (ESV) (cf. Luke 6.22; 10.3; Rom. 8.17; 2 Tim. 2.3; 3.12; 1 Pet. 2.20-24; Heb. 5.8; 13.11-14) **Service** - But Jesus called them to him and said, "You know that the rulers of the Gentiles lord it over them, and their great ones exercise authority over them. It shall not be so among you. But whoever would be great among you must be your servant, and whoever would be first among you must be your slave even as the Son of Man came not to be served but to serve, and to give his life as a ransom for many." - Matt. 20.25-28 (ESV) (cf. 1 John 4.16-18; Gal. 2.10)

APPENDIX 11
Living in the Already and the Not Yet Kingdom
Rev. Dr. Don L. Davis

The Spirit: The pledge of the inheritance **(arrabon)**
The Church: The foretaste **(aparche)** of the Kingdom
"In Christ": The rich life **(en Christos)** we share as citizens of the Kingdom

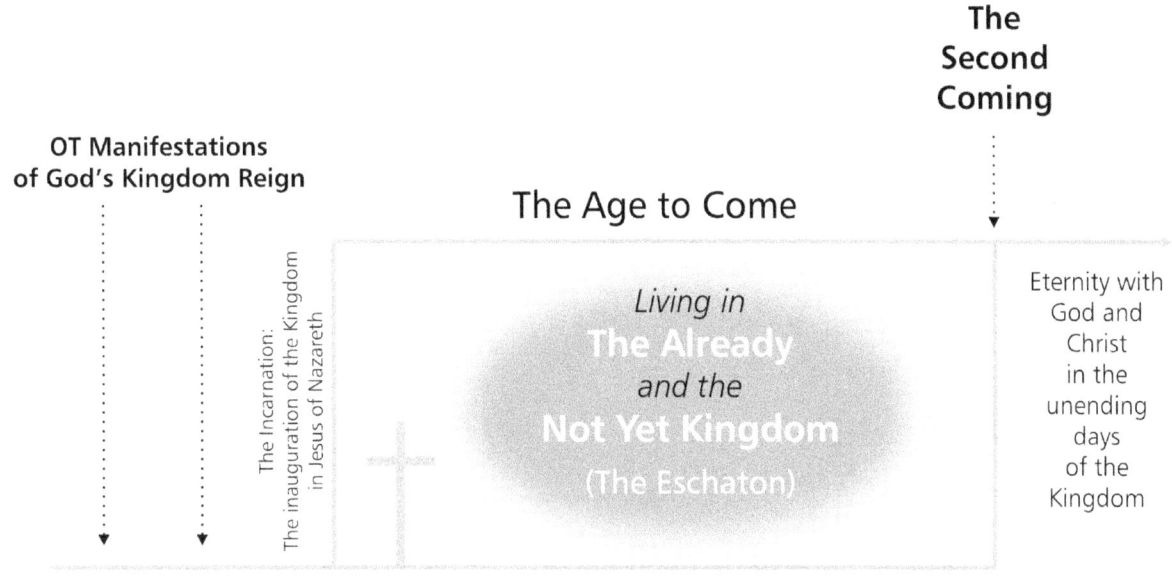

Internal enemy: The flesh (*sarx*) and the sin nature
External enemy: The world (*kosmos*) the systems of greed, lust, and pride
Infernal enemy: The devil (*kakos*) the animating spirit of falsehood and fear

Jewish View of Time

This Present Age   The Age to Come

The Coming of Messiah
The restoration of Israel
The end of Gentile oppression
The return of the earth to Edenic glory
Universal knowledge of the Lord

APPENDIX 12
Jesus of Nazareth: The Presence of the Future
Rev. Dr. Don L. Davis

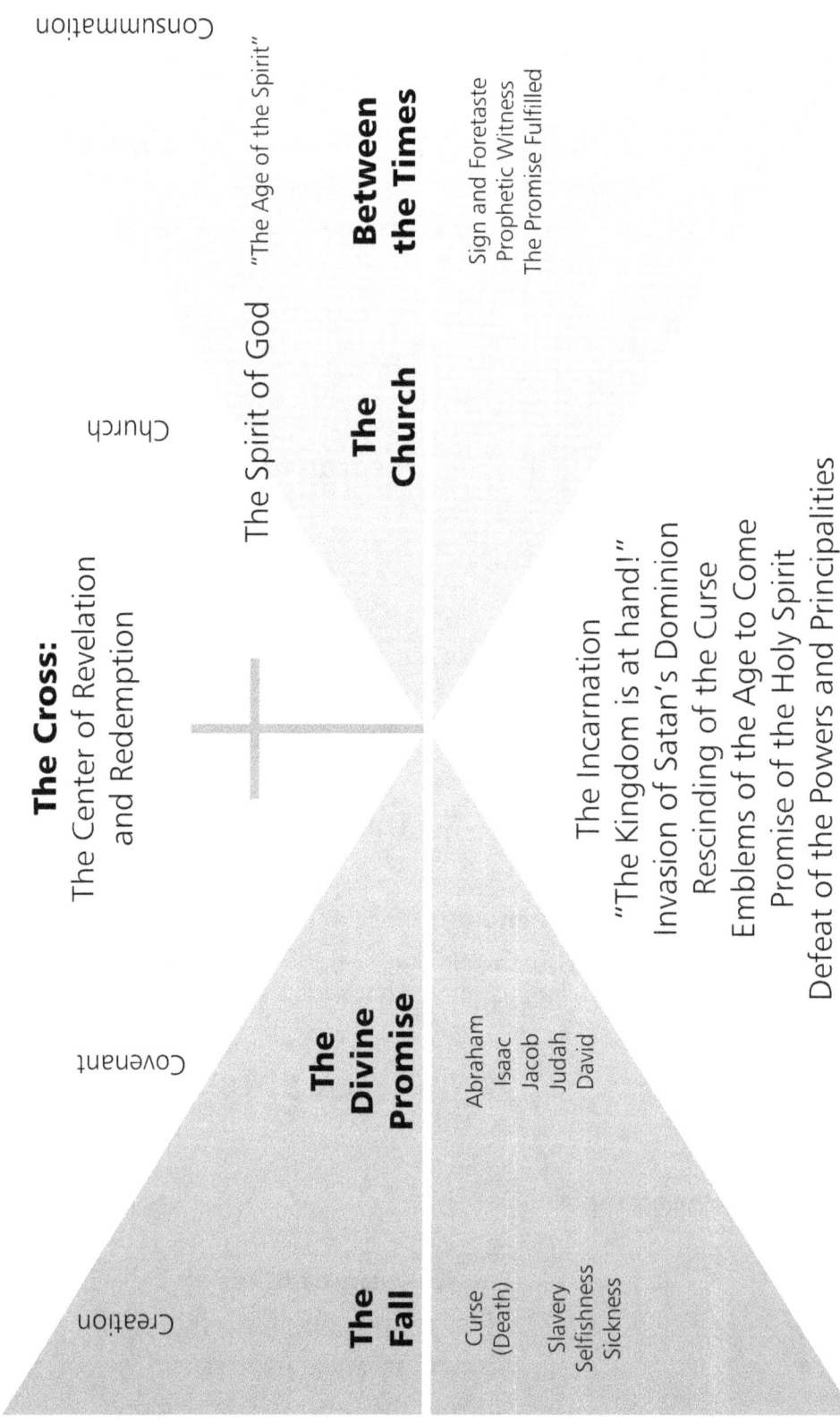

APPENDIX 13

Traditions
(Paradosis)
Dr. Don L. Davis and Rev. Terry G. Cornett

Strong's Definition

Paradosis. Transmission, i.e. (concretely) a precept; specifically, the Jewish traditionary law

Vine's Explanation

denotes "a tradition," and hence, by metonymy, (a) "the teachings of the rabbis," . . . (b) "apostolic teaching," . . . of instructions concerning the gatherings of believers, of Christian doctrine in general . . . of instructions concerning everyday conduct.

1. **The concept of tradition in Scripture is essentially positive.**

   Jer. 6.16 (ESV) - Thus says the Lord: "Stand by the roads, and look, and ask for the ancient paths, where the good way is; and walk in it, and find rest for your souls. But they said, 'We will not walk in it'" (cf. Exod. 3.15; Judg. 2.17; 1 Kings 8.57-58; Ps. 78.1-6).

   2 Chron. 35.25 (ESV) - Jeremiah also uttered a lament for Josiah; and all the singing men and singing women have spoken of Josiah in their laments to this day. They made these a rule in Israel; behold, they are written in the Laments (cf. Gen. 32.32; Judg. 11.38-40).

   Jer. 35.14-19 (ESV) - The command that Jonadab the son of Rechab gave to his sons, to drink no wine, has been kept, and they drink none to this day, for they have obeyed their father's command. I have spoken to you persistently, but you have not listened to me. I have sent to you all my servants the prophets, sending them persistently, saying, 'Turn now every one of you from his evil way, and amend your deeds, and do not go after other gods to serve them, and then you shall dwell in the land that I gave to you and your fathers.' But you did not incline your ear or listen to me. The sons of Jonadab the son of Rechab have kept the command that their father gave them, but this people has not obeyed me. Therefore, thus says the

Traditions (continued)

Lord, the God of hosts, the God of Israel: Behold, I am bringing upon Judah and all the inhabitants of Jerusalem all the disaster that I have pronounced against them, because I have spoken to them and they have not listened, I have called to them and they have not answered." But to the house of the Rechabites Jeremiah said, "Thus says the Lord of hosts, the God of Israel: Because you have obeyed the command of Jonadab your father and kept all his precepts and done all that he commanded you, therefore thus says the Lord of hosts, the God of Israel: Jonadab the son of Rechab shall never lack a man to stand before me."

2. **Godly tradition is a wonderful thing, but not all tradition is godly.**

   Any individual tradition must be judged by its faithfulness to the Word of God and its usefulness in helping people maintain obedience to Christ's example and teaching.[1] In the Gospels, Jesus frequently rebukes the Pharisees for establishing traditions that nullify rather than uphold God's commands.

   Mark 7.8 (ESV) - You leave the commandment of God and hold to the tradition of men" (cf. Matt. 15.2-6; Mark 7.13).

   Col. 2.8 (ESV) - See to it that no one takes you captive by philosophy and empty deceit, according to human tradition, according to the elemental spirits of the world, and not according to Christ.

3. **Without the fullness of the Holy Spirit, and the constant edification provided to us by the Word of God, tradition will inevitably lead to dead formalism.**

   Those who are spiritual are filled with the Holy Spirit, whose power and leading alone provides individuals and congregations a sense of freedom and vitality in all they practice and believe. However, when the practices and teachings of any given tradition are no longer infused by the power of the Holy Spirit and the Word of God, tradition loses its effectiveness, and may actually become counterproductive to our discipleship in Jesus Christ.

   Eph. 5.18 (ESV) - And do not get drunk with wine, for that is debauchery, but be filled with the Spirit.

---

[1] "All Protestants insist that these traditions must ever be tested against Scripture and can never possess an independent apostolic authority over or alongside of Scripture." (J. Van Engen, "Tradition," *Evangelical Dictionary of Theology*, Walter Elwell, Gen. ed.) We would add that Scripture is itself the "authoritative tradition" by which all other traditions are judged. See "Appendix A, The Founders of Tradition: Three Levels of Christian Authority," p. 4.

Traditions (continued)

Gal. 5.22-25 (ESV) - But the fruit of the Spirit is love, joy, peace, patience, kindness, goodness, faithfulness, gentleness, self-control; against such things there is no law. And those who belong to Christ Jesus have crucified the flesh with its passions and desires. If we live by the Spirit, let us also walk by the Spirit.

2 Cor. 3.5-6 (ESV) - Not that we are sufficient in ourselves to claim anything as coming from us, but our sufficiency is from God, who has made us competent to be ministers of a new covenant, not of the letter but of the Spirit. For the letter kills, but the Spirit gives life.

4. **Fidelity to the Apostolic Tradition (teaching and modeling) is the essence of Christian maturity.**

    2 Tim. 2.2 (ESV) - and what you have heard from me in the presence of many witnesses entrust to faithful men who will be able to teach others also.

    1 Cor. 11.1-2 (ESV) - Be imitators of me, as I am of Christ. Now I commend you because you remember me in everything and maintain the traditions even as I delivered them to you (cf. 1 Cor. 4.16-17, 2 Tim. 1.13-14, 2 Thess. 3.7-9, Phil. 4.9).

    1 Cor. 15.3-8 (ESV) - For I delivered to you as of first importance what I also received: that Christ died for our sins in accordance with the Scriptures, that he was buried, that he was raised on the third day in accordance with the Scriptures, and that he appeared to Cephas, then to the twelve. Then he appeared to more than five hundred brothers at one time, most of whom are still alive, though some have fallen asleep. Then he appeared to James, then to all the apostles. Last of all, as to one untimely born, he appeared also to me.

5. **The Apostle Paul often includes an appeal to the tradition for support in doctrinal practices.**

    1 Cor. 11.16 (ESV) - If anyone is inclined to be contentious, we have no such practice, nor do the churches of God (cf. 1 Cor. 1.2, 7.17, 15.3).

Traditions (continued)

> 1 Cor. 14.33-34 (ESV) - For God is not a God of confusion but of peace. As in all the churches of the saints, the women should keep silent in the churches. For they are not permitted to speak, but should be in submission, as the Law also says.

6. When a congregation uses received tradition to remain faithful to the "Word of God," they are commended by the apostles.

> 1 Cor. 11.2 (ESV) - Now I commend you because you remember me in everything and maintain the traditions even as I delivered them to you.

> 2 Thess. 2.15 (ESV) - So then, brothers, stand firm and hold to the traditions that you were taught by us, either by our spoken word or by our letter.

> 2 Thess. 3.6 (ESV) - Now we command you, brothers, in the name of our Lord Jesus Christ, that you keep away from any brother who is walking in idleness and not in accord with the tradition that you received from us.

Appendix A

The Founders of Tradition: Three Levels of Christian Authority

Exod. 3.15 (ESV) - God also said to Moses, "Say this to the people of Israel, 'The Lord, the God of your fathers, the God of Abraham, the God of Isaac, and the God of Jacob, has sent me to you.' This is my name forever, and thus I am to be remembered throughout all generations."

1. The Authoritative Tradition: the Apostles and the Prophets (The Holy Scriptures)

Eph. 2.19-21 (ESV) - So then you are no longer strangers and aliens, but you are fellow citizens with the saints and members of the household of God, built on the foundation of the apostles and prophets, Christ Jesus himself being the cornerstone, in whom the whole structure, being joined together, grows into a holy temple in the Lord.

~ The Apostle Paul

Traditions (continued)

Those who gave eyewitness testimony to the revelation and saving acts of Yahweh, first in Israel, and ultimately in Jesus Christ the Messiah. This testimony is binding for all people, at all times, and in all places. It is the authoritative tradition by which all subsequent tradition is judged.

2. The Great Tradition: the Ecumenical Councils and their Creeds[2]

[2] See Appendix B, "Defining the Great Tradition."

What has been believed everywhere, always, and by all.

~ Vincent of Lerins

The Great Tradition is the core dogma (doctrine) of the Church. It represents the teaching of the Church as it has understood the Authoritative Tradition (the Holy Scriptures), and summarizes those essential truths that Christians of all ages have confessed and believed. To these doctrinal statements the whole Church, (Catholic, Orthodox, and Protestant)[3] gives its assent. The worship and theology of the Church reflects this core dogma, which finds its summation and fulfillment in the person and work of Jesus Christ. From earliest times, Christians have expressed their devotion to God in its Church calendar, a yearly pattern of worship which summarizes and reenacts the events of Christ's life.

[3] Even the more radical wing of the Protestant reformation (Anabaptists) who were the most reluctant to embrace the creeds as dogmatic instruments of faith, did not disagree with the essential content found in them. "They assumed the Apostolic Creed–they called it 'The Faith,' Der Glaube, as did most people." See John Howard Yoder, Preface to Theology: Christology and Theological Method. Grand Rapids: Brazos Press, 2002. pp. 222-223.

3. Specific Church Traditions: the Founders of Denominations and Orders

The Presbyterian Church (U.S.A.) has approximately 2.5 million members, 11,200 congregations and 21,000 ordained ministers. Presbyterians trace their history to the 16th century and the Protestant Reformation. Our heritage, and much of what we believe, began with the French lawyer John Calvin (1509-1564), whose writings crystallized much of the Reformed thinking that came before him.

~ The Presbyterian Church, U.S.A.

Christians have expressed their faith in Jesus Christ in various ways through specific movements and traditions which embrace and express the Authoritative Tradition and the Great Tradition in unique ways. For instance,

Traditions (continued)

Catholic movements have arisen around people like Benedict, Francis, or Dominic, and among Protestants people like Martin Luther, John Calvin, Ulrich Zwingli, and John Wesley. Women have founded vital movements of Christian faith (e.g., Aimee Semple McPherson of the Foursquare Church), as well as minorities (e.g., Richard Allen of the African Methodist Episcopal Church or Charles H. Mason of the Church of God in Christ, who also helped to spawn the Assemblies of God), all which attempted to express the Authoritative Tradition and the Great Tradition in a specific way consistent with their time and expression.

The emergence of vital, dynamic movements of the faith at different times and among different peoples reveal the fresh working of the Holy Spirit throughout history. Thus, inside Catholicism, new communities have arisen such as the Benedictines, Franciscans, and Dominicans; and outside Catholicism, new denominations have emerged (Lutherans, Presbyterians, Methodists, Church of God in Christ, etc.). Each of these specific traditions have "founders," key leaders whose energy and vision helped to establish a unique expression of Christian faith and practice. Of course, to be legitimate, these movements must adhere to and faithfully express both the Authoritative Tradition and the Great Tradition. Members of these specific traditions embrace their own unique practices and patterns of spirituality, but these unique features are not necessarily binding on the Church at large. They represent the unique expressions of that community's understanding of and faithfulness to the Authoritative and Great Traditions.

Specific traditions seek to express and live out this faithfulness to the Authoritative and Great Traditions through their worship, teaching, and service. They seek to make the Gospel clear within new cultures or sub-cultures, speaking and modeling the hope of Christ into new situations shaped by their own set of questions posed in light of their own unique circumstances. These movements, therefore, seek to contextualize the Authoritative tradition in a way that faithfully and effectively leads new groups of people to faith in Jesus Christ, and incorporates those who believe into the community of faith that obeys his teachings and gives witness of him to others.

Traditions (continued)

Appendix B

Defining the "Great Tradition"

The Great Tradition (sometimes called the "classical Christian tradition") is defined by Robert E. Webber as follows:

> *[It is] the broad outline of Christian belief and practice developed from the Scriptures between the time of Christ and the middle of the fifth century*
>
> ~ Webber. **The Majestic Tapestry**.
> Nashville: Thomas Nelson Publishers, 1986. p. 10.

This tradition is widely affirmed by Protestant theologians both ancient and modern.

> *Thus those ancient Councils of Nicea, Constantinople, the first of Ephesus, Chalcedon, and the like, which were held for refuting errors, we willingly embrace, and reverence as sacred, in so far as relates to doctrines of faith, for they contain nothing but the pure and genuine interpretation of Scripture, which the holy Fathers with spiritual prudence adopted to crush the enemies of religion who had then arisen.*
>
> ~ John Calvin. **Institutes**. IV, ix. 8.

> *. . . most of what is enduringly valuable in contemporary biblical exegesis was discovered by the fifth century.*
>
> ~ Thomas C. Oden. **The Word of Life**.
> San Francisco: HarperSanFrancisco, 1989. p. xi

> *The first four Councils are by far the most important, as they settled the orthodox faith on the Trinity and the Incarnation.*
>
> ~ Philip Schaff. **The Creeds of Christendom**. Vol. 1.
> Grand Rapids: Baker Book House, 1996. p. 44.

Our reference to the Ecumenical Councils and Creeds is, therefore, focused on those Councils which retain a widespread agreement in the Church among Catholics, Orthodox, and Protestants. While Catholic and Orthodox share common agreement on the first seven councils, Protestants tend to affirm and use primarily the first four. Therefore, those councils which continue to be shared by the whole Church are completed with the Council of Chalcedon in 451.

Traditions (continued)

It is worth noting that each of these four Ecumenical Councils took place in a pre-European cultural context and that none of them were held in Europe. They were councils of the whole Church and they reflected a time in which Christianity was primarily an eastern religion in it's geographic core. By modern reckoning, their participants were African, Asian, and European. The councils reflected a church that ". . . has roots in cultures far distant from Europe and preceded the development of modern European identity, and [of which] some of its greatest minds have been African" (Oden, *The Living God*, San Francisco: HarperSanFrancisco, 1987, p. 9).

Perhaps the most important achievement of the Councils was the creation of what is now commonly called the Nicene Creed. It serves as a summary statement of the Christian faith that can be agreed on by Catholic, Orthodox, and Protestant Christians.

The first four Ecumenical Councils are summarized in the following chart:

Name/Date/Location	Purpose
First Ecumenical Council 325 A.D. Nicea, Asia Minor	Defending against: *Arianism* Question answered: *Was Jesus God?* Action: *Developed the initial form of the Nicene Creed to serve as a summary of the Christian faith*
Second Ecumenical Council 381 A.D. Constantinople, Asia Minor	Defending against: *Macedonianism* Question answered: *Is the Holy Spirit a personal and equal part of the Godhead?* Action: *Completed the Nicene Creed by expanding the article dealing with the Holy Spirit*
Third Ecumenical Council 431 A.D. Ephesus, Asia Minor	Defending against: *Nestorianism* Question answered: *Is Jesus Christ both God and man in one person?* Action: *Defined Christ as the Incarnate Word of God and affirmed his mother Mary as* **theotokos** *(God-bearer)*
Fourth Ecumenical Council 451 A.D. Chalcedon, Asia Minor	Defending against: *Monophysitism* Question answered: *How can Jesus be both God and man?* Action: *Explained the relationship between Jesus' two natures (human and Divine)*

APPENDIX 14
33 Blessings in Christ
Rev. Dr. Don L. Davis

Did you know that 33 things happened to you at the moment you became a believer in Jesus Christ? Lewis Sperry Chafer, the first president of Dallas Theological Seminary, listed these benefits of salvation in his *Systematic Theology, Volume III* (pp. 234-266). These points, along with brief explanations, give the born-again Christian a better understanding of the work of grace accomplished in his life as well as a greater appreciation of his new life.

1. In the eternal plan of God, the believer is:

    a. *Foreknown* - Acts 2.23; 1 Pet. 1.2, 20. God knew from all eternity every step in the entire program of the universe.

    b. *Predestined* - Rom. 8.29-30. A believer's destiny has been appointed through foreknowledge to the unending realization of all God's riches of grace.

    c. *Elected* - Rom. 8.38; Col. 3.12. He/she is chosen of God in the present age and will manifest the grace of God in future ages.

    d. *Chosen* - Eph. 1.4. God has separated unto himself his elect who are both foreknown and predestined.

    e. *Called* - 1 Thess. 5.23-24. God invites man to enjoy the benefits of his redemptive purposes. This term may include those whom God has selected for salvation, but who are still in their unregenerate state.

2. A believer has been *redeemed* - Rom. 3.24. The price required to set him/her free from sin has been paid.

3. A believer has been *reconciled* - 2 Cor. 5.18-21; Rom. 5.10. He/she is both restored to fellowship by God and restored to fellowship with God.

4. A believer is related to God through *propitiation* - Rom. 3.24-26. He/she has been set free from judgment by God's satisfaction with his Son's death for sinners.

5. A believer has been *forgiven* all trespasses - Eph. 1.7. All his/her sins are taken care of - past, present, and future.

6. A believer is vitally *conjoined to Christ* for the judgment of the old man "unto a new walk" - Rom. 6.1-10. He/she is brought into a union with Christ.

33 Blessings in Christ (continued)

7. A believer is *"free from the law"* - Rom. 7.2-6. He/she is both dead to its condemnation, and delivered from its jurisdiction.

8. A believer has been made a *child of God* - Gal. 3.26. He/she is born anew by the regenerating power of the Holy Spirit into a relationship in which God the First Person becomes a legitimate Father and the saved one becomes a legitimate child with every right and title - an heir of God and a joint heir with Jesus Christ.

9. A believer has been *adopted as an adult child* into the Father's household - Rom. 8.15, 23.

10. A believer has been *made acceptable to God* by Jesus Christ - Eph. 1.6. He/she is made *righteous* (Rom. 3.22), *sanctified* (set apart) positionally (1 Cor. 1.30, 6.11); *perfected forever in his/her standing and position* (Heb. 10.14), and *made acceptable* in the Beloved (Col. 1.12).

11. A believer has been *justified* - Rom. 5.1. He/she has been declared righteous by God's decree.

12. A believer is *"made right"* - Eph. 2.13. A close relation is set up and exists between God and the believer.

13. A believer has been *delivered from the power of darkness* - Col. 1.13; 2.13. A Christian has been delivered from Satan and his evil spirits. Yet the disciple must continue to wage a warfare against these powers.

14. A believer has been *translated into the Kingdom of God* - Col. 1.13. The Christian has been transferred from Satan's kingdom to Christ's Kingdom.

15. A believer is *planted* on the Rock, Jesus Christ - 1 Cor. 3.9-15. Christ is the foundation on which the believer stands and on which he/she builds his/her Christian life.

16. A believer is *a gift from God to Jesus Christ* - John 17.6, 11, 12, 20. He/she is the Father's love gift to Jesus Christ.

17. A believer is *circumcised in Christ* - Col. 2.11. He/she has been delivered from the power of the old sin nature.

18. A believer has been made a *partaker of the Holy and Royal Priesthood* - 1 Pet. 2.5, 9. He/she is a priest because of his/her relation to Christ, the High Priest, and will reign on earth with Christ.

33 Blessings in Christ (continued)

19. A believer is part of a *chosen generation, a holy nation and a peculiar people* - 1 Pet. 2.9. This is the company of believers in this age.

20. A believer is a *heavenly citizen* - Phil. 3.20. Therefore he/she is called a stranger as far as his/her life on earth is concerned (1 Pet. 2.13), and will enjoy his/her true home in heaven forever.

21. A believer is in *the family and household of God* - Eph. 2.1, 9. He/she is part of God's "family" which is composed only of true believers.

22. A believer is in *the fellowship of the saints*. John 17.11, 21-23. He/she can be a part of the fellowship of believers with one another.

23. A believer is in *a heavenly association* - Col. 1.27; 3.1; 2 Cor. 6.1; Col. 1.24; John 14.12-14; Eph. 5.25-27; Titus 2.13. He/she is *a partner with Christ* now in life, position, service, suffering, prayer, betrothal as a bride to Christ, and expectation of the coming again of Christ.

24. A believer has *access to God* - Eph. 2.18. He/she has access to God's grace which enables him/her to grow spiritually, and he/she has unhindered approach to the Father (Heb. 4.16).

25. A believer is within *the "much more" care of God* - Rom. 5.8-10. He/she is an object of God's love (John 3.16), God's grace (Eph. 2.7-9), God's power (Eph. 1.19), God's faithfulness (Phil. 1.6), God's peace (Rom. 5.1), God's consolation (2 Thess. 2.16-17), and God's intercession (Rom. 8.26).

26. A believer is *God's inheritance* - Eph. 1.18. He/she is given to Christ as a gift from the Father.

27. A believer *has the inheritance of God himself* and all that God bestows - 1 Pet. 1.4.

28. A believer has *light in the Lord* - 2 Cor. 4.6. He/she not only has this light, but is commanded to walk in the light.

29. A believer is *vitally united to the Father, the Son and the Holy Spirit* - 1 Thess. 1.1; Eph. 4.6; Rom. 8.1; John 14.20; Rom. 8.9; 1 Cor. 2.12.

30. A believer is blessed with *the earnest or firstfruits of the Spirit* - Eph. 1.14; 8.23. He/she is born of the Spirit (John 3.6), and baptized by the Spirit (1 Cor. 12.13), which is a work of the Holy Spirit by which the believer is joined to Christ's body and comes to be "in Christ," and therefore is a partaker of all that Christ is.

33 Blessings in Christ (continued)

The disciple is also indwelt by the Spirit (Rom. 8.9), sealed by the Spirit (2 Cor. 1.22), making him/her eternally secure, and filled with the Spirit (Eph. 5.18) whose ministry releases his Power and effectiveness in the heart in which he dwells.

31. A believer is *glorified* - Rom. 8.18. He/she will be a partaker of the infinite story of the Godhead.

32. A believer is *complete in God* - Col. 2.9, 10. He/she partakes of all that Christ is.

33. A believer *possesses every spiritual blessing* - Eph. 1.3. All the riches tabulated in the other 32 points made before are to be included in this sweeping term, "all spiritual blessings."

Come Thou Fount of every blessing
Tune my heart to sing Thy grace;
Streams of mercy, never ceasing,
Call for songs of loudest praise
Teach me some melodious sonnet,
Sung by flaming tongues above.
Praise the mount! I'm fixed upon it,
Mount of God's unchanging love.

Here I raise my Ebenezer;
Hither by Thy help I'm come;
And I hope, by Thy good pleasure,
Safely to arrive at home.
Jesus sought me when a stranger,
Wandering from the fold of God;
He, to rescue me from danger,
Interposed His precious blood.

O to grace how great a debtor
Daily I'm constrained to be!
Let that grace now like a fetter,
Bind my wandering heart to Thee.
Prone to wander, Lord, I feel it,
Prone to leave the God I love;
Here's my heart, O take and seal it,
Seal it for Thy courts above.

Come, Thou Fount of Every Blessing, Robert Robinson, 1757

APPENDIX 15
Paul's Partnership Theology
Our Union with Christ and Partnership in Kingdom Ministry
*Adapted from Brian J. Dodd. **Empowered Church Leadership**. Downers Grove: InterVarsity Press, 2003.*

The Apostolic fondness for Greek terms compounded with the prefix syn (with or co-)

English Translation of the Greek Term	Scripture References
Co-worker (*Synergos*)	Rom 16.3, 7, 9, 21; 2 Cor. 8.23; Phil. 2.25; 4.3; Col. 4.7, 10, 11, 14; Philem. 1, 24
Co-prisoner (*Synaichmalotos*)	Col. 4.10; Philem. 23
Co-slave (*Syndoulous*)	Col. 1.7; 4.7
Co-soldier (*Systratiotes*)	Phil. 2.25; Philem. 2
Co-laborer (*Synathleo*)	Phil. 4.2-3

APPENDIX 16
Six Kinds of New Testament Ministry for Community
Rev. Dr. Don L. Davis

Type	Greek	Text	Task
Proclamation	*evanggelion*	Rom. 1.15-17	Preaching the Good News
Teaching	*didasko*	Matt. 28.19	To make disciples of Jesus
Worship	*latreuo*	John 4.20-24	Ushering into God's presence
Fellowship	*agape*	Rom. 13.8-10	The communion of saints
Witness	*martyria*	Acts 1.8	Compelling testimony to the lost
Service	*diakonia*	Matt. 10.43-45	Caring for the needs of others

APPENDIX 17
Spiritual Gifts Specifically Mentioned in the New Testament
Rev. Terry G. Cornett

Administration	1 Cor. 12.28	The ability to bring order to Church life.
Apostleship	1 Cor. 12.28; Eph. 4.11	The ability to establish new churches among the unreached, nurture them to maturity, and exercise the authority and wisdom necessary to see them permanently established and able to reproduce; and/or A gift unique to the founding of the Church age which included the reception of special revelation and uniquely binding leadership authority
Discernment	1 Cor. 12.10	The ability to serve the Church through a Spirit-given ability to distinguish between God's truth (his presence, working, and doctrine) and fleshly error or satanic counterfeits
Evangelism	Eph. 4.11	The passion and the ability to effectively proclaim the Gospel so that people understand it
Exhortation	Rom. 12.8	The ability to give encouragement or rebuke that helps others obey Christ
Faith	1 Cor. 12.9	The ability to build up the Church through a unique ability to see the unrealized purposes of God and unwaveringly trust God to accomplish them
Giving	Rom. 12.8	The ability to build up a church through taking delight in the consistent, generous sharing of spiritual and physical resources
Healing	1 Cor. 12.9; 12.28	The ability to exercise faith that results in restoring people to physical, emotional, and spiritual health
Interpretation	1 Cor. 12.10	The ability to explain the meaning of an ecstatic utterance so that the Church is edified
Knowledge	1 Cor. 12.8	The ability to understand scriptural truth, through the illumination of the Holy Spirit, and speak it out to edify the body; and/or The supernatural revelation of the existence, or nature, of a person or thing which would not be known through natural means

Spiritual Gifts Specifically Mentioned in the New Testament (continued)

Leadership	Rom. 12.8	Spiritually-inspired courage, wisdom, zeal, and hard work which motivate and guide others so that they can effectively participate in building the Church
Mercy	Rom. 12.8	Sympathy of heart which enables a person to empathize with and cheerfully serve those who are sick, hurting, or discouraged
Ministering (or Service, or Helping, or Hospitality)	Rom. 12.7; 1 Pet. 4.9	The ability to joyfully perform any task which benefits others and meets their practical and material needs (especially on behalf of the poor or afflicted)
Miracles	1 Cor. 12.10; 12.28	The ability to confront evil and do good in ways that make visible the awesome power and presence of God
Pastoring	Eph. 4.11	The desire and ability to guide, protect, and equip the members of a congregation for ministry
Prophecy	1 Cor. 12.28; Rom. 12.6	The ability to receive and proclaim openly a revealed message from God which prepares the Church for obedience to him and to the Scriptures
Teaching	1 Cor. 12.28; Rom. 12.7; Eph. 4.11	The ability to explain the meaning of the Word of God and its application through careful instruction
Tongues	1 Cor. 12.10; 12.28	Ecstatic utterance by which a person speaks to God (or others) under the direction of the Holy Spirit
Wisdom	1 Cor. 12.8	Spirit-revealed insight that allows a person to speak godly instruction for solving problems; and/or Spirit-revealed insight that allows a person to explain the central mysteries of the Christian faith

APPENDIX 18
Paul's Team Members
Don L. Davis

Achaicus, A Corinthian who visited Paul at Philippi, 1 Cor. 16.17.

Archippus, Colossian disciple whom Paul exhorted to fulfill his ministry, Col. 4.17; Philem. 2.

Aquila, Jewish disciple Paul found at Corinth, Acts 18.2, 18, 26; Rom. 16.3; 1 Cor. 16.19; 2 Tim. 4.19.

Aristarchus, With Paul on 3rd journey, Acts 19.29; 20.4; 27.2; Col. 4.10; Philem. 24.

Artemas, Companion of Paul at Nicopolis, Titus 3.12.

Barnabas, A Levite, cousin of John Mark, and companion with Paul in several of his journeys, cf. Acts 4.36, 9.27; 11.22, 25, 30; 12.25; chs. 13, 14, and 15; 1 Cor. 9.6; Gal. 2.1, 9, 13; Col. 4.13.

Carpus, Disciple of Troas, 2 Tim. 4.13.

Claudia, Female disciple of Rome, 2 Tim. 4.21.

Clement, Fellow-laborer at Phillipi, Phil. 4.3.

Crescens, A disciple at Rome, 2 Tim. 4.10.

Demas, A laborer of Paul at Rome, Col. 4.14; Philem. 24; 2 Tim. 4.10.

Epaphras, Fellow laborer and prisoner, Col. 1.7, 4.12; Philem. 23.

Epaphroditus, Messenger between Paul and the churches, Phil. 2.25, 4.18.

Eubulus, Disciple of Rome, 2 Tim. 4.21.

Euodia, Christian woman of Philippi, Phil. 4.2

Fortunatus, Part of the Corinthian team, 1 Cor. 16.17.

Gaius, 1) A Macedonian companion, Acts 19.29; 2) A disciple/companion in Derbe, Acts 20.4.

Jesus (Justus), A Jewish disciple at Colossae, Col. 4.11.

John Mark, Companion of Paul and cousin of Barnabas, Acts 12.12, 15; 15.37, 39; Col. 4.10; 2 Tim. 4.11; Philem. 24.

Linus, A Roman Companion of Paul, 2 Tim. 4.21.

Luke, Physician and fellow-traveler with Paul, Col. 4.14; 2 Tim. 4.11; Philem. 24.

Paul's Team Members (continued)

Onesimus, Native of Colossae and slave of Philemon who served Paul, Col. 4.9; Philem. 10.

Hermogenes, A team member who abandoned Paul in prison, 2 Tim. 1.15.

Phygellus, One with Hermogenes turned from Paul in Asia, 2 Tim. 1.15.

Priscilla (Prisca), Wife of Aquila of Pontus and fellow-worker in the Gospel, Acts 18.2, 18, 26; Rom. 16.3; 1 Cor. 16.19.

Pudens, A Roman companion of Paul, 2 Tim. 4.21.

Secundus, Companion of Paul on his way from Greece to Syria, Acts 20.4.

Silas, Disciple, fellow laborer, and prisoner with Paul, Acts 15.22, 27, 32, 34, 40; 16.19, 25, 29; 17.4, 10, etc.

Sopater, Accompanied Paul to Syria, Acts 20.4.

Sosipater, Kinsman of Paul, Rom. 16.21.

Silvanus, Probably same as Silas, 2 Cor. 1.19; 1 Thess. 1.1; 2 Thess. 1.1.

Sosthenes, Chief Ruler of the Synagogue of Corinth, laborer with Paul there, Acts 18.17.

Stephanus, One of the first believers of Achaia and visitor to Paul, 1 Cor. 1.16; 16.15; 16.17.

Syntyche, One of Paul's female "fellow workers" in Philippi, Phil. 4.2.

Tertius, Slave and person who wrote the Epistle to the Romans, Rom. 16.22.

Timothy, A young man of Lystra with a Jewish mother and Greek father who labored on with Paul in his ministry, Acts 16.1;17.14, 15; 18.5; 19.22; 20.4; Rom. 16.21; 1 Cor. 4.17; 16.10; 2 Cor. 1.1, 19; Phil. 1.1; 2.19; Col. 1.1; 1 Thess. 1.1; 3.2, 6; 2 Thess. 1.1; 1 Tim. 1.2, 18; 6.20; 2 Tim. 1.2; Philem. 1; Heb. 13.23.

Titus, Greek disciple and co-laborer of Paul, 2 Cor. 2.13; 7.6, 13, 14; 8.6, 16, 23; 12.18; Gal. 2.1, 3; 2 Tim. 4.10; Titus 1.4.

Trophimus, A Ephesian disciple who accompanied Paul to Jerusalem from Greece, Acts 20.4; 21.29; 2 Tim. 4.20.

Tryphena and Tryphosa, Female disciples of Rome, probably twins, who Paul calls laborers in the Lord, Rom. 16.12.

Tychicus, A disciple of Asia Minor who accompanied Paul in various trips, Acts 20.4; Eph. 6.21; Col. 4.7; 2 Tim. 4.12; Titus 3.12.

Urbanus, Roman disciple and aid to Paul, Rom. 16.9.

APPENDIX 19
Nurturing Authentic Christian Leadership
Rev. Dr. Don L. Davis

Cliff On-One-Side	Cliff On-the-Other-Side
Laying on hands too quickly	Always postponing delegation to the indigenous
Ignoring culture in leadership training	Elevating culture above truth
Demoting doctrine and theology	Supposing doctrine and theology as only criteria
Highlighting skills and gifts above availability and character	Substituting availability and character for genuine giftedness
Emphasizing administrative abilities above spiritual dynamism	Ignoring administration's role in spiritual vitality and power
Equating readiness with Christian perfection	Ignoring the importance of biblical standards
Limiting candidacy for leadership based on gender and ethnicity	Setting quotas of leadership based on gender and ethnicity
Seeing everyone as a leader	Seeing virtually no one as worthy to lead

APPENDIX 20
The Role of Women in Ministry
Dr. Don L. Davis

While it is plain that God has established a clearly designed order of responsibility within the home, it is equally clear that women are called and gifted by God, led by his own Spirit to bear fruit worthy of their calling in Christ. Throughout the NT, commands are directed specifically to women to submit, with the particular Greek verb *hupotasso*, occurring frequently which means "to place under" or "to submit" (cf. 1 Tim. 2.11). The word also translated into our English word "subjection" is from the same root. In such contexts these Greek renderings ought not to be understood in any way except as positive admonitions towards God's designed framework for the home, where women are charged to learn quietly and submissively, trusting and working within the Lord's own plan.

This ordering of the woman's submission in the home, however, must not be misinterpreted to mean that women are disallowed from ministering their gifts under the Spirit's direction. Indeed, it is the Holy Spirit through Christ's gracious endowment who assigns the gifts as he wills, for the edification of the Church (1 Cor. 12.1-27; Eph. 4.1-16). The gifts are not given to believers on the criteria of gender; in other words, there is no indication from the Scriptures that some gifts are for men only, and the others reserved for women. On the contrary, Paul affirms that Christ provided gifts as a direct result of his own personal victory over the devil and his minions (cf. Eph. 4.6ff.). This was his own personal choice, given by his Spirit to whomever he wills (cf. 1 Cor. 12.1-11). In affirming the ministry of women we affirm the right of the Spirit to be creative in all saints for the well-being of all and the expansion of his Kingdom, as he sees fit, and not necessarily as we determine (Rom. 12.4-8; 1 Pet. 4.10-11).

Furthermore, a careful study of the Scriptures as a whole indicates that God's ordering of the home in no way undermines his intention for men and women to serve Christ as disciples and laborers together, under Christ's leading. The clear NT teaching of Christ as head of the man, and the man of the woman (see 1 Cor. 11.4) shows God's esteem for godly spiritual representation within the home. The apparent forbidding of women to hold teaching/ruling positions appears to be an admonition to protect God's assigned lines of responsibility and authority within the home. For instance, the particular Greek term in the highly debated passage in 1 Timothy 2.12, *andros*, which has often times been translated "man," may also be

The Role of Women in Ministry (continued)

translated "husband." With such a translation, then, the teaching would be that a wife ought not to rule over her husband.

This doctrine of a woman who, in choosing to marry, makes herself voluntarily submissive to "line up under" her husband is entirely consistent with the gist of the NT teaching on the role of authority in the Christian home. The Greek word *hupotasso*, which means to "line up under" refers to a wife's voluntary submission to her own husband (cf. Eph. 5.22, 23; Col. 3.18; Titus 2.5; 1 Pet. 3.1). This has nothing to do with any supposed superior status or capacity of the husband; rather, this refers to God's design of godly headship, authority which is given for comfort, protection, and care, not for destruction or domination (cf. Gen. 2.15-17; 3.16; 1 Cor. 11.3). Indeed, that this headship is interpreted in light of Christ's headship over the Church signifies the kind of godly headship that must be given, that sense of tireless care, service, and protection required from godly leadership.

Of course, such an admonition for a wife to submit to a husband would not in any way rule out that women be involved in a teaching ministry (e.g., Titus 2.4), but, rather, that in the particular case of married women, that their own ministries would come under the protection and direction of their respective husbands (Acts 18.26). This would assert that a married woman's ministry in the Church would be given serving, protective oversight by her husband, not due to any notion of inferior capacity or defective spirituality, but for the sake of, as one commentator has put it, "avoiding confusion and maintaining orderliness" (cf. 1 Cor. 14.40).

In both Corinth and Ephesus (which represent the contested Corinthian and Timothy epistolary comments), it appears that Paul's restriction upon women's participation was prompted by occasional happenings, issues which grew particularly out of these contexts, and therefore are meant to be understood in those lights. For instance, the hotly-contested test of a women's "silence" in the church (see both 1 Cor. 14 and 1 Tim. 2) does not appear in any way to undermine the prominent role women played in the expansion of the Kingdom and development of the Church in the first century. Women were involved in the ministries of prophecy and prayer (1 Cor. 11.5), personal instruction (Acts 18.26), teaching (Titus 2.4,5), giving testimony (John 4.28, 29), offering hospitality (Acts 12.12), and serving as co-laborers with the Apostles in the cause of the Gospel (Phil. 4.2-3). Paul did not relegate women to an inferior role or hidden status but served side-by-side with women for the sake of Christ "I urge Euodia and I urge Syntyche to live in harmony in the Lord. Indeed, true companion, I ask you also to help these women

The Role of Women in Ministry (continued)

who have shared my struggle in *the cause of* the Gospel, together with Clement also and the rest of my fellow workers, whose names are in the book of life" (Phil. 4.2-3).

Furthermore, we must be careful in subordinating the personage of women *per se* (that is, their nature as women) versus their subordinated role in the marriage relationship. Notwithstanding the clear description of the role of women as heirs together of the grace of life in the marriage relationship (1 Pet. 3.7), it is equally plain that the Kingdom of God has created a dramatic shift in how women are to be viewed, understood, and embraced in the kingdom community. It is plain that in Christ there is now no difference between rich and poor, Jew and Gentile, barbarian, Scythian, bondman and freemen, as well as man and woman (cf. Gal. 3.28; Col. 3.11). Women were allowed to be disciples of a Rabbi (which was foreign and disallowed at the time of Jesus), and played prominent roles in the NT church, including being fellow laborers side by side with the Apostles in ministry (e.g., see Euodia and Syntyche in Phil. 4.1ff.), as well as hosting a church in their houses (cf. Phoebe in Rom. 16.1-2, and Apphia in Philem. 1).

In regards to the issue of pastoral authority, I am convinced that Paul's understanding of the role of equippers (of which the pastor-teacher is one such role, cf. Eph. 4.9-15) is not gender specific. In other words, the decisive and seminal text for me on the operation of gifts and the status and function of offices are those NT texts which deal with the gifts (1 Cor. 12.1-27; Rom. 12.4-8; 1 Pet. 4.10-11, and Eph. 4.9-15). There is no indication in any of these formative texts that gifts are gender-specific. In other words, for the argument to hold decisively that women were never to be in roles that were pastoral or equipping in nature, the simplest and most effective argument would be to show that the Spirit simply would never even consider giving a woman a gift which was not suited to the range of callings which she felt a calling towards. Women would be forbidden from leadership because the Holy Spirit would never grant to a woman a calling and its requisite gifts because she was a woman. Some gifts would be reserved for men, and women would never receive those gifts.

A careful reading of these and other related texts show no such prohibition. It appears that it is up to the Holy Spirit to give any person, man or woman, any gift that suits him for any ministry he wishes them to do, as he wills (1 Cor. 12.11 "But one and the same Spirit works all these things, distributing to each one individually as he wills"). Building upon this point, Terry Cornett has even written a fine theological essay showing how the NT Greek for the word "apostle" is

The Role of Women in Ministry (continued)

unequivocally applied to women, most clearly shown in the rendering of the female noun, "Junia" applied to "apostle" in Romans 16.7, as well as allusions to co-laboring, for instance, with the twins, Tryphena and Tryphosa, who "labored" with Paul in the Lord (16.12).

Believing that every God-called, Christ-endowed, and Spirit-gifted and led Christian ought to fulfill their role in the body, we affirm the role of women to lead and instruct under godly authority that submits to the Holy Spirit, the Word of God, and is informed by the tradition of the Church and spiritual reasoning. We ought to expect God to give women supernatural endowments of grace to carry out his bidding on behalf of his Church, and his reign in the Kingdom of God. Since men and women both reflect the *Imago Dei* (i.e., image of God), and both stand as heirs together of God's grace (cf. Gen. 1.27; 5.2; Matt. 19.4; Gal. 3.28; 1 Pet. 3.7), they are given the high privilege of representing Christ together as his ambassadors (2 Cor. 5.20), and through their partnership to bring to completion our obedience to Christ's Great Commission of making disciples of all nations (Matt. 28.18-20).

APPENDIX 21
Discerning the Call: The Profile of a Godly Christian Leader
Rev. Dr. Don L. Davis

	Commission	Character	Community	Competence
Definition	Recognizes the call of God and replies with prompt obedience to his lordship and leading	Reflects the character of Christ in their personal convictions, conduct, and lifestyle	Regards multiplying disciples in the body of Christ as the primary role of ministry	Responds in the power of the Spirit with excellence in carrying out their appointed tasks and ministry
Key Scripture	2 Tim. 1.6-14; 1 Tim. 4.14; Acts 1.8; Matt. 28.18-20	John 15.4-5; 2 Tim. 2.2; 1 Cor. 4.2; Gal. 5.16-23	Eph. 4.9-15; 1 Cor. 12.1-27	2 Tim. 2.15; 3.16-17; Rom. 15.14; 1 Cor. 12
Critical Concept	The Authority of God: God's leader acts on God's recognized call and authority, acknowledged by the saints and God's leaders	The Humility of Christ: God's leader demonstrates the mind and lifestyle of Christ in his or her actions and relationships	The Growth of the Church: God's leader uses all of his or her resources to equip and empower the body of Christ for his/her goal and task	The Power of the Spirit: God's leader operates in the gifting and anointing of the Holy Spirit
Central Elements	A clear call from God Authentic testimony before God and others Deep sense of personal conviction based on Scripture Personal burden for a particular task or people Confirmation by leaders and the body	Passion for Christlikeness Radical lifestyle for the Kingdom Serious pursuit of holiness Discipline in the personal life Fulfills role-relationships as bondslave of Jesus Christ Provides an attractive model for others in their conduct, speech, and lifestyle (the fruit of the Spirit)	Genuine love for and desire to serve God's people Disciples faithful individuals Facilitates growth in small groups Pastors and equips believers in the congregation Nurtures associations and networks among Christians and churches Advances new movements among God's people locally	Endowments and gifts from the Spirit Sound discipling from an able mentor Skill in the spiritual disciplines Ability in the Word Able to evangelize, follow up, and disciple new converts Strategic in the use of resources and people to accomplish God's task
Satanic Strategy to Abort	Operates on the basis of personality or position rather than on God's appointed call and ongoing authority	Substitutes ministry activity and/or hard work and industry for godliness and Christlikeness	Exalts tasks and activities above equipping the saints and developing Christian community	Functions on natural gifting and personal ingenuity rather than on the Spirit's leading and gifting
Key Steps	Identify God's call Discover your burden Be confirmed by leaders	Abide in Christ Discipline for godliness Pursue holiness in all	Embrace God's Church Learn leadership's contexts Equip concentrically	Discover the Spirit's gifts Receive excellent training Hone your performance
Results	Deep confidence in God arising from God's call	Powerful Christlike example provided for others to follow	Multiplying disciples in the Church	Dynamic working of the Holy Spirit

APPENDIX 22

Suffering: The Cost of Discipleship and Servant-Leadership

Don L. Davis

To be a disciple is to bear the stigma and reproach of the One who called you into service (2 Tim. 3.12). Practically, this may mean the loss of comfort, convenience, and even life itself (John 12.24-25).

All of Christ's Apostles endured insults, rebukes, lashes, and rejections by the enemies of their Master. Each of them sealed their doctrines with their blood in exile, torture, and martyrdom. Listed below are the fates of the Apostles according to traditional accounts.

- Matthew suffered martyrdom by being slain with a sword at a distant city of Ethiopia.

- Mark expired at Alexandria, after being cruelly dragged through the streets of that city.

- Luke was hanged upon an olive tree in the classic land of Greece.

- John was put in a caldron of boiling oil, but escaped death in a miraculous manner, and was afterward branded at Patmos.

- Peter was crucified at Rome with his head downward.

- James, the Greater, was beheaded at Jerusalem.

- James, the Less, was thrown from a lofty pinnacle of the temple, and then beaten to death with a fuller's club.

- Bartholomew was flayed alive.

- Andrew was bound to a cross, whence he preached to his persecutors until he died.

- Thomas was run through the body with a lance at Coromandel in the East Indies.

- Jude was shot to death with arrows.

- Matthias was first stoned and then beheaded.

- Barnabas of the Gentiles was stoned to death at Salonica.

- Paul, after various tortures and persecutions, was at length beheaded at Rome by the Emperor Nero.

APPENDIX 23
Our Declaration of Dependence: Freedom in Christ

It is important to teach morality within the realm of freedom (i.e., Gal. 5.1, "It is for freedom Christ has set you free"), and always in the context of using your freedom in the framework of bringing God glory and advancing Christ's Kingdom. I emphasize the "6-8-10" principles of 1 Corinthians, and apply them to all moral issues.

1. 1 Cor. 6.9-11, Christianity is about transformation in Christ; no amount of excuses will get a person into the Kingdom.

2. 1 Cor. 6.12a, We are free in Christ, but not everything one does is edifying or helpful.

3. 1 Cor. 6.12b, We are free in Christ, but anything that is addictive and exercising control over you is counter to Christ and his Kingdom.

4. 1 Cor. 8.7-13, We are free in Christ, but we ought never to flaunt our freedom, especially in the face of Christians whose conscience would be marred and who would stumble if they saw us doing something they found offensive.

5. 1 Cor. 10.23, We are free in Christ; all things are lawful for us, but neither is everything helpful, nor does doing everything build oneself up.

6. 1 Cor. 10.24, We are free in Christ, and ought to use our freedom to love our brothers and sisters in Christ, and nurture them for other's well being (cf. Gal. 5.13).

7. 1 Cor. 10.31, We are free in Christ, and are given that freedom in order that we might glorify God in all that we do, whether we eat or drink, or anything else.

8. 1 Cor. 10.32-33, We are free in Christ, and ought to use our freedom in order to do what we can to give no offense to people in the world or the Church, but do what we do in order to influence them to know and love Christ, i.e., that they might be saved.

This focus on freedom, in my mind, places all things that we say to adults or teens in context. Often, the way in which many new Christians are discipled is through a

Our Declaration of Dependence - Freedom in Christ (continued)

rigorous taxonomy (listing) of different vices and moral ills, and this can at times give them the sense that Christianity is an anti-act religion (a religion of simply not doing things), and/or a faith overly concerned with not sinning. Actually, the moral focus in Christianity is on freedom, a freedom won at a high price, a freedom to love God and advance the Kingdom, a freedom to live a surrendered life before the Lord. The moral responsibility of urban Christians is to live free in Jesus Christ, to live free unto God's glory, and to not use their freedom from the law as a license for sin.

The core of the teaching, then, is to focus on the freedom won for us through Christ's death and resurrection, and our union with him. We are now set free from the law, the principle of sin and death, the condemnation and guilt of our own sin, and the conviction of the law on us. We serve God now out of gratitude and thankfulness, and the moral impulse is living free in Christ. Yet, we do not use our freedom to be wiseguys or knuckle-heads, but to glorify God and love others. This is the context in which we address the thorny issues of homosexuality, abortion, and other social ills. Those who engage in such acts feign freedom, but, lacking a knowledge of God in Christ, they are merely following their own internal predispositions, which are not informed either by God's moral will or his love.

Freedom in Christ is a banner call to live holy and joyously as urban disciples. This freedom will enable them to see how creative they can be as Christians in the midst of so-called "free" living which only leads to bondage, shame, and remorse.

APPENDIX 24

"You Got To Serve Somebody!"

Over half of the metaphors chosen by Jesus describe someone who is under the authority of another. Often the word selected is one member of a familiar role pair, such as child (of a father, *pater*), servant (of a master, *kyrios*), or disciple (of a teacher, *didaskalos*). Other images of those under authority include the shepherd (*poimen*) who tends a flock that belongs to another, the worker (*ergates*) hired by the landowner (*oikodespotes*), the apostle (*apostolos*) commissioned by his superior, and the sheep (*probaton*) obeying the voice of the shepherd. It is interesting to note that even though the disciples are being prepared for spiritual leadership in the Church, Jesus places far more emphasis on their responsibility to God's authority, than on the authority which they themselves will exercise. There is far more instruction about the role of *following* than about the role of *leading* [emphasis added].

~ David Bennett, **The Metaphors of Ministry**, p. 62.

APPENDIX 25
Spiritual Service Checklist
Rev. Dr. Don L. Davis

1. *Salvation*: Has this person believed the Gospel, confessed Jesus as Lord and Savior, been baptized, and formally joined our church as a member?

2. *Personal integrity*: Are they walking with God, growing in their personal life, and demonstrating love and faithfulness in their family, work, and in the community?

3. *Equipped in the Word*: How equipped is this person in the Word of God to share and teach with others?

4. *Support of our church*: Do they support the church through their presence, pray for the leaders and members, and give financially to its support?

5. *Submission to authority*: Does this person joyfully submit to spiritual authority?

6. *Identification of spiritual gifts*: What gifts, talents, abilities, or special resources does this person have for service, and what is their particular burden for ministry now?

7. *Present availability*: Are they open to be assigned to a task or project where we could use their service to build up the body?

8. *Reputation amongst leaders*: How do the other leaders feel about this person's readiness for a new role of leadership?

9. *Resources needed to accomplish*: If appointed to this role, what particular training, monies, resources, and/or input will they need to accomplish the task?

10. *Formal commissioning*: When and how will we make known to others that we have appointed this person to their task or project?

11. *Timing and reporting*: Also, if we dedicate this person to this role/task, when will they be able to start, and how long ought they serve before we evaluate them.

12. *Evaluate and re-commission*: When will we evaluate the performance of the person, and determine what next steps we ought to take in their leadership role at the church?

APPENDIX 26
Lording Over versus Serving Among
Differing Styles and Models of Leadership
*Adapted from George Mallone, **Furnace of Renewal**.*

Secular Authority	Servant Authority
Functions on the basis of power	Functions on basis of love and obedience
Primarily rules by giving orders	Serves as one who is under orders of another
Unwilling to fail: blame-shifts for leverage	Unafraid to receive responsibility for failure
Sees itself as absolutely necessary	Willing to be used and expended for the body
Drives others (cow-punching mentality)	Leads others (shepherding mentality)
Subjects others to threat of loss and pain	Builds others by encouragement and challenge
Consolidates power for maximum impact	Stewards authority for greatest good
Has gold, makes rules	Follows the Golden Rule
Uses position for personal advancement	Exercises authority to please the Master
Expects benefits from service	Expects to expend oneself in service to others
Strength, not character, is decisive	Character, not strength, carries most weight

APPENDIX 27
From Deep Ignorance to Credible Witness
Rev. Dr. Don L. Davis

Level	Description		
8	**Witness** - Ability to give witness and teach 2 Tim. 2.2 Matt. 28.18-20 1 John 1.1-4 Prov. 20.6 2 Cor. 5.18-21	*And the things you have heard me say in the presence of many witnesses entrust to reliable men who will also be qualified to teach others.* - 2 Tim. 2.2	
7	**Lifestyle** - Consistent appropriation and habitual practice based on beliefs Heb. 5.11-6.2 Eph. 4.11-16 2 Pet. 3.18 1 Tim. 4.7-10	*And Jesus increased in wisdom and in stature, and in favor with God and man.* - Luke 2.52	
6	**Demonstration** - Expressing conviction in corresponding conduct, speech, and behavior James 2.14-26 2 Cor. 4.13 2 Pet. 1.5-9 1 Thess. 1.3-10	*Nevertheless, at your word I will let down the net.* - Luke 5.5	
5	**Conviction** - Committing oneself to think, speak, and act in light of information Heb. 2.3-4 Heb. 11.1, 6 Heb. 3.15-19 Heb. 4.2-6	*Do you believe this?* - John 11.26	
4	**Discernment** - Understanding the meaning and implications of information John 16.13 Eph. 1.15-18 Col. 1.9-10 Isa. 6.10; 29.10	*Do you understand what you are reading?* - Acts 8.30	
3	**Knowledge** - Ability to recall and recite information 2 Tim. 3.16-17 1 Cor. 2.9-16 1 John 2.20-27 John 14.26	*For what does the Scripture say?* - Rom. 4.3	
2	**Interest** - Responding to ideas or information with both curiosity and openness Ps. 42.1-2 Acts 9.4-5 John 12.21 1 Sam. 3.4-10	*We will hear you again on this matter.* - Acts 17.32	
1	**Awareness** - General exposure to ideas and information Mark 7.6-8 Acts 19.1-7 John 5.39-40 Matt. 7.21-23	*At that time, Herod the tetrarch heard about the fame of Jesus.* - Matt. 14.1	
0	**Ignorance** - Unfamiliarity with information due to naivete, indifference, or hardness Eph. 4.17-19 Ps. 2.1-3 Rom. 1.21; 2.19 1 John 2.11	*Who is the Lord that I should heed his voice?* - Exod. 5.2	

APPENDIX 28

Ethics of the New Testament: Living in the Upside-Down Kingdom of God
True Myth and Biblical Fairy Tale
Dr. Don L. Davis

The Principle of Reversal

The Principle Expressed	Scripture
The poor shall become rich, and the rich shall become poor	Luke 6.20-26
The law breaker and the undeserving are saved	Matt. 21.31-32
Those who humble themselves shall be exalted	1 Pet. 5.5-6
Those who exalt themselves shall be brought low	Luke 18.14
The blind shall be given sight	John 9.39
Those claiming to see shall be made blind	John 9.40-41
We become free by being Christ's slave	Rom. 12.1-2
God has chosen what is foolish in the world to shame the wise	1 Cor. 1.27
God has chosen what is weak in the world to shame the strong	1 Cor. 1.27
God has chosen the low and despised to bring to nothing things that are	1 Cor. 1.28
We gain the next world by losing this one	1 Tim. 6.7
Love this life and you'll lose it; hate this life, and you'll keep the next	John 12.25
You become the greatest by being the servant of all	Matt. 10.42-45
Store up treasures here, you forfeit heaven's reward	Matt. 6.19
Store up treasures above, you gain Heaven's wealth	Matt. 6.20
Accept your own death to yourself in order to live fully	John 12.24
Release all earthly reputation to gain Heaven's favor	Phil. 3.3-7
The first shall be last, and the last shall become first	Mark 9.35
The grace of Jesus is perfected in your weakness, not your strength	2 Cor. 12.9
God's highest sacrifice is contrition and brokenness	Ps. 51.17
It is better to give to others than to receive from them	Acts 20.35
Give away all you have in order to receive God's best	Luke 6.38

APPENDIX 29

Substitute Centers to a Christ-Centered Vision

Goods and Effects Which Our Culture Substitutes as the Ultimate Concern

Rev. Dr. Don L. Davis

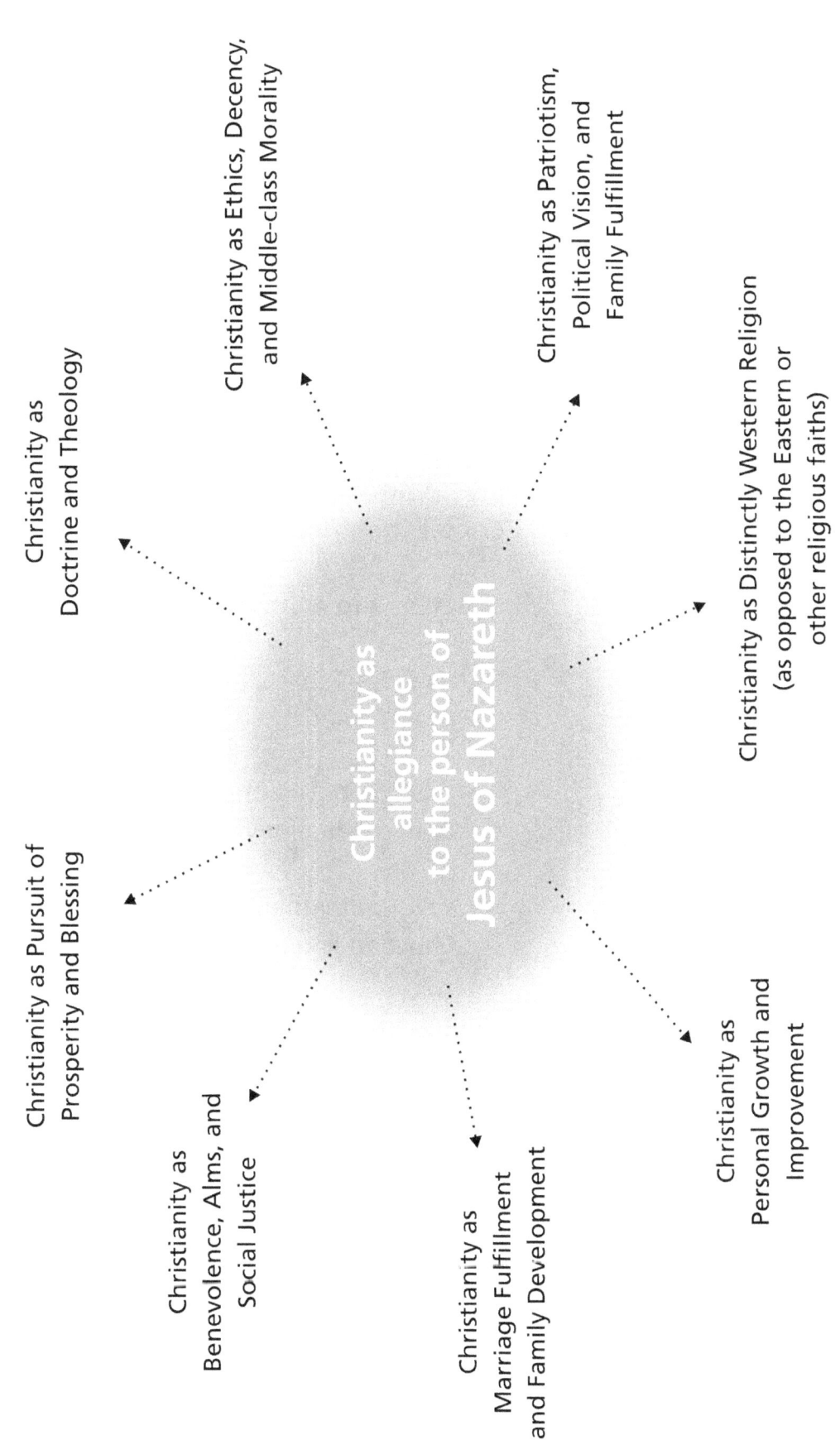

- Christianity as Doctrine and Theology
- Christianity as Ethics, Decency, and Middle-class Morality
- Christianity as Patriotism, Political Vision, and Family Fulfillment
- Christianity as Distinctly Western Religion (as opposed to the Eastern or other religious faiths)
- Christianity as Personal Growth and Improvement
- Christianity as Marriage Fulfillment and Family Development
- Christianity as Benevolence, Alms, and Social Justice
- Christianity as Pursuit of Prosperity and Blessing

Center: Christianity as allegiance to the person of Jesus of Nazareth

APPENDIX 30
Dealing With Old Ways
Adapted from Paul Hiebert

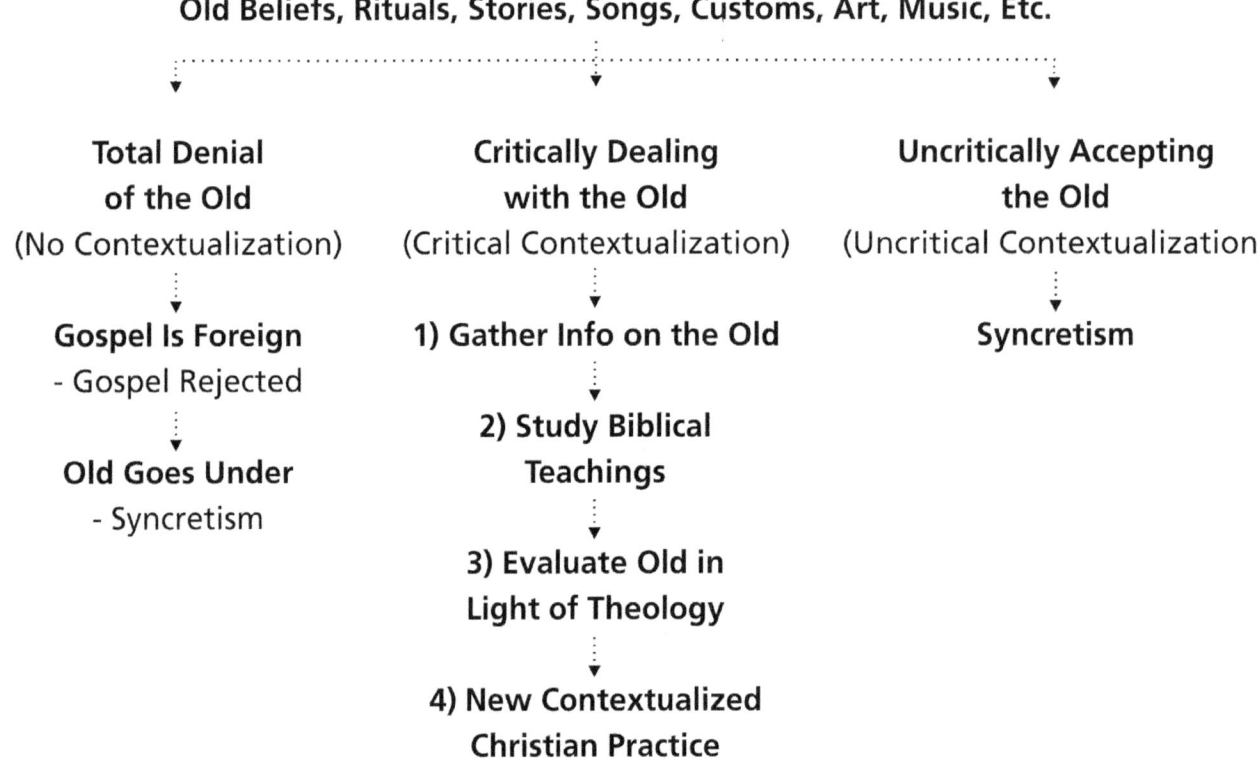

APPENDIX 31
Three Contexts of Urban Christian Leadership Development
Rev. Dr. Don L. Davis

Ephesians 4.11 (ESV) - And he himself gave some to be apostles, some prophets, some evangelists, and some pastors and teachers, **12.** for the equipping of the saints for the work of ministry, for the edifying of the body of Christ

Three Contexts of Leadership Function

I. Forming, Leading, and Reproducing Dynamic Small Group Life and Ministry
  - Inreach (discipling, fellowship, care giving, etc.)
  - Outreach (evangelism, service, witness)

II. Facilitating and Reproducing Vital Congregational Life and Ministry

III. Nurturing and Cultivating Inter-congregational Support, Cooperation, and Collaboration

God has appointed leaders in the Church to equip Christians for "the work of the ministry," that they might walk worthy of the Lord in all things, bear abundant fruit in Christ, to win, follow-up, and disciple members within their *oikos* (their family, friends, and associates), and to be zealous in good works to reveal the Kingdom's life

Less than all of us

"Us" (My church)

More than all of us

God has given to the Church leaders of unique gifting - apostles, prophets, evangelists, pastors and teachers in order that the "Church Assembled" might be edified and equipped to fulfill its mission and ministry as it scatters, as individuals, into the world. **Luke 10.2-3 (ESV)**, And he said to them, "The harvest is plentiful but the laborers are few. Therefore pray earnestly to the Lord of the harvest to send out laborers into his harvest. **[3]** Go your way; behold, I am sending you out as lambs in the midst of wolves").

Any recognized part of a larger assembly, e.g., Cell group, Women's study, Prayer group, BibleStudy, Sunday School class, Street Ministry team, Prison outreach team, etc.

The church together as one, from house church to mega-church (i.e., Any distinct gathering of believers who identify with one another, give and serve together, under one pastoral head, where their presence and allegiance are shown and known)

Congregational Form

The Locale Church

"The Church Assembled"

According to some biblical linguists, the phrase in the NT for the church in assembly, *en ekklesia*, applies to the local expressions of the people of God when they "come together as a church," cf. 1 Cor. 11.18. The people of God can thus be called the "church/assembly," that is, those who by faith in Jesus Christ and his Holy Spirit now represent his called ones in a particular place and locale.

Clusters of churches which band together in partnership for mutual support, refreshment, service, and mission (e.g., Associations, denominations, conferences, etc.)

APPENDIX 32
Four Contexts of Urban Christian Leadership Development
Rev. Dr. Don L. Davis

1. Personal Friendships, Mentoring, and Discipleship

2. Small Group Nurture and Cell Groups

3. Congregational Life and Governance

4. Inter-congregational Cooperation and Collaboration

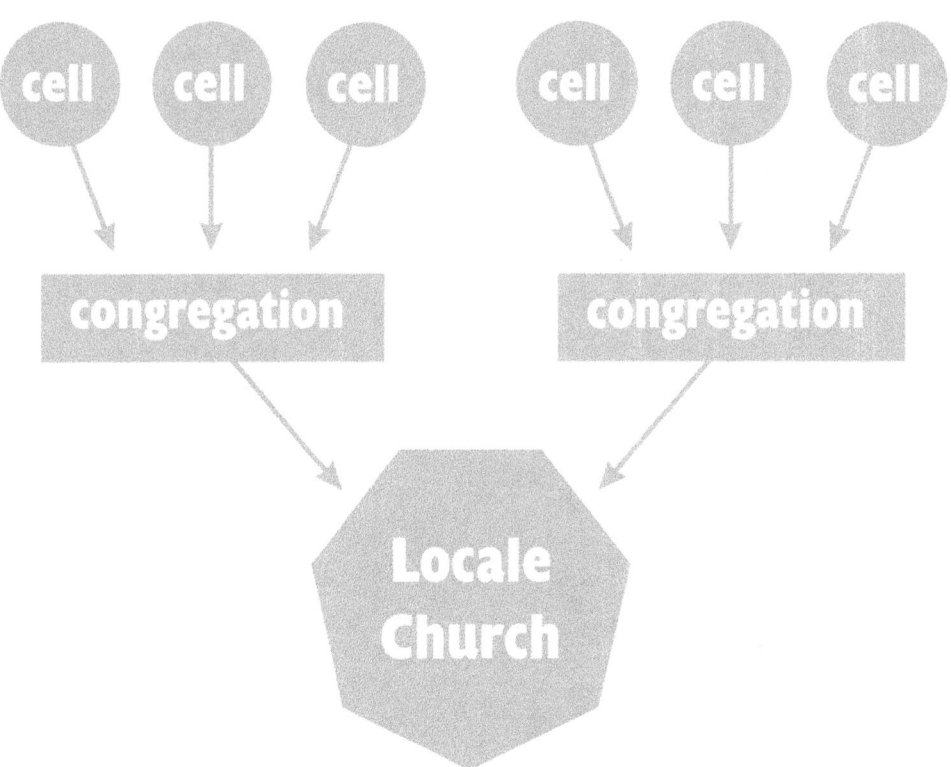

APPENDIX 33

Investment, Empowerment, and Assessment

How Leadership as Representation Provides Freedom to Innovate

Rev. Dr. Don L. Davis

INVEST: Preparation and Resources

Selection and Investment of Leaders and Team Members

Ministry oversight provides support, resources and authority here

- Formal leadership selection
- Acknowledgment of personal call
- Determination of task and assignment
- Training in spiritual warfare
- Authorization to act defined and given
- Necessary resources given and logistics planned
- Commissioning: deputization formally recognized

EMPOWER

Freedom to innovate under the oversight of godly local leadership and the guidance of the Holy Spirit

Ministry oversight provides resources, prayer, and counsel

ASSESS: Evaluate and Review

Accountability for Results Within an Agreed Upon Time Frame

Ministry oversight measure results here

- Evaluation by sending authority
- Review of results in light of task
- Faithfulness and loyalty assessed
- Overall evaluation of plan and strategy
- Critical evaluation of leadership performance
- Formal determination of operation's "success"
- Reassignment in light of evaluation

APPENDIX 34
Representin'
Jesus as God's Chosen Representative
Rev. Dr. Don L. Davis

To represent another

Is to be selected to stand in the place of another, and thereby fulfill the assigned duties, exercise the rights and serve as deputy for, as well as to speak and act with another's authority on behalf of their interests and reputation.

Jesus Fulfills The Duties Of Being an Emissary

1. Receiving an *Assignment*, **John 10.17-18**
2. Resourced with an *Entrustment*, **John 3.34; Luke. 4.18**
3. Launched into *Engagement*, **John 5.30**
4. Answered with an *Assessment*, **Matthew 3.16-17**
5. New assignment after *Assessment*, **Philippians 2.9-11**

The Temptation of Jesus Christ
Challenge to and Contention with God's Rep

Mark 1.12-13 (ESV) The Spirit immediately drove him out into the wilderness. **[13]** *And he was in the wilderness forty days, being tempted by Satan. And he was with the wild animals,* and the angels were ministering to him.

The Baptism of Jesus Christ
Commissioning and Confirmation of God's Rep

Mark 1.9-11 (ESV) *In those days Jesus came from Nazareth of Galilee and was baptized by John in the Jordan.* **[10]** And when he came up out of the water, immediately he saw the heavens opening and the Spirit descending on him like a dove. **[11]** And a voice came from heaven, "You are my beloved Son; with you I am well pleased."

The Public Preaching Ministry of Jesus Christ
Communication and Conveyance by God's Rep

Mark 1.14-15 (ESV) Now after John was arrested, Jesus came into Galilee, proclaiming the gospel of God, **[15]** and saying, "The time is fulfilled, and the kingdom of God is at hand; repent and believe in the gospel."

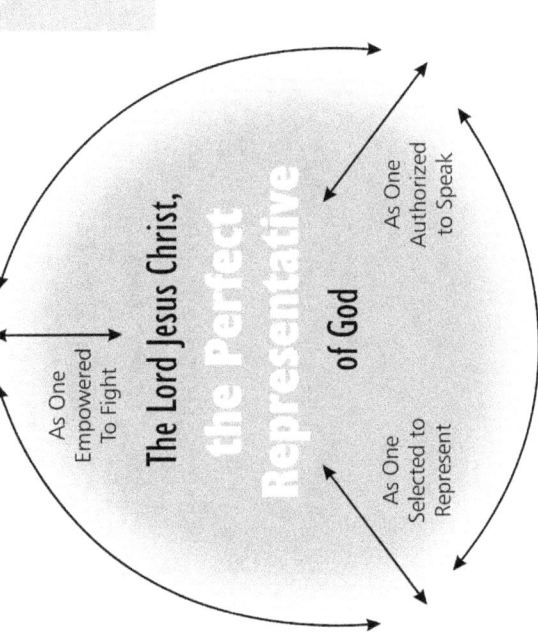

The Lord Jesus Christ, **the Perfect Representative** of God
- As One Empowered To Fight
- As One Authorized to Speak
- As One Selected to Represent

APPENDIX 35

Delegation and Authority in Christian Leadership

Rev. Dr. Don L. Davis

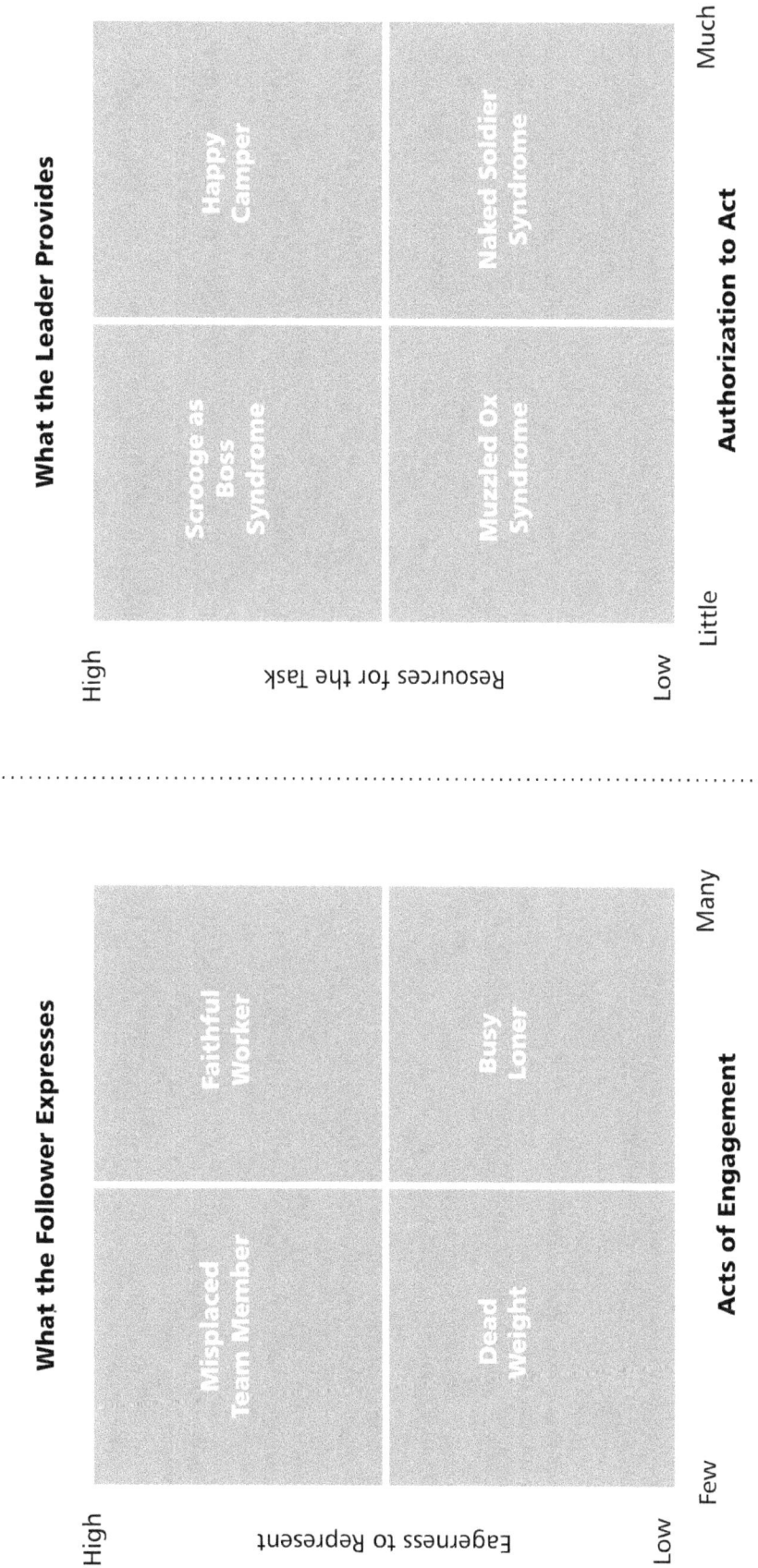

APPENDIX 36
Re-presenting Messiah
Don L. Davis

Central Diagram

Re-present Messiah Yeshua with passion and clarity
with fidelity to Scripture
in sync with historic orthodoxy
without cultural distortion
without theological bias

Triangle sides:
- Rediscover the Hebraic roots of the biblical Messianic hope (return)
- Recognize the socio-cultural captivity of Christian profession (exile)

"Gentilization" of modern Christian faith expressions
- Contextualization: freedom in Christ to enculturate the gospel
- Common modern portrayal of Messianic hope as Gentile faith
- Tendency of tradition/culture to usurp biblical authority
- Present day eclipse of biblical framework by "captivities"

Strange fires on the altar: examples of socio-cultural captivities
- Nationalism
- Capitalism
- Scientific rationalism
- Denominationalism
- Personal existentialism
- Asceticism/moralism
- Ethnocentrism
- Nuclear family life

Jesus' critique of socio-cultural captivity
- Bondage to religious tradition, Matt. 15.3-9
- Ignorance of Scripture and God's power, Matt. 22.29
- Zealous effort without knowledge, Romans 10.1-3

Hermeneutic habits that lead toward a syncretistic faith
- Selective choice of texts
- Tradition viewed as canon
- Cultural readings of texts
- Preaching and teaching based on eisegesis and audience
- Uncritical approaches to one's own doctrine and practice
- Apologetics for socio-cultural identity

"Paradigm paralysis" & biblical faith
- Blind to one's own historical conditionedness
- Limited vantage point and perspective
- Privilege and power: political manipulation
- Inability to receive criticism
- Persecution of opposite viewpoints and new interpretations of faith

---

Rediscover the Hebraic roots (right side)
- Rediscovery of the Jewish origins of biblical faith, John 4.22
- YHWH as God of lovingkindness in covenant faithfulness
- Messianic fulfillment in OT: prophecy, type, story, ceremony, and symbol
- Hebraic roots of the Promise: YHWH as a Warrior God
- People of Israel as community of Messianic hope
- Psalms and Prophets emphasize divine rulership of Messiah

Tracing the Seed
- Seed of the Woman, Gen. 3.15
- Seed of Shem, Gen. 9.26-27
- Seed of Abraham, Gen. 12.3
- Seed of Isaac and Jacob, Gen. 26.2-5; 28.10-15
- Seed of Judah, Gen. 49.10
- Seed of David, 2 Sam. 7

- Suffering Servant of YHWH: humiliation and lowliness of God's Davidic king
- Glimmers of Gentile salvation and global transformation

Recognize the socio-cultural captivity (bottom)
- Live the adventure of NT apocalyptic myth (possession)
- Apocalyptic as the "mother tongue and native language" of the apostles and early Church as eschatological community
- Yeshua Messiah as the Cosmic Warrior: YHWH as God who wins ultimate victory over his enemies
- Messiah Yeshua as Anointed One and Binder of the Strong Man: the Messianic Age to come inaugurated in Jesus of Nazareth
- "Already/Not Yet" Kingdom orientation: The Reign of God as both manifest but not consummated
- The Evidence and Guarantee of the Age to Come: The Spirit as down payment, first fruits, and seal of God

APPENDIX 37

"You Can Pay Me Now, Or You Can Pay Me Later"
Don L. Davis

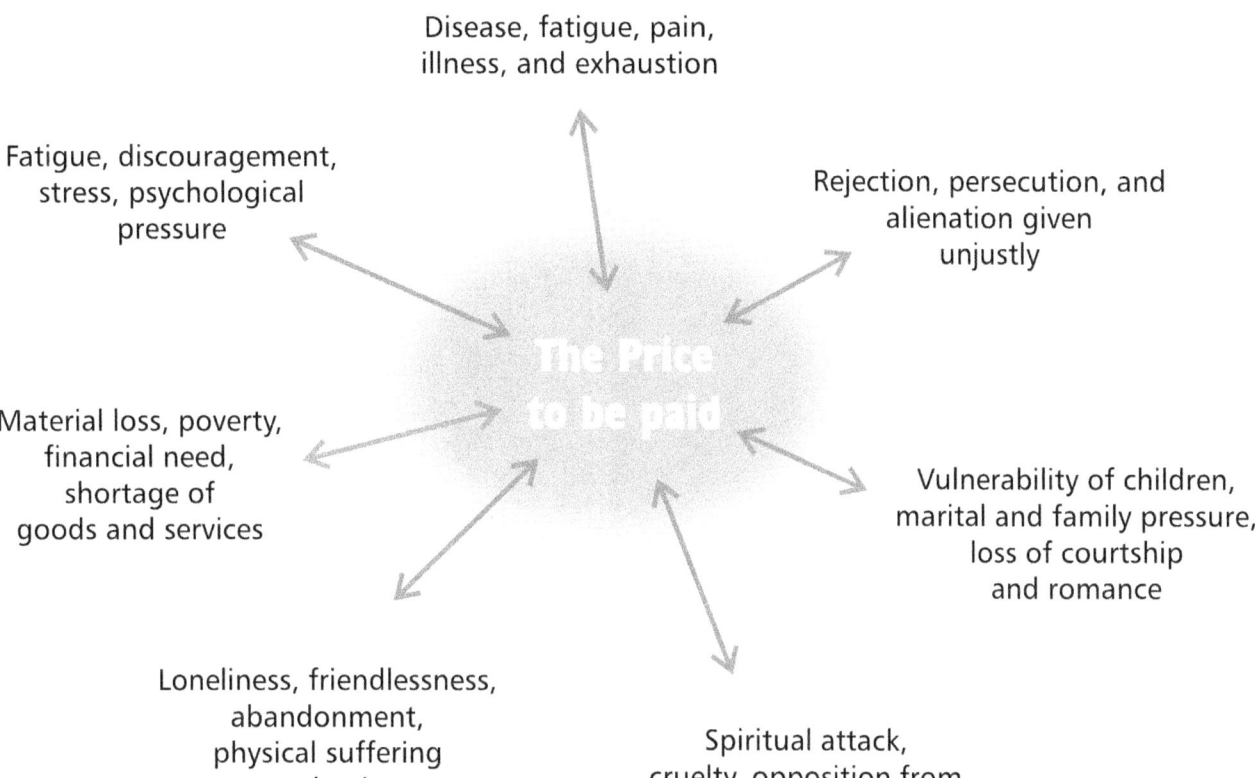

APPENDIX 38
Hindrances to Christ-Like Servanthood
Don L. Davis

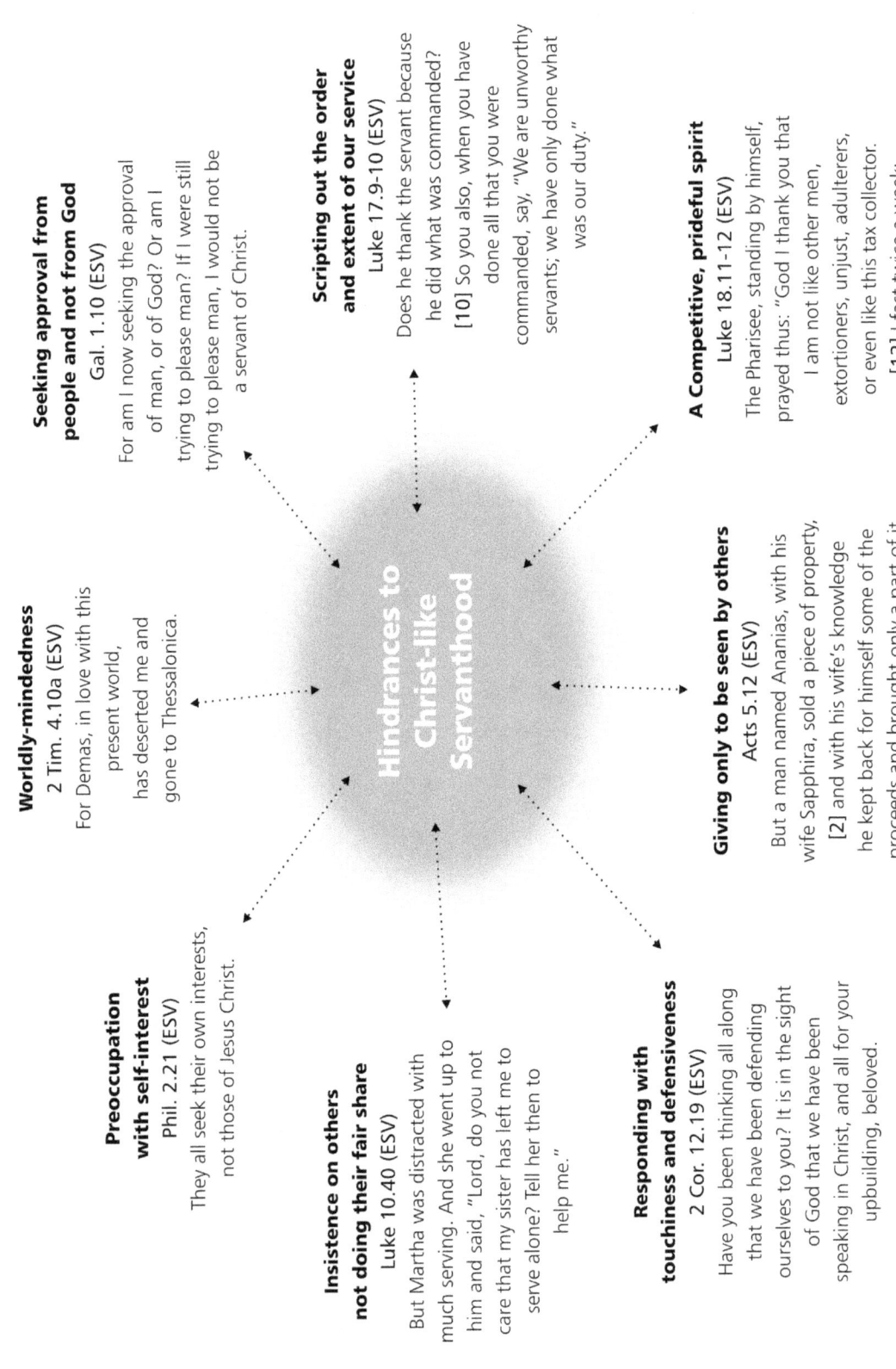

Hindrances to Christ-like Servanthood

Seeking approval from people and not from God
Gal. 1.10 (ESV)
For am I now seeking the approval of man, or of God? Or am I trying to please man? If I were still trying to please man, I would not be a servant of Christ.

Scripting out the order and extent of our service
Luke 17.9-10 (ESV)
Does he thank the servant because he did what was commanded? [10] So you also, when you have done all that you were commanded, say, "We are unworthy servants; we have only done what was our duty."

A Competitive, prideful spirit
Luke 18.11-12 (ESV)
The Pharisee, standing by himself, prayed thus: "God I thank you that I am not like other men, extortioners, unjust, adulterers, or even like this tax collector. [12] I fast twice a week; I give tithes of all that I get."

Giving only to be seen by others
Acts 5.1-2 (ESV)
But a man named Ananias, with his wife Sapphira, sold a piece of property, [2] and with his wife's knowledge he kept back for himself some of the proceeds and brought only a part of it and laid it at the apostles' feet.

Responding with touchiness and defensiveness
2 Cor. 12.19 (ESV)
Have you been thinking all along that we have been defending ourselves to you? It is in the sight of God that we have been speaking in Christ, and all for your upbuilding, beloved.

Insistence on others not doing their fair share
Luke 10.40 (ESV)
But Martha was distracted with much serving. And she went up to him and said, "Lord, do you not care that my sister has left me to serve alone? Tell her then to help me."

Preoccupation with self-interest
Phil. 2.21 (ESV)
They all seek their own interests, not those of Jesus Christ.

Worldly-mindedness
2 Tim. 4.10a (ESV)
For Demas, in love with this present world, has deserted me and gone to Thessalonica.

APPENDIX 39
The Ministry of Praise and Worship
Rev. Dr. Don L. Davis

The Special Call to the Ministry of Praise and Worship

*The praise which overcomes is not merely occasional or spasmodic praise, praise that fluctuates with moods and circumstances. It is continuous praise, praise that is a vocation, a way of life. "I will bless [praise] the Lord at **all times**; his praise shall **continually** be in my mouth" (Psalms 34.1). Blessed are they that dwell in thy house; they will be still [always] praising thee" (Psalms 84.4). It has been pointed out that in heaven praise is so important that it constitutes the total occupation of a certain order of beings (Revelation 4.8). God gave to King David such a revelation of the importance and power of praise upon earth that, following the heavenly pattern, he set aside and dedicated an army of four thousand Levites whose sole occupation was to praise the Lord! (1 Chronicles 23.5). They did nothing else. One of the last official acts of King David before his death was the organization of a formal program of praise. Each morning and each evening a contingent of these four thousand Levites engaged in this service. "And to stand every morning to thank and praise the Lord, and likewise at evening," (1 Chronicles 23.30, New Scofield). To the shame and defeat of the Church, the significance of the massive praise content of the Word has been largely overlooked. To be most effective, then, praise must be massive, continuous, a fixed habit, a full-time occupation, a diligently pursued vocation, a total way of life. This principle is emphasized in Psalm 57.7: "My hearted is fixed, O God, my heart is fixed; I will sing and give praise." This suggests a premeditated and predetermined habit of praise. "My heart is FIXED." This kind of praise depends on something more than temporary euphoria.*

~ Paul Billheimer, **Destined for the Throne**, pp. 121-22.

I. Exalted God-centered Purpose, Ps. 150.5; Rev. 4.11; Ps. 29.1-2

    A. "That's why we praise him, that's why we sing!"

        1. To express our joy in God in the Holy Spirit

        2. To acknowledge the grace of God in the person of Jesus Christ

        3. To experience the presence of God

        4. To see the beauty of God in the midst of his people

The Ministry of Praise and Worship (continued)

    B. Worship is not

        1. Good music alone

        2. Professionally performed liturgies

        3. Outstanding gear and equipment

    C. Worship represents the expression of the saved heart who approaches the Father through the Son in the power of the Holy Spirit for his praise and glory alone! (John 4.24)

    D. Worship leading is imitating a GE light bulb

        1. When it is most effective, you never notice it, only the effects of its working

        2. When it is not working is the only time you give attention to it!

II. The Goal: to Acknowledge and Extol the Excellence of God in Every Dimension of Our Lives, Our Praises of God, 1 Pet. 2.8-9

Principles of Effective Worship Leading

I. To Be an Effective Worship Leader One Must Understand the Nature, Design, and Importance of Worship

    A. Worship as spiritual inquiry (*darash*), Ezra 4.2, 6.21

    B. Worship as reverent obedience (*yare*), Exod.14.31; Deut.31.12-13

    C. Worship as loyal service (*abad*), Exod. 5.18; Num. 8.25

    D. Worship as personal ministry (*sharat*), Deut. 10.8, 18.5-7

    E. Worship as genuine humility (*shaha*), most common Isa. 49.7; Gen.47.31; Exod. 34.8 cf. Isa. 66.2

The Ministry of Praise and Worship (continued)

F. Worship as prostration in prayer (*segid*), Dan.3.5-7, 10-12, 14-18, 28

G. Worship as nearness to God (*nagash*), Ps. 69.18; Isa. 58.2

II. **To Be an Effective Worship Leader One Must above All Else Become an Effective Worshiper**

   A. Modeling: the cardinal principle of Christian discipleship

   1. Luke 6.40
   2. 1 Tim. 4.6-16
   3. 1 Cor. 11.1
   4. 1 Cor. 15.1-4
   5. Phil. 3.12-15
   6. Phil. 4.6-9
   7. 1 Pet. 5.1-4

   B. God desires that we worship him in spirit and in truth (John 4.34)

   C. With wholehearted passion: the big three

   1. Moses, Exod. 33-34
   2. David, Ps. 27.1ff; 34.1-3; 104
   3. Paul, Phil.1.18-21

III. **To Be an Effective Worship Leader One Must Understand the Principles and Practice of Worship as They Have Displayed Themselves in the History of the Saints**

   A. Liturgical Theology

   1. Liturgical theology does not focus primarily on the data of the Bible

The Ministry of Praise and Worship (continued)

  2. It concentrates on the history of the Church, that is, what the Church has done in its historical practice to bring glory and honor to God

  3. Use of reason and sociology

B. Tendencies toward shallowness: the problem of ignoring historical worship practice of the Church

  1. Create the rut of ignoring everything that has gone on before, concentrate on what we like and have done

  2. Ignore the power of the Spirit to work in the past

  3. Deny the anointing that God has given to his people throughout every era

  4. Short-change those you lead by isolating them from their brothers and sisters of long ago

C. Views regarding Liturgical Theology

  1. *Anabaptist view*: reproduce NT practice unchanged

  2. *Lutheran, Anglican, Reformed view*: biblical principles and changing conditions

  3. *Jewish synagogue practice*: innovation (things included in the Jewish synagogue practice which were not contained in the OT)

  4. *Historic Christian practice*: cultural, fluid, in line with Scripture

D. Doxological Theology (cf. Robert Webber)

  1. How Jewish and Christian worship can inform theology

  2. Explaining precisely what is the tie between theology and worship, Phil. 2.5-11

  3. Historical outline of theology through detailed study of worship

The Ministry of Praise and Worship (continued)

E. Key subject of liturgical theology: the liturgical calendar (the story of God in the service of the Church)

1. Judaism

    a. Elaborate calendar of holy days in Judaism (similar in some respects to the Catholic calendar)

    b. One weekly (Sabbath), one monthly (the new moon)

    c. Leviticus 23 as biblical description of some of the key festivals and feasts

    d. All days of festival included feasts except the Day of Atonement (a fast)

    e. Feast of Purim added later, along with Dedication (cf. John 10.22)

    f. Worship as ritual drama (remembrance and re-enactment)

2. Gentile Christianity (after the first century)

    a. Exempted from literal law obedience (the council of Jerusalem, Acts 15)

    b. Destruction of the Temple in AD 70, prominence of Gentile form

    c. Christian calendar consisted of Christian holy-days shortly thereafter

    d. The Lord's Day, Sunday

    e. Fasts on Wednesday and Friday (opposed to Jewish on Monday and Thursday)

    f. Borrowed from Judaism – Easter (*Pascha*, i.e., the Passover)

    g. Ascension Day, Epiphany, and Christmas

    h. Trinity Sunday (10th c., western)

F. Summary of Liturgical Theology: celebrates the course of the Revelation story culminating in the life, death, exaltation, and return of Christ

The Ministry of Praise and Worship (continued)

IV. To Be an Effective Worship Leader One Must Comprehend Specifically and Biblically the Power and Significance of Music

A. The power of music

1. As a spiritual force

2. As a cultural phenomenon

3. As an emotional response

4. As a form of communication

5. As a artistic expression

B. Love music as an expression of your heart to the Lord: Psalm 150 (worship is to be unbroken, undiluted, high-energy, wholehearted, and uncompromising)

C. Learning to be a member of a band: the power of contribution

1. Band vs. individual

2. Contribution's elements

   a. Developing an ear for "our sound:" playing a role on a team

   b. Dashes and pinches: the "Lazy Susan" approach to contribution

   c. Learning to downshift: providing sound only when it contributes

   d. Your goal: "I intend to play on my instrument all that and no more which each song requires to give the overall sense and impression that we together intend to make."

D. Master and employ to the full the *Basic Building Blocks* of music.

1. Rhythm - Beat

2. Tempo

The Ministry of Praise and Worship (continued)

      3. Melody

      4. Harmony

      5. Lyrics

      6. Dynamics

  E. The importance of regular practice

      1. Alone

      2. Together

  F. Familiarity: becoming best friends with your instrument

V. To Be an Effective Worship Leader One Must Concentrate on Developing Mastery in Musicianship and Identify Gifts and Passions in Worship

  A. Mastery comes with discipline: 1 Tim. 4.7-8

  B. Identify what your best gifts are (under the scrutiny of loving critique!)

      1. Is it my voice?

      2. Is it my instrumentation?

      3. Is it both? Is it neither? Is it something else altogether?

  C. Design your worship themes, sets of music, and approaches to the service

      1. In conjunction with the theme: forming links, connections, and associations

          a. Invocation and opening praise: beckoning the saints to worship ("Come, Now is the Time to Worship")

The Ministry of Praise and Worship (continued)

      b. Joyous celebration in the presence of the Lord ("We Bring the Sacrifice of Praise")

      c. Adoration and worship ("We Declare Your Majesty")

      d. Commitment and benediction ("Lift Up Your Hearts")

  2. In conjunction with the proclaimed Word of the Lord

  3. In conjunction with the styles

  4. In conjunction with your time constraints

D. Shaping each song within your music set

  1. A song as a story: introductions, middles, transitions, and ends

  2. The art of transposition, changed tempo, voices dropping out, etc.

  3. From trickle to stream to rapids to ocean

  4. Avoiding the "wall of sound" problem associated with young musicians

E. Learning to help every worship team member make their unique contribution to the worship experience through who they are and what they do

  1. Don't simply play or sing; listen to yourself and contribute

  2. The cycle of unending noise

      a. We're playing loud; I cannot hear myself

      b. I turn myself up; others can't hear themselves, they turn themselves up

      c. We're all playing even louder now; I cannot hear myself

      d. Etc.

The Ministry of Praise and Worship (continued)

F. Note the difference between merely playing well vs. enhancing the body's worship

1. Between performing a concert and leading worship

2. Between highlighting your play and contributing to the feeling and mood of the song

3. Between beautifying our song together and playing your instrument

G. Obtain and use the Appropriate Gear

1. Make the financial and emotional investment

   a. From the church: becoming a part of the church's budget

   b. From the musician: investing wisely in the right materials

2. Quality

   a. Avoid the cheapest gear

   b. Don't go broke on the high end

   c. Middle-of-the-road is not bad today: modest investments can produce CD quality return

3. Tastiness: the art of tweaking

4. "Less is more:" If in doubt, dumb down for greatest impact

VI. To Be an Effective Worship Leader One Must Know How to Build and Sustain a Focused Worship Team

A. The many voices, contributions, and gifts in coordination = greatest worship experience for the congregation

B. The importance of worship as a *community event*

The Ministry of Praise and Worship (continued)

C. The Trinitarian Principle applied to worship: unity, diversity, and equality

1. The symphony as model for worship in the Church of Jesus Christ

2. European styles dominate in American churches

3. The Nicene Creed: the Church is one, holy, apostolic, and catholic

    a. Hundreds of styles of praise

    b. Offered to God in scores of languages

    c. Ethno-musicology - the science of human music and learning

    d. No form is superior; all forms are acceptable if done in conjunction with the biblical edicts

4. Dangerous to ignore this principle: hegemony of European styles and power

D. Have clear standards and policies for everyone involved

E. Be careful not to become too professional; emphasize quality but allow for full participation by the body

F. Offer clear and encouraging leadership at all times

G. Recruit from a broad base of people

H. Organize for maximum success and effectiveness

The Ministry of Praise and Worship (continued)

VII. To Be an Effective Worship Leader One Must Creatively Use Resources to Blend the Old and New (the Ancient and the Modern) in Worship and Praise

A. The broadness of expression in the Church of Jesus Christ

1. The biblical plethora: Revelation 5 (from every tribe, language, kindred, and nation)

2. Within these many different styles are reflected, expressed, and enjoyed

   a. Differences according to time: traditional styles versus contemporary styles

   b. Differences according to culture: southern gospel to hip-hop

   c. Differences according to volume

   d. Differences according to meanings of music

3. The "fight" is real and meaningful

4. Not "either/or" but "both/and"

B. Why is a blended worship approach so important?

1. Variety is truly the spice of life, and the nature of God's person and working

2. To hear the Lord's voice afresh: the case for contemporary

3. To remember the Lord's work in our past: the case for traditional

C. One person's garbage is another person's wealth: the tyranny and phases of ethnocentrism (see Acts 10: Peter and the Jewish band's reaction to Cornelius)

1. Phase one: ours is *preferred* over theirs

2. Phase two: ours is *better* than theirs

3. Phase three: ours is *right*, theirs is somewhat iffy

The Ministry of Praise and Worship (continued)

    4. Phase four: mine is God-ordained and *superior*, and everyone else's is odd and wrong

D. Blending: an affirmation of the importance of difference of expression and the holding of tradition in our worship experience in God. How do you blend?

    1. In the songs you select

    2. In the styles you play

    3. In the instrumentation you select

    4. In the vocal arrangements you choose

E. Respecting difference while allowing for preferences and self-expression: the constant challenge of the worship leader

    1. Integrate the service with genuine appreciation of styles

    2. Tease out meaning by playing the same music in differing styles

VIII. The Summary of Worship: Glorifying God in God-Pleasing Harmony

A. Members of the household of God: worship as the expression of saved spirits

B. Built on the foundation of the apostles and prophets, with Jesus Christ as the Chief and Precious Cornerstone: worship as the response to God's historical self-revelation through his Word

C. Joined together as a holy temple in the Lord: worship as the people of God becoming a holy sanctuary where his praises dwell

D. Built together into a dwelling place for God by the Spirit: we ourselves are the place where God's praises originate and where he dwells

E. All that we are and do can harmonize together as leaders, congregation, and worship team into a praise offering sweet and pure enough for our God to dwell!

Eph. 2.19-22 (ESV)
So then you are no longer strangers and aliens, but you are fellow citizens with the saints and members of the household of God, [20] built on the foundation of the apostles and prophets, Christ Jesus himself being the cornerstone, [21] in whom the whole structure, being joined together, grows into a holy temple in the Lord. [22] In him you also are being built together into a dwelling place for God by the Spirit.

APPENDIX 40
The Church Year (Western Church)
The Urban Ministry Institute

The purpose of the liturgical calendar is to relive the major events in Jesus' life in real time.

Date	Event	Purpose
Begins late Nov. or early Dec.	Advent	A season of anticipation and repentance which focuses on **the First and Second Comings of Christ**. The dual focus means that Advent both begins and ends the Christian year (Isa. 9.1-7, 11.1-16; Mark 1.1-8).
Dec. 25	Christmas	Celebrates **the Birth of Christ** (Luke 2.1-20).
Jan. 6	Epiphany	The Feast of Epiphany on January 6 commemorates the coming of the Magi which reveals Christ's mission to the world. The entire season of Epiphany then emphasizes **the way in which Christ revealed himself to the world as the Son of God** (Luke 2.32; Matt. 17.1-6; John 12.32).
The seventh Wednesday before Easter	Ash Wednesday	A day of fasting and repentance that reminds us that we are disciples about to begin **the journey with Jesus that ends in the cross** (Luke 9.51). Ash Wednesday begins the observance of Lent.
40 days before Easter (excluding Sundays)	Lent	A time for reflection on **the suffering and death of Jesus**. Lent also emphasizes "death to self" so that, like Jesus, we prepare ourselves to obey God no matter what sacrifice it involves. Lenten observance calls for people to fast as a way of affirming this attitude of obedience (Luke 5.35; 1 Cor. 9.27; 2 Tim. 2.4; Heb. 11.1-3).
Moveable depending on the date of Easter Sunday which occurs in March or April	Holy Week	*Palm Sunday* The Sunday before Easter which commemorates **the Triumphal Entry of Christ** (John 12.12-18). *Maundy* Thursday* The Thursday before Easter which commemorates the giving of **the New Commandment and the Lord's Supper** prior to Christ's Death (Mark 14.12-26; John 13). (* From the Latin *mandatum novarum* - "new commandment.") *Good Friday* The Friday before Easter which commemorates **the crucifixion of Christ** (John 18-19). *Easter Sunday* The Sunday which celebrates **the resurrection of Christ** (John 20).
40 days after Easter	Ascension Day	Celebrates **the Ascension of Christ** to heaven at which time God "seated him at his right hand in the heavenly realms, far above all rule and authority, power and dominion, and every title that can be given, not only in the present age but also in the one to come" (Eph. 1.20b-21; 1 Pet. 3.22; Luke 24.17-53).
7th Sunday after Easter	Pentecost	The day which commemorates the coming of the Holy Spirit to the Church. **Jesus is now present with all his people** (John 16; Acts 2).
Nov. 1st	All Saints Day	A time to remember those heroes of the faith who have come before us (especially those who died for the Gospel). **The living Christ is now seen in the world through the words and deeds of his people** (John 14.12; Heb. 11; Rev. 17.6).

The Church Year (continued)

The Church Year Follows the Ordering of the Gospels and Acts

- It begins with the birth of Christ (Advent to Epiphany).
- It then focuses on the revelation of his mission to the world (Epiphany).
- It reminds us that Jesus set his face toward Jerusalem and the cross (Ash Wednesday and Lent).
- It chronicles his final week, his crucifixion and his resurrection (Holy Week).
- It affirms his Ascension to the Father's right hand in glory (Ascension Day).
- It celebrates the birth of his Church through the ministry of his Spirit (Pentecost).
- It remembers the history of his Church throughout the ages (All Saints Day).
- Advent both ends the cycle and begins it again. It looks forward to his Second Coming as the conclusion of the Church year but also prepares to remember again his first coming and thus starts the Church year afresh.

Birth
⇩
Ministry
⇩
Passion
⇩
Ascension
⇩
Descent of the Spirit
⇩
The Church through the Ages
⇩
Second Coming

Colors Associated With the Church Year

Christmas Season (Christmas Day through start of Epiphany) - *White and Gold*

Epiphany Season - *Green*

Ash Wednesday and Lent - *Purple*

Holy Week

   Palm Sunday - *Purple*

   Maundy Thursday - *Purple*

   Good Friday - *Black*

   Easter Sunday - *White and Gold*

Ascension Day - *White and Gold*

Pentecost - *Red*

All Saints Day - *Red*

Advent Season (Fourth Sunday before Christmas through Christmas Eve) - *Purple*

The Meaning of the Colors

Black
Mourning, Death

Gold
Majesty, Glory

Green
Hope, Life

Purple
Royalty, Repentance

Red
Holy Spirit (flame)
Martyrdom (blood)

White
Innocence, Holiness, Joy

APPENDIX 41
A Guide to Determining Your Worship Profile
Taken from Robert Webber, Planning Blended Worship, Nashville: Abingdon Press, 1998

1. Which of the following categories best describes your church?

    ____ Affected by Catholic and mainline worship renewal

    ____ Affected by the Pentecostal, charismatic, or praise and worship renewal

    ____ Affected by the movement to blend traditional and contemporary worship

    ____ Not affected by any of the worship renewal movements

2. Identify the age make-up of the people in your church

    ____% of people in our church are boosters (born before 1945)

    ____% of people in our church are boomers (born between 1945 and 1961)

    ____% of people in our church are from generation X (born after 1961)

3. Of the 8 common elements of worship renewal, which ones have made an impact on the worship of your church? Evaluate each of the areas on a scale of 1 (least impact) to 10 (most impact). Then take time to discuss those areas that are weakest.

a.	Our church draws from a biblical understanding of worship.	1 2 3 4 5 6 7 8 9 10
b.	The worship of our church draws from the past, especially the early Church.	1 2 3 4 5 6 7 8 9 10
c.	Our church has experienced a new focus on Sunday worship.	1 2 3 4 5 6 7 8 9 10
d.	Our church draws from the music of the whole Church.	1 2 3 4 5 6 7 8 9 10
e.	Our church has restored the use of the arts.	1 2 3 4 5 6 7 8 9 10
f.	Our church follows the calendar of the Christian year effectively.	1 2 3 4 5 6 7 8 9 10
g.	Our church has experienced the restoration of life in the sacred actions of worship.	1 2 3 4 5 6 7 8 9 10
h.	The worship of our church empowers its outreach ministries.	1 2 3 4 5 6 7 8 9 10

A Guide to Determining Your Worship Profile (continued)

4. Evaluate the content, structure, and style of your worship. Again, use a scale of 1 ("That does not describe our church at all.") to 10 ("Yes, that is our church!"). Discuss areas of greatest weakness.

   a. The content of our worship is the full story of Scripture. 1 2 3 4 5 6 7 8 9 10

   b. The structure of our worship is the universally accepted fourfold pattern. 1 2 3 4 5 6 7 8 9 10

   c. The style of our worship is appropriate to our congregation and to the people we attract. 1 2 3 4 5 6 7 8 9 10

5. Answer the following:

   a. The approach to worship in our church is based upon: Conceptual language/Symbolic language

   b. The communication style of our church will relate best to: Boosters/Boomers/Generation X

   All of the above

6. I would describe our church as: An old paradigm church/A new paradigm church

7. Draw from each of the previous questions to create a worship profile of the church. Do so by completing each of the following sentences:

   a. Our church has been affected by (which stream of worship renewal)

   b. Our age group is primarily

   c. Of the eight aspects of worship renewal, we draw on

   d. The content of our worship is

   e. The structure of our worship is

   f. The style of our worship is

   g. Our approach to communication is

8. To complete this study, comment on the kinds of changes you would like to see occur in the worship of your church.

APPENDIX 42

Understanding Leadership as Representation

The Six Stages of Formal Proxy

Don L. Davis

Commissioning (1)
Formal Selection and Call to Represent

- Chosen to be an emissary, envoy, or proxy
- Confirmed by appropriate other who recognize the call
- Is recognized to be a member of a faithful community
- Calling out of a group to a particular role of representation
- Calling to a particular task or mission
- Delegation of position or responsibility

> Luke 10.1 (ESV) After this the Lord appointed seventy-two others and sent them on ahead of him, two by two, into every town and place where he himself was about to go. . .
>
> Luke 10.16 (ESV) "The one who hears you hears me, and the one who rejects you rejects me, and the one who rejects me rejects him who sent me."
>
> John 20.21 (ESV) Jesus said to them again, "Peace be with you. As the Father has sent me, even so I am sending you."

Equipping (2)
Appropriate Resourcing and Training to Fulfill the Call

- Assignment to a supervisor, superior, mentor, or instructor
- Disciplined instruction of principles underlying the call
- Constant drill, practice, and exposure to appropriate skills
- Recognition of gifts and strengths
- Expert coaching and ongoing feedback

Entrustment (3)
Corresponding Authorization and Empowerment to Act

- Delegation of authority to act and speak on commissioner's behalf
- Scope and limits of representative power provided
- Formal deputization (right to enforce and represent)
- Permission given to be an emissary (to stand in stead of)
- Release to fulfill the commission and task received

Mission (4)
Faithful and Disciplined Engagement of the Task

- Subordination of one's will to accomplish the assignment
- Obedience: carrying out the orders of those who sent you
- Fulfilling the task that was given to you
- Maintaining loyalty to those who sent you
- Freely acting within one's delegated authority to fulfill the task
- Using all means available to do one's duty, whatever the cost
- Full recognition of one's answerability to the one(s) who commissioned

Reckoning (5)
Official Evaluation and Review of One's Execution

- Reporting back to sending authority for critical review
- Formal comprehensive assessment of one's execution and results
- Judgment of one's loyalties and faithfulness
- Sensitive analysis of what we accomplished
- Readiness to ensure that our activities and efforts produce results

Reward (6)
Public Recognition and Continuing Response

- Formal publishing of assessment's results
- Acknowledgment and recognition of behavior and conduct
- Corresponding reward or rebuke for execution
- Review made basis for possible reassignment or recommissioning
- Assigning new projects with greater authority

Leadership As Representation

- The Revealed Will of God
- The Fulfillment of the Task and Mission
- Consent of Your Leaders

CONVICTION • CHARACTER • CONSENSUS

APPENDIX 43
Fit to Represent
Multiplying Disciples of the Kingdom of God

Rev. Dr. Don L. Davis • Luke 10.16 (ESV) - The one who hears you hears me, and the one who rejects you rejects me, and the one who rejects me rejects him who sent me.

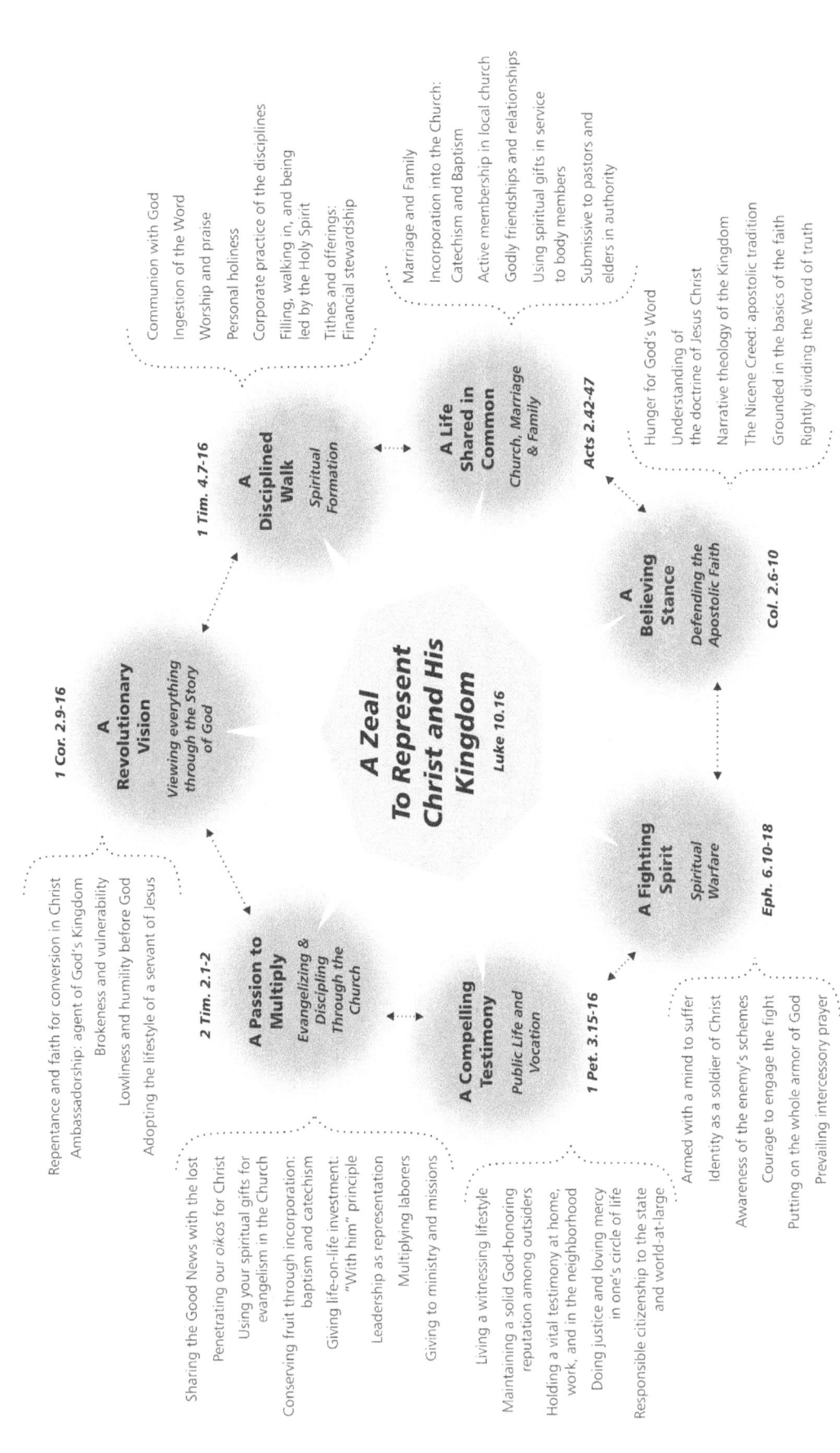

APPENDIX 44
Documenting Your Work
A Guide to Help You Give Credit Where Credit Is Due
The Urban Ministry Institute

Avoiding Plagiarism

Plagiarism is using another person's ideas as if they belonged to you without giving them proper credit. In academic work it is just as wrong to steal a person's ideas as it is to steal a person's property. These ideas may come from the author of a book, an article you have read, or from a fellow student. The way to avoid plagiarism is to carefully use "notes" (textnotes, footnotes, endnotes, etc.) and a "Works Cited" section to help people who read your work know when an idea is one you thought of, and when you are borrowing an idea from another person.

Using Citation References

A citation reference is required in a paper whenever you use ideas or information that came from another person's work.

All citation references involve two parts:

- Notes in the body of your paper placed next to each quotation which came from an outside source.

- A "Works Cited" page at the end of your paper or project which gives information about the sources you have used

Using Notes in Your Paper

There are three basic kinds of notes: parenthetical notes, footnotes, and endnotes. At The Urban Ministry Institute, we recommend that students use parenthetical notes. These notes give the author's last name(s), the date the book was published, and the page number(s) on which you found the information. Example:

> In trying to understand the meaning of Genesis 14.1-24, it is important to recognize that in biblical stories "the place where dialogue is first introduced will be an important moment in revealing the character of the speaker . . ." (Kaiser and Silva 1994, 73). This is certainly true of the character of Melchizedek who speaks words of blessing. This identification of Melchizedek as a positive spiritual influence is reinforced by the fact that he is the King of Salem, since Salem means "safe, at peace" (Wiseman 1996, 1045).

Documenting Your Work (continued)

A "Works Cited" page should be placed at the end of your paper. This page:

- lists every source you quoted in your paper
- is in alphabetical order by author's last name
- includes the date of publication and information about the publisher

Creating a Works Cited Page

The following formatting rules should be followed:

1. Title

The title "Works Cited" should be used and centered on the first line of the page following the top margin.

2. Content

Each reference should list:

- the author's full name (last name first)
- the date of publication
- the title and any special information (Revised edition, 2nd edition, reprint) taken from the cover or title page should be noted
- the city where the publisher is headquartered followed by a colon and the name of the publisher

3. Basic form

- Each piece of information should be separated by a period.
- The second line of a reference (and all following lines) should be indented.
- Book titles should be underlined (or italicized).
- Article titles should be placed in quotes.

Example:

> Fee, Gordon D. 1991. *Gospel and Spirit: Issues in New Testament Hermeneutics.* Peabody, MA: Hendrickson Publishers.

Documenting Your Work (continued)

4. Special Forms

A book with multiple authors:

> Kaiser, Walter C., and Moisés Silva. 1994. *An Introduction to Biblical Hermeneutics: The Search for Meaning.* Grand Rapids: Zondervan Publishing House.

An edited book:

> Greenway, Roger S., ed. 1992. *Discipling the City: A Comprehensive Approach to Urban Mission.* 2nd ed. Grand Rapids: Baker Book House.

A book that is part of a series:

> Morris, Leon. 1971. *The Gospel According to John.* Grand Rapids: Wm. B. Eerdmans Publishing Co. The New International Commentary on the New Testament. Gen. ed. F. F. Bruce.

An article in a reference book:

> Wiseman, D. J. "Salem." 1982. In *New Bible Dictionary.* Leicester, England - Downers Grove, IL: InterVarsity Press. Eds. I. H. Marshall and others.

(An example of a "Works Cited" page is located on the next page.)

For Further Research

Standard guides to documenting academic work in the areas of philosophy, religion, theology, and ethics include:

> Atchert, Walter S., and Joseph Gibaldi. 1985. *The MLA Style Manual.* New York: Modern Language Association.

> *The Chicago Manual of Style.* 1993. 14th ed. Chicago: The University of Chicago Press.

> Turabian, Kate L. 1987. *A Manual for Writers of Term Papers, Theses, and Dissertations.* 5th edition. Bonnie Bertwistle Honigsblum, ed. Chicago: The University of Chicago Press.

Documenting Your Work (continued)

Works Cited

Fee, Gordon D. 1991. *Gospel and Spirit: Issues in New Testament Hermeneutics.* Peabody, MA: Hendrickson Publishers.

Greenway, Roger S., ed. 1992. *Discipling the City: A Comprehensive Approach to Urban Mission.* 2nd ed. Grand Rapids: Baker Book House.

Kaiser, Walter C., and Moisés Silva. 1994. *An Introduction to Biblical Hermeneutics: The Search for Meaning.* Grand Rapids: Zondervan Publishing House.

Morris, Leon. 1971. *The Gospel According to John.* Grand Rapids: Wm. B. Eerdmans Publishing Co. *The New International Commentary on the New Testament.* Gen. ed. F. F. Bruce.

Wiseman, D. J. "Salem." 1982. In *New Bible Dictionary.* Leicester, England-Downers Grove, IL: InterVarsity Press. Eds. I. H. Marshall and others.

Mentoring
The Capstone Curriculum

Before the Course Begins

- First, read carefully the Introduction of the Module found on page 5, and browse through the Mentor's Guide in order to gain an understanding of the content that will be covered in the course. The Student's Workbook is identical to your Mentor's Guide. Your guide, however, also contains a section of additional material and resources for each lesson, called *Mentor's Notes*. References to these instructions are indicated by a symbol in the margin: 📖. The Quizzes, Final Exam, and Answer Keys can all be found on the TUMI Satellite Gateway. (This is available to all approved satellites.)

- Second, you are strongly encouraged to view the teaching on both DVDs prior to the beginning of the course.

- Third, you should read any assigned readings associated with the curriculum, whether textbooks, articles or appendices.

- Fourth, it may be helpful to review the key theological themes associated with the course by using Bible dictionaries, theological dictionaries, and commentaries to refresh your familiarity with major topics covered in the curriculum.

- Fifth, please know that the students *are not tested on the reading assignments*. These are given to help the students get a fuller understanding of what the module is teaching, but it is not required that your students be excellent readers to understand what is being taught. For those of you who are receiving this module in any translation other than English, the required reading might not be available in your language. Please select a book or two that is available in your language - one that you think best represents what is being taught in this module - and assign that to your students instead.

- Finally, begin to think about key questions and areas of ministry training that you would like to explore with students in light of the content that is being covered.

Before Each Lesson

Prior to each lesson, you should once again watch the teaching content that is found on the DVD for that class session, and then create a *Contact* and *Connection* section for this lesson.

Preparing the Contact Section

Review the Mentor's Guide to understand the lesson objectives and gather ideas for possible Contact activities. (Two to three Contacts are provided which you may use, or feel free to create your own, if that is more appropriate.)

Then, create a Contact section that introduces the students to the lesson content and captures their interest. As a rule, Contact methods fall into three general categories.

Attention Focusers capture student attention and introduce them to the lesson topic. Attention focusers can be used by themselves with motivated learners or combined with one of the other methods described below. Examples:

- Singing an opening song related to the lesson theme.

- Showing a cartoon or telling a joke that relates to an issue addressed by the lesson.

- Asking students to stand on the left side of the room if they believe that it is easier to teach people how to be saved from the Gospels and to stand on the right side if they believe it is easier to teach people from the Epistles.

Story-telling methods either have the instructor tell a story that illustrates the importance of the lesson content or ask students to share their experiences (stories) about the topic that will be discussed. Examples:

- In a lesson on the role of the pastor, a Mentor may tell the story of conducting a funeral and share the questions and challenges that were part of the experience.

- In a lesson about evangelism, the Mentor may ask students to describe an experience they have had of sharing the Gospel.

Problem-posing activities raise challenging questions for students to answer and lead them toward the lesson content as a source for answering those questions, or they may ask students to list the unanswered questions that they have about the topic that will be discussed. Examples:

- Presenting case studies from ministry situations that call for a leadership decision and having students discuss what the best response would be.

- Problems framed as questions such as "When preaching at a funeral, is it more important for a minister to be truthful or compassionate? Why?"

Regardless of what method is chosen, the key to a successful Contact section is making a transition from the Contact to the Content of the lesson. When planning the Contact section, Mentors should write out a transition statement that builds a bridge from the Contact to the lesson content. For example, if the lesson content was on the truth that the Holy Spirit is a divine Person who is a full member of the Godhead, the Contact activity might be to have students quickly draw a symbol that best represents the Holy Spirit to them. After having them share their drawings and discuss why they chose what they did, the Mentor might make a transition statement along the following lines:

> *Because the Holy Spirit is often represented by symbols like fire or oil in Scripture rather than with a human image like the Father or the Son, it is sometimes difficult to help people understand that the Spirit is a full person within the Godhead who thinks, acts, and speaks as personally as God the Father or Jesus Christ. In this lesson, we want to establish the scriptural basis for understanding that the Spirit is more than just a symbol for "God's power" and think about ways that we can make this plain to people in our congregations.*

This is a helpful transition statement because it directs the students to what they can expect from the lesson content and also prepares them for some of the things that might be discussed in the Connection section that comes later. Although you may adapt your transition statement based on student responses during the Contact section, it is important, during the planning time, to think about what will be said.

Three useful questions for evaluating the Contact section you have created are:

- Is it creative and interesting?
- Does it take into account the needs and interests of this particular group?
- Does it focus people toward the lesson content and arouse their interest in it?

Again, review the Mentor's Guide to understand the lesson objectives and gather ideas for possible Connection activities.

Preparing the Connection Section

Then, create a Connection section that helps students form new associations between truth and their lives (implications) and discuss specific changes in their beliefs, attitudes, or actions that should occur as a result (applications). As you plan, be a little wary of making the Connection section overly specific. Generally this lesson section should come to students as an invitation to discover, rather than as a finished product with all the specific outcomes predetermined.

At the heart of every good Connection section is a question (or series of questions) that asks students how knowing the truth will change their thinking, attitudes, and behaviors. (We have included some Connection questions in order to "prime the pump" of your students, to spur their thinking, and help them generate their own questions arising from their life experience.) Because this is theological and ministry training, the changes we are most concerned with are those associated with the way in which the students train and lead others in their ministry context. Try and focus in on helping students think about this area of application in the questions you develop.

The Connection section can utilize a number of different formats. Students can discuss the implications and applications together in a large Mentor-led group or in small groups with other students (either open discussion or following a pre-written set of questions). Case studies, also, are often good discussion starters. Regardless of the method, in this section both the Mentor and the learning group itself should be seen as a source of wisdom. Since your students are themselves already Christian leaders, there is often a wealth of experience and knowledge that can be drawn on from the students themselves. Students should be encouraged to learn from each other as well as from the Mentor.

Several principles should guide the Connection discussions that you lead:

- First, the primary goal in this section is to bring to the surface the questions that students have. In other words, the questions that occur to students during the lesson take priority over any questions that the Mentor prepares in advance–although the questions raised by an experienced Mentor will still be a useful learning tool. A corollary to this is to assume that the question raised by one student is very often the unspoken question present among the entire group.

- Second, try and focus the discussion on the concrete and the specific rather than the purely theoretical or hypothetical. This part of the lesson is meant to focus on the actual situations that are being faced by the specific students in your classroom.

- Third, do not be afraid to share the wisdom that you have gained through your own ministry experience. You are a key resource to students and they should expect that you will make lessons you have learned available to them. However, always keep in mind that variables of culture, context, and personality may mean that what has worked for you may not always work for everyone. Make suggestions, but dialogue with students about whether your experience seems workable in their context, and if not, what adaptations might be made to make it so.

Three useful questions for evaluating the Connection section you have created are:

- Have I anticipated in advance what the general areas of implication and application are likely to be for the teaching that is given in the lesson?

- Have I created a way to bring student questions to the surface and give them priority?

- Will this help a student leave the classroom knowing what to do with the truth they have learned?

Finally, because the Ministry Project is the structured application project for the entire course, it will be helpful to set aside part of the Connection section to have students discuss what they might choose for their project and to evaluate progress and/or report to the class following completion of the assignment.

Steps in Leading a Lesson

- Take attendance.

- Lead the devotion.

- Say or sing the Nicene Creed and pray.

- Administer the quiz.

- Check Scripture memorization assignment.

- Collect any assignments that are due.

Opening Activities

- Use a Contact provided in the Mentor's Guide, or create your own.

Teach the Contact Section

- Present the Content of the lesson using the video teaching.

  Using the Video Segments
  Each lesson has two video teaching segments, each approximately 25 minutes in length. After teaching the Contact section (including the transition statement), play the first video segment for the students. Students can follow this presentation using their Student Workbook which contains a general outline of the material presented and Scripture references and other supplementary materials referenced by the speaker. Once the first segment is viewed, work with the students to confirm that the content was understood.

  Ensuring that the Content is Understood
  Segue
  Using the Mentor's Guide, check for comprehension by asking the questions listed in the "Student Questions and Response" section. Clarify any incomplete understandings that students may demonstrate in their answers.

  Ask students if there are any questions that they have about the content and discuss them together as a class. NOTE - The questions here should focus on

Oversee the Content Section

understanding the content itself rather than on how to apply the learning. Application questions will be the focus of the upcoming Connection section.

Take a short class break and then repeat this process with the second video segment.

Teach the Connection Section

- Summary of Key Concepts
- Student Application and Implications
- Case Studies
- Restatement of Lesson's Thesis
- Resources and Bibliographies
- Ministry Connections
- Counseling and Prayer

Remind Students of Upcoming Assignments

- Scripture Memorization
- Assigned Readings
- Other Assignments

Close Lesson

- Close with prayer
- Be available for any individual student's questions or needs following the class

Please see the next page for an actual "Module Lesson Outline."

The quizzes, the final exam, and their answer keys are located at the back of this book.

Module Lesson Outline

    Lesson Title — Introduction
    Lesson Objectives
    Devotion
    Nicene Creed and Prayer
    Quiz
    Scripture Memorization Review
    Assignments Due

    Contact (1-3) — Contact

    Video Segment 1 Outline — Content
    Segue 1 (Student Questions and Response)
    Video Segment 2 Outline
    Segue 2 (Student Questions and Response)

    Summary of Key Concepts — Connection
    Student Application and Implications
    Case Studies
    Restatement of Lesson's Thesis
    Resources and Bibliographies
    Ministry Connections
    Counseling and Prayer

    Scripture Memorization — Assignments
    Reading Assignment
    Other Assignments
    Looking Forward to the Next Lesson

Effective Worship Leading
Worship, Word, and Sacrament

MENTOR'S NOTES 1

📖 1
Page 13
Lesson Introduction

Welcome to the Mentor's Guide for Lesson 1, *Effective Worship Leading: Worship, Word, and Sacrament*. The overall focus of the Practicing Christian Leadership module is on Christian leadership, the kind of leadership that can establish, equip, and empower disciples in the city for ministry. This module seeks to highlight the ways in which Christian leaders provide care for the spiritual well-being and welfare of others, those whom they either formally or informally lead in the body of Christ.

Immediately, it would be helpful for you to understand, review, and teach to your students the general outlines of what is involved in Christian leadership as understood formally in the New Testament. There are two designations in the New Testament for leader, generally. The first, "presbyters" or elder (Gk. *presbuteros*), which carries the connotation of someone who is both older and a believer, either for an older man or woman (1 Tim. 5.1, 2). It is used also for both Church leaders (Acts 14.23; 15.2, 4, 6) as well as members of the Sanhedrin (Acts 4.5). This term focuses on the dignity, station, and credibility of the role of Christian leadership. It speaks, likewise of authority and responsibility; elders had authority to distribute the funds of the body for the well-being of others (Acts 11.30), determine issues of doctrine and ethical practice (Acts 15.2-6, 22; 16.2), and to receive updates from the evangelists and apostles on the progress of their work (Acts 20.17; 21.18). They were to be entrusted with authority, respected in their service, and charged with prayer for the sick and those requiring care (1 Tim. 5.17; 1 Pet. 5.1-4; James 5.14).

The second formal sense of leadership has to do with overseers, or bishops (Gk. *episkopos*). This term related to the Christian leader's responsibility to guard or give watch over the flock of God, in the same way that a shepherd watches over his sheep. In like manner, all of the duties of a shepherd are applied to the role of the bishop, to nurture, feed, guard, and protect the flock of God (cf. Acts 20.28; 1 Tim. 3.2; Titus 1.7). When we compare the Scriptures of Acts 20.17, 28 and Titus 1.5, 7 show that the terms for "elder" and "overseer" are used in a way to show that they refer to the same position in the Church. Some have described that *presbuteros* stresses the dignity of Christian leadership and *episkopos* focuses on the work Christian leaders do. This is a helpful designation thoroughly consistent with the meaning of the terms in Scripture.

For a full listing of the qualifications of these formal offices please refer carefully to 1 Timothy 3.1-7 and Titus 1.5-9. People of the highest moral, spiritual, and theological character are to be appointed to positions of Christian leadership in the Church. The reason for this high character is plain; elders and bishops were charged with leading the flock of the Lord (Acts 20.28), teaching and nurturing them in the Word of God (1 Tim. 3.2), and providing general oversight in the affairs of the community, especially protecting them from the errors and attacks of unscrupulous deceivers and the deceits of the enemy (1 Tim. 5.17; Titus 1.9). The fact that elders are often mentioned as more than one says that we must conceive of Christian leadership as a plurality in the body of Christ; God will raise up a sufficient number of qualified spiritual laborers to care for his people (see Acts 14.23; Phil. 1.1; Titus 1.5). To these two designations we can also add the role of deacons (Gk. *diakonos*), or "servants" or "ministers" whose roles seemed to focus on providing support to the elders, while assuming responsibility for ministering to the material needs of the body (cf. Acts 6.1-6). These leaders were to be people of high character and devotion to the Lord (1 Tim. 3.8-13).

All in all, through elders, bishops, and deacons, the Church of God has been supplied through the grace of God with a remarkable resource of spiritual laborers to protect, feed, and care for the body of Christ.

In the objectives section of the Student Workbook you will notice that these aims are clearly stated, and you ought to emphasize them throughout the lesson, during the discussions and interaction with the students. The more you can highlight the objectives throughout the class period, the better the chances are that they will understand and grasp the magnitude of these objectives. Indeed, the more aware you are of the objectives, the more integrated and helpful the teaching material will be for your students throughout the sessions.

Do not hesitate to discuss these objectives briefly before you enter into the class period. Draw the students' attention to the objectives, for, in a real sense, this is the heart of your educational aim for the class period in this lesson. Everything

📖 2
*Page 13
Lesson Objectives*

discussed and done ought to point back to these objectives. Find ways to highlight these at every turn, to reinforce them and reiterate them as you go.

In a real sense, focusing on the objectives gives you a constellation to navigate the flow and content of the class by. Refer to them often with the students, and relate the various points of interest and conversation to them as you lead them.

In regards to the textbooks, it is important for you to understand the way in which these relate to the overall handling of the course. Your key texts for the course are the following:

> Cothen, Joe H. (Revision editors J. H. Cothen and Jerry N. Barlow), *Equipped for Good Work*.
>
> Carter, Kenneth H. Jr., *The Gifted Pastor: Finding and Using Your Spiritual Gifts*.
>
> Engle, Paul E., ed. *Baker's Wedding Handbook*.
>
> ------, ed. *Baker's Worship Handbook*.
>
> ------, ed. *Baker's Funeral Handbook*.
>
> Ward, Charles G., Ed. *The Billy Graham Christian Worker's Handbook: A Topical Guide with Biblical Answers to the Urgent Concerns of Our Day*.

Here are a few observations about these texts:

1. The books are given in order to both enrich and supplement the overall experience of learning in the class. Different from normal academic treatments, the textbooks are important but play a complimentary role in connection to the course material.

2. Wherever possible, highlight different insights and ideas from the text as they correlate and interact with the subject of the day, or the general ideas you are dealing with in regards to their questions, or the course in general.

3. Remind the students of the importance of them acquiring a solid core of texts that they can use for their ministries in the future. This is especially true in this module regarding the Billy Graham Christian Worker's Handbook, as well as

the Baker Series (i.e., *Baker's Worship Handbook, Baker's Wedding Handbook,* and *Baker's Funeral Handbook*). While the students may think this is overkill, and while they may not use these in the classic sense as textbooks in this course, it is important for you to remind them of the purpose of the Capstone Curriculum. It was designed to provide an urban leader with all the resources needed to either plant or lead urban churches. These texts are critical for those who go into more formal leadership roles, so encourage the students to use these prime resources wisely. They constitute a good beginning of Christian worker's or pastor's practical library for ministry, covering the vast majority of situations they will encounter, from marriage to baby dedications to funerals to counseling sessions.

4. Your ability to refer to the ideas in the reading assignments during your class sessions will help the students understand the importance of gleaning from them insights that will enhance their ability to lead. Again, for some who are studying formally for pastoral ministry, such encouragements will be less necessary. For those lay leaders who are taking the course for enrichment, you will have to encourage them to "sharpen their saw" with an intent to be prepared for whatever the Lord might have for them to do.

5. From a practical standpoint, the books in this module address many contemporary questions that your students are likely to have great interest in. Encourage them to become acquainted with them, especially the *Baker Handbook Series* and the *Graham Christian Worker's Handbook* as they deal with a broad number of important topics the students will encounter as they minister to and counsel others. They are aptly named, handbooks to deal with specific issues, concerns, and problems. Encourage them to use them in this way.

6. Both Cothen's and Carter's books deal with the subject matter of the sessions in a more direct and complimentary way. Make certain that you read the week's assignment ahead of time, and make a note to yourself to refer to the reading at some time during the class session. This will help the students not only see the relevance of the reading to the study assignment, but will force them to think critically how the materials connect with the themes of the day.

In all things, the operative principle ought to be what Paul said to Timothy:

> 2 Timothy 2.20-21 - Now in a great house there are not only vessels of gold and silver but also of wood and clay, some for honorable use, some for dishonorable. [21] Therefore, if anyone cleanses himself from what is dishonorable, he will be a vessel for honorable use, set apart as holy, useful to the master of the house, ready for every good work.

All students must be prepared for the work which the Lord may call them to. It is in this spirit that we encourage you to exhort your students to strive for excellence and depth.

3
Page 13 Devotion

This devotion focuses on the concept of representation, which is a critical metaphor for all leadership in Scripture, expressed and shown in both the Old and New Testaments. A number of texts highlight this emphasis; notice how each one gives a sense of representation in spiritual leadership:

> 2 Cor. 5.20 - Therefore, we are ambassadors for Christ, God making his appeal through us. We implore you on behalf of Christ, be reconciled to God.

> Job 33.23 - If there be for him an angel, a mediator, one of the thousand, to declare to man what is right for him.

> Prov. 13.17 - A wicked messenger falls into trouble, but a faithful envoy brings healing.

> Mal. 2.7 - For the lips of a priest should guard knowledge, and people should seek instruction from his mouth, for he is the messenger of the Lord of hosts.

> John 20.21 - Jesus said to them again, "Peace be with you. As the Father has sent me, even so I am sending you."

> Luke 10.16 - The one who hears you hears me, and the one who rejects you rejects me, and the one who rejects me rejects him who sent me.

Acts 26.17-18 - delivering you from your people and from the Gentiles - to whom I am sending you [18] to open their eyes, so that they may turn from darkness to light and from the power of Satan to God, that they may receive forgiveness of sins and a place among those who are sanctified by faith in me.

2 Cor. 3.6 - who has made us competent to be ministers of a new covenant, not of the letter but of the Spirit. For the letter kills, but the Spirit gives life.

Eph. 6.20 - for which I am an ambassador in chains, that I may declare it boldly, as I ought to speak.

Enabling your students to see that they, in fact, represent the risen and exalted Lord Jesus in their leadership is one of the critical empowering elements of this module. What they are engaged in is not merely good efforts or care; they stand in the place of and for the glory of the Lord Jesus, and he himself will reward their faithful obedience in serving the needs of his people. This corresponds directly to the way in which our Lord obeyed the Father, and therefore God highly exalted him (Phil. 2.5-11). In the same way, we honor Christ, and so he will honor us (John 12.24-25). This was applied as well to receiving the apostles' words as Christ's own instruction (cf. 1 Thess. 4.8 - Therefore whoever disregards this, disregards not man but God, who gives his Holy Spirit to you.)

Notice this sense of representation again in the following texts:

Matt. 10.40 - Whoever receives you receives me, and whoever receives me receives him who sent me.

Mark 9.37 - Whoever receives one such child in my name receives me, and whoever receives me, receives not me but him who sent me.

Luke 9.48 - and said to them, "Whoever receives this child in my name receives me, and whoever receives me receives him who sent me. For he who is least among you all is the one who is great."

John 12.44 - And Jesus cried out and said, "Whoever believes in me, believes not in me but in him who sent me."

John 12.48 - The one who rejects me and does not receive my words has a judge; the word that I have spoken will judge him on the last day.

John 13.20 - Truly, truly, I say to you, whoever receives the one I send receives me, and whoever receives me receives the one who sent me.

📖 4
Page 26
Student Questions and Response

The segue questions are designed to ensure that the students understand the critical aims and facts presented in the first video segment. Your role as mentor is to use the questions to review the key concepts and insights presented in the video, as well as draw out the students to see that they understand them as presented.

It will be necessary, of course, for you to gauge your time well, especially if your students are intrigued with the concepts, and want to discuss their implications at length. Your class session and its length should guide you in the kind of freedom you give yourself and your students to interact on the various concerns and issues that emerge from your dialogue. Allow for the proper time to focus in on the main points, and still have enough time for a break before the next video segment is started.

📖 5
Page 37
Summary of Key Concepts

This section of a module offers you an opportunity to review the key concepts of the entire lesson, including both segments and any other ideas which have emerged in your study of the theme. The statements listed below, therefore, represent the fundamental truths which the students should take away from this materials in this lesson, that is, from the videos and your guided discussion with them. Make sure that these concepts are clearly defined and carefully considered, for their quiz work and exams will be taken from these items directly.

📖 6
Page 38
Student Application and Implications

In helping your students think through their own situations, you might want to design some questions or use those provided below as water to "prime the pump" of their interests, so to speak. It is important that you help the students develop habits of critical thinking, the ability to ponder not only what the facts are but also (and more importantly) what the meaning of those facts are in light of their own lives and ministries. So, please see this sections and its questions in the proper light. What is significant here is not that you merely ask the questions written below, but that you, in conversation with your students, start to help them identify that cadre of issues, concerns, questions, and ideas that flow directly from their experience.

Do not hesitate to spend the majority of time on some question that arose from the video, or some special concern that is especially relevant in their ministry context right now. The goal of this section is for you to enable them to think critically and theologically in regards to their own lives and ministry contexts. Again, the questions below are provided as guides and primers, and ought not to be seen as absolute necessities. Pick and choose among them, or come up with your own. The key is relevance now, to their context and to their questions.

A part of a good classroom situation is that the students are clear regarding their responsibilities for class, that is, that they know all facets of the assignment, that all their questions regarding those assignments are known and answered, and that you as mentor or instructor are prepared to lead them to the next theme and study.

Make certain that the students understand the assignment for next week, especially what they are responsible for in their summaries of the texts they are to read. This is not difficult; the goal is that they would read the material as best as they can and write a few sentences on what they take them to mean. This is a critical intellectual skill for your students to learn, so make sure that you encourage them in this process. Of course, for those students who might find this difficult, assure them of the intent behind this assignment, and emphasize their understanding of the material being the key, not their writing skills. We want to improve their skills, but not at the expense of their encouragement and edification. Nor, however, do we want to sell them short. Strike to find the midpoint between challenge and encouragement here.

*7
*Page 42
Assignments*

Effective Christian Education
Incorporating, Parenting, and Discipling

MENTOR'S NOTES 2

📖 1
Page 47
Lesson Introduction

Welcome to the Mentor's Guide for Lesson 2, *Effective Christian Education: Incorporating, Parenting, and Discipling*. The overall focus of this lesson deals with the responsibility of the Christian leader to bring newly converted believers into the body, and spiritually parent them for the purpose of their own edification and establishment in the faith. G. W. Icenogle makes this clear in his fine book on the biblical foundations for small group ministry:

> *In a real sense, your goal is to help the students learn that accepting their responsibility as Christian leaders involves their commitment to walking with believers from birth to childhood to maturity. To be a Christian leader is to be a spiritual parent. Jesus designated the Twelve to be apostles. An apostle is 'one who is sent forth.' The etymology of the word implies 'one who is sent from.' Jesus first called the small group to come and follow, then to go and minister. In relationship with Jesus, this inner group of twelve grew out of discipleship into apostleship. The following and learning flowed into them being sent and ministering. Implied in the life-cycle of the faithful small group is the process of journey, growth, transformation and progression into ministry. Mission is always the fulfillment of learning. In his overwhelming bestseller* **The Master Plan of Evangelism**, *Robert Coleman described this small group movement as eight stages of discipleship: selection, association, consecration, impartation, demonstration, delegation, supervision and reproduction. Coleman asserts the overarching importance of the Twelve as a small group community in their discipleship with Jesus.*

~ G. W. Icenogle. **Biblical Foundations for Small Group Ministry: An Integrative Approach**. (electronic version). Downers Grove, IL: InterVarsity Press, 1994.

The truths within this lesson are designed to get your students thinking critically about the need to take responsibility for incorporating (i.e., bringing into the family) new believers into the Church, and once incorporated, taking responsibility for their care and feeding as newborn babes in Christ. Please notice again in the objectives that these truths are clearly stated. As usual, your responsibility as Mentor is to emphasize these concepts throughout the lesson, especially during the discussions and interaction with the students. The more you can highlight the objectives throughout the class period, the better the chances are that they will understand and grasp the magnitude of these objectives.

This devotion deals with the call to grow up to Christian maturity. In a real sense, a believer grows in three senses, or put another way, experiences three dimensions of being saved by Jesus Christ. First and foundationally speaking, a Christian is saved as a result of the sacrifice of Christ, which allows us to think of our salvation in Christ as a past event (Titus 3.4-5; cf. Eph. 2.5-8). In this first sense, we have already been saved from the wrath of God and the punishment we so justly deserved by the shed blood of Jesus Christ. We called on the name of the Lord Jesus (Rom. 10.9-13) and entered into the Kingdom of God by faith (Mark 10.23-27). Simultaneously, we were sealed by the Holy Spirit, and baptized (placed into) the Church as the body of Christ (1 Cor. 12.13; Gal. 3.26-28).

We are also "being saved" as we yield ourselves to the Holy Spirit, who makes us slaves of righteousness through his power and brings release from the power and reign of sin (Gal. 5.16ff.; Rom. 6.6, 12-14, 19). As we yield to the Holy Spirit we continue to grow towards Christian maturity (Eph. 4.13; Col. 1.28). Believers are described, then, by the Apostle Paul as "those who are *being saved*" (cf. 2 Cor. 2.15; cf. 1 Cor. 1.18). Moreover, Peter also challenges disciples of Jesus to grow up in their salvation, making their calling and election sure (see 1 Pet. 2.2; 2 Pet.1.4-10, cf. Heb. 6.9). We work out in our lives what God through his Spirit is working within us (Phil. 2.12-13 with Eph. 2.10). In this sense, as babies born anew in Christ, we are now to grow up into Christ into all things a fully mature believers (Eph. 4.9-16), and then become teachers of others (Heb. 5.11-14).

Of course, our salvation will only be completely consummated at the Second Coming of our Lord where, in the future, we experience the full "redemption of the body" from our susceptibility to corruption and death to our conformity to the body of the risen Jesus (Phil. 3.20-21), and the entrance of the "new heavens and a new earth in which righteousness has its home" (2 Pet. 3.13).

To ask believers to "act their age" is an exhortation to maturity, to disdain remaining a spiritual infant, to call believers to attain to the full measure of the stature of Christ which is God's will for the believer in the midst of his people. Things which are both understandable and excusable for a baby or an infant would be scandalous for a teenager or young adult, let alone a fully grown and mature

2
Page 47
Devotion

person. Encourage your students to become fully mature in Jesus Christ, and to be willing to pay the requisite price in discipline, self-sacrifice, and obedience to attain to that level of excellence and maturity.

📖 3
*Page 49
Scripture
Memorization
Review*

The memorized Word carries with it deep promises of blessing, benefit, and fruitfulness in the life of a follower of Jesus Christ, and is an indispensable weapon in the arsenal of the man or woman of God in ministry.

> Ps. 119.9-11 - How can a young man keep his way pure? By guarding it according to your word. [10] With my whole heart I seek you; let me not wander from your commandments! [11] I have stored up your word in my heart, that I might not sin against you.

> Job 22.22 - Receive instruction from his mouth, and lay up his words in your heart.

> Ps. 37.31 - The law of his God is in his heart; his steps do not slip.

> Ps. 40.8 - I desire to do your will, O my God; your law is within my heart.

> Ps. 119.97 - Oh how I love your law! It is my meditation all the day.

> Jer. 15.16 - Your words were found, and I ate them, and your words became to me a joy and the delight of my heart, for I am called by your name, O Lord, God of hosts.

> Col. 3.16 - Let the word of Christ dwell in you richly, teaching and admonishing one another in all wisdom, singing psalms and hymns and spiritual songs, with thankfulness in your hearts to God.

If at all possible, memorize the Scriptures with the students, and challenge them to be faithful in their review of the verses, which is the key to ensuring that they not only keep them, but also allow the Holy Spirit to bring these texts to their remembrance. (It will be easier for the Spirit to bring them back if they are hidden in the heart already.)

Remind the students of the words of Christ:

> John 16.13 - When the Spirit of truth comes, he will guide you into all the truth, for he will not speak on his own authority, but whatever he hears he will speak, and he will declare to you the things that are to come.

> John 14.26 - But the Helper, the Holy Spirit, whom the Father will send in my name, he will teach you all things and bring to your remembrance all that I have said to you.

Again, in the questions below you will find the focus is upon mastering the data and the facts associated with the claims made in the first video segment, which focused on the nuts-and-bolts of bringing a new believer into the family of God. Our ability or inability to welcome new believers can dramatically impact whether or not they continue to grow to maturity as God desires for them. Help your students come to grips with the significance of this challenge, and spend much of your discussion time concentrating on all the various issues related to the healthy transition and welcome of a person into the body after they have placed their faith in Christ.

Of course, as always, make certain that you watch the clock here, covering the questions below and those posed by your students, and watch for any tangents which may lead you from rehearsing the critical facts and main points.

*4
Page 58
Student Questions and Response*

If you have time to cover extra material, you might want to concentrate some discussion on the first two chapters of Paul's first letter to the Thessalonians. Perhaps no epistle in the NT so forcefully and powerfully gives us a picture of what it means to be a spiritual parent than these chapters. Paul's deep burden for them extended to his likening himself to their spiritual mother (2.8), their father (2.10ff.), and their brother (chapters 3-5). The principles to be gleaned here on the nature of the kind of affection and care that an authentic Christian leader has for newborn and immature believers are priceless, and cannot be over-emphasized. You may want to review these chapters in 1 Thessalonians, and use some of the ideas you glean from those chapters in the discussions you lead with the students.

*5
Page 70
Summary of Key Concepts*

📖 6
Page 73
Case Studies

The case studies included in these modules are designed to enable your students to "win a battle on the blackboard," so to speak, since many (if not most) of them are induced from actual experiences and situations in urban ministry. What is important for the students to be able to do (and you as well, as their facilitator) is to place themselves imaginatively within the situation, and then actually confront the issues as best they can, given their knowledge and experience. You can either engage these as a class, as small groups, or as individuals. Discuss the various strategies that are possible, and show the students that in many cases there may be more than one right answer to the nagging problem encountered in the case study.

What is critical is that you allow the students to field test their ability to apply biblical principles and their ministry experience to solving a real life issue of Christian growth and maturity. The goal, of course, is not that the students find the one correct solution to the challenge, but that they incorporate in their solutions the insight and lessons that they have learned from Scripture and the interaction within your learning sessions together.

📖 7
Page 76
Counseling and Prayer

It is hard to overestimate the strength of your example in helping your students understand the power of prayer in every phase of their lives and ministries. Even a few of the more categorical promises about the importance of prayer can underscore the significance of this claim:

> Phil. 4.6-7 - Do not be anxious about anything, but in everything by prayer and supplication with thanksgiving let your requests be made known to God. [7] And the peace of God, which surpasses all understanding, will guard your hearts and your minds in Christ Jesus.

> Ps. 34.5 - Those who look to him are radiant, and their faces shall never be ashamed.

> Ps. 34.7 - The angel of the Lord encamps around those who fear him, and delivers them.

> Ps. 55.17 - Evening and morning and at noon I utter my complaint and moan, and he hears my voice.

Ps. 55.22 - Cast your burden on the Lord, and he will sustain you; he will never permit the righteous to be moved.

Ps. 62.8 - Trust in him at all times, O people; pour out your heart before him; God is a refuge for us. *Selah*.

Prov. 3.5-6 - Trust in the Lord with all your heart, and do not lean on your own understanding. [6] In all your ways acknowledge him, and he will make straight your paths.

Prov. 16.3 - Commit your work to the Lord, and your plans will be established.

Jer. 33.3 - Call to me and I will answer you, and will tell you great and hidden things that you have not known.

Matt. 7.7-8 - Ask, and it will be given to you; seek, and you will find; knock, and it will be opened to you. [8] For everyone who asks receives, and the one who seeks finds, and to the one who knocks it will be opened.

Eph. 6.18 - Praying at all times in the Spirit, with all prayer and supplication. To that end keep alert with all perseverance, making supplication for all the saints.

Col. 4.2 - Continue steadfastly in prayer, being watchful in it with thanksgiving.

1 Thess. 5.17-18 - Pray without ceasing, [18] give thanks in all circumstances; for this is the will of God in Christ Jesus for you.

1 Pet. 4.7 - The end of all things is at hand; therefore be self-controlled and sober-minded for the sake of your prayers.

Jude 1.20-21 - But you, beloved, build yourselves up in your most holy faith; pray in the Holy Spirit; [21] keep yourselves in the love of God, waiting for the mercy of our Lord Jesus Christ that leads to eternal life.

In light of these plain injunctions and promises to prayer, never therefore become overly familiar or dismissive of the need to pray with and for your students. Prayer is a wonderfully practical and helpful way to apply truth; by taking specific needs to

God in light of a truth, the students can solidify those ideas in their soul, and receive back from the Lord the answers they need in order to be sustained in the midst of their ministries. Of course, everything is somehow dependent on the amount of time you have in your session, and how you have organized it. Nevertheless, your ability and earnestness to take their needs before the Lord in prayer is a model and a habit that will never be lost nor neglected in their own discipleship. Prayer is a forceful and potent part of any spiritual encounter and teaching, and if you can, it should always have its place, even if it is a short summary prayer of what God has taught us, and a determination to live out its implications as the Holy Spirit teaches us.

Effective Church Discipline
Exhorting, Rebuking, and Restoring

MENTOR'S NOTES 3

Page 81
Lesson Introduction

Welcome to the Mentor's Guide for Lesson 3, *Effective Church Discipline: Exhorting, Rebuking, and Restoring*. This lesson concentrates on the role of the Christian leader to both exhort and encourage believers in the body of Christ to remain faithful to Christ. The inability to identify the kinds of input that a believer needs, and then to provide them with the appropriate care is a great problem in much small group, pastoral, and one-on-one ministry today. Undergirding all attempts to care for believers is the assumption that we have understood precisely what they require, and that we have provided for that need in the right measure, at the right time, and with the appropriate emphasis called for. This lesson introduces us to the very real possibilities that Christian leaders, especially those who are equipping disciples among the urban poor, will encounter those who need encouragement, and at times, exhortation and even rebuke.

It will be important for you to help your students in this lesson understand that one's temperament and style are only of marginal importance in this expression of Christian leadership. Whether they are introverted or outgoing, whether they prefer an indirect approach or more confrontational style, the biblical injunction of exhortation and discipline stands clear and important. As you explore these concepts you must help your students to understand the *scriptural grounds* for these demands. In a day when privacy and individualism are at all time peak levels in society and the Church, it will be tempting to overlook this part of Christian leadership, or delegate it to those who do not mind engaging in conflict for the sake of growth. After all, not all of us were born with a staff sergeant's personality, and the Christian Church is not the personal boot camp of an aggressive, buttinsky kind of spiritual leader.

What will become plain as you look at the texts, however, is that the contour of authentic Christian leadership involves the pole of challenge as well as the pole of affection, the pole of confrontation as well as the pole of encouragement. We will not define this in terms of "balance" since the appropriate response is not a matter of weighing how many encouragements you have given over against how many exhortations. Rather, led by the Spirit of God and sensitive to the people we lead and the situations they face, we provide the appropriate care which matches their spirit of openness, their level of responsiveness, and the facts we are encountering together. We will seek to take our cues and models on Paul's example, where he exhorted the Thessalonians to employ such a multi-faceted approach to discipling and care. Note his instruction:

> 1 Thess. 5.14-15 - And we urge you, brothers, admonish the idle, encourage the fainthearted, help the weak, be patient with them all. [15] See that no one repays anyone evil for evil, but always seek to do good to one another and to everyone.

We are to admonish the *idle* not the *fainthearted*, and we are to *help* the weak, not *admonish* them. Truly, one size in Christian care does not fit all. This lesson is a challenge to the leader to be filled with the Spirit in such a way that they can discern what kind of response is called for, at what time, for what end, and in what way.

This devotion highlights a critical element in all genuinely Christian exhortation or discipline. The focus is not upon imposing guilt, condemnation, and shame on the offender or recalcitrant believer, but rather on the restoration and re-inclusion of the person within the family of God and the fellowship of the body. The example of Peter's betrayal may be one of the most vivid examples of this principle, largely because of the Herculean size of the offense. Peter betrayed the Lord, not once, but three times, denying even to have known him or to have associated with him in any way. What could be more horrible, in the family of terrible acts, than this?

What is instructive in this example is that the Lord, knowing fully that Peter would commit these acts, had already interceded for him, and made plans for this incident not to isolate or shame him, but to propel him to a position of servanthood and care for his fellow disciples. Having experienced the forgiveness and grace of our Lord, Peter would be in a good position to empathize with the situation of others who would need the forgiveness of the Lord.

Several key principles can be emphasized throughout this lesson touching upon the forgiveness of Christ and our responsibility to show humility and grace to others, even as the Lord has done so to us:

2
Page 82
Devotion

No restoration is to be done in a spirit of meanness or bitterness, but we are to forgive as we have been forgiven in Christ.

> Eph. 4.31-32 - Let all bitterness and wrath and anger and clamor and slander be put away from you, along with all malice. [32] Be kind to one another, tenderhearted, forgiving one another, as God in Christ forgave you.

Our prayer must that our debts be forgiven in the same way that we ourselves forgive the debts of others.

> Matt. 6.12 - and forgive us our debts, as we also have forgiven our debtors. (Cf. Matt. 6.14-15 - For if you forgive others their trespasses, your heavenly Father will also forgive you, [15] but if you do not forgive others their trespasses, neither will your Father forgive your trespasses.)

We are to forgive not merely to seven times, but seventy-times seven!

> Matt. 18.21-35 - If we neither judge nor condemn, we will not then be judged and condemned, Luke 6.37 Judge not, and you will not be judged; condemn not, and you will not be condemned; forgive, and you will be forgiven.

We do not return kind for kind, even from enemies, but overcome evil with good.

> Rom. 12.20-21 - To the contrary, "if your enemy is hungry, feed him; if he is thirsty, give him something to drink; for by so doing you will heap burning coals on his head." [21] Do not be overcome by evil, but overcome evil with good.

This impartial love is truly an imitation of God.

> Eph. 5.1 - Therefore be imitators of God, as beloved children.

We are to forgive in the same way we have been forgiven by our Lord.

> Col. 3.12-13 - Put on then, as God's chosen ones, holy and beloved, compassion, kindness, humility, meekness, and patience, [13] bearing with one another and, if one has a complaint against another, forgiving each other; as the Lord has forgiven you, so you also must forgive.

Evil must not be returned against evil, but blessing instead.

> 1 Pet. 3.8-9 - Finally, all of you, have unity of mind, sympathy, brotherly love, a tender heart, and a humble mind. [9] Do not repay evil for evil or reviling for reviling, but on the contrary, bless, for to this you were called, that you may obtain a blessing.

God is willing to restore the offender if they acknowledge their wrong to him.

> 1 John 1.9 - If we confess our sins, he is faithful and just to forgive us our sins and to cleanse us from all unrighteousness.

The Peter example reveals the mercy and grace of Christ, as well as the redemptive power of restoration.

The following "contacts" are launching points for engaging the difficult subjects of offense, exhortation, and discipline in the Church. These have been carefully selected to mirror actual situations and perspectives being encountered today. While it may be tempting to spend prolonged time on any one of them, their purpose is to bring to the surface of your student's minds and attentions the critical problems and issues connected with the issue of forgiveness, restoration, restitution, and discipline. Use your time wisely, but do not hesitate to begin the lesson in earnest with clear, engaging, and important dialogue on these questions. In some way, the issues covered in this lesson are at the heart of successful pastoral care in urban congregations, so it is appropriate to be generous and yet wise in your allowance of time to consider them.

*3
Page 83
Contact*

It is critical for students to recognize throughout this lesson that every Christian in some sense, is called to participate in the process of exhorting, healing, and restoring those who are caught in sin, or who are walking the edge of being backslidden. D. N. Freedman's commentary on the text in Matthew 18 illumines for us the role that exhortation and discipline are to have upon the entire Christian Church.

*4
Page 94
Outline point IV*

The narratives that focused on Peter, Church, and the disciples naturally flow into the discourse on Church life and order. The discourse has two major parts: (1) the need to care for children (vv 1–5) and for "the little ones," the lowly church members who are easily neglected (vv 6–14); (2) the need to apply church discipline to the recalcitrant sinful member of the church (vv 15–20) but always with a readiness to forgive (vv 21–35). Jesus tells the would-be leaders in the Church that they must be willing to assume the powerlessness and vulnerability of a little child; indeed, they must give special attention to such unprotected people. This includes not only literal children but all the spiritual little ones who are easily led astray by the bad example of others. All disciples (note the lack of any restriction to Church leaders) must be good shepherds, leading the straying sheep back to the Father. But what of the arrogant sinner who remains in the Church and refuses private correction? Matthew provides a three-step procedure (based on Lev. 19.17–18 and Deut. 19.15 and seen also at Qumran), culminating in excommunication. Once again, we meet the phrases "church" and "bind and loose" (cf. 16.18–19), but here the church is the local community, and its action refers to expelling or admitting members. Such a serious decision is made in the presence and by the authority of Jesus (v 20). But the parable of the unforgiving servant (vv 21–35) reminds us that the final word on Church discipline must be forgiveness within the family of God.

~ D. N. Freedman. **The Anchor Bible Dictionary**. Vol. 4. New York: Doubleday, 1996. p. 633.

Page 98
Student Questions and Response

As in all segue questions, the ones below concentrate on helping your students get a grasp on the nature of exhortation and spiritual discipline. The weightiness of this subject will require the best thinking and reflection of your students. This subject seems to suffer from both over-exposure and complete neglect. The questions below will enable your students to concentrate on the basic outline of the New Testament's focus on exhortation, at least those covered in general form in the first video segment. Seek to ensure that your students grasp both the basic facts as well as the critical principles underlying these themes, and help them to prepare the next segment's more specific focus on the nature of spiritual discipline in the Church.

The heart and soul of exhortation and Church discipline is the authentication of the offense, that is, the ability to substantiate (prove) any of the charges against the one so accused. The fact that Jesus gave a procedure where every claim could be established clearly, discretely, and definitely is instructive. For example, when the Apostle Paul wrote the Corinthians, he warned that on his third visit to them they would have to establish any matter against him by the testimony of two or three witnesses (2 Cor. 13.1-10). It appears that they fully intended to hear charges about his authenticity as an apostle, which he was more than willing to demonstrate with power when he arrived. Of course, the demand that Paul gave regarding two or three witnesses is firmly grounded in Scripture, found both in Deuteronomy 19.15 and, more importantly, in our Lord's instructions to the disciples about exercising discipline in the body (Matt. 18.16; see also John 8.17; 1 Tim. 5.19; Heb. 10.28; 1 John 5.8).

This is significant in every regard for your students. Nothing covered in the lesson above can be glossed over or failed to be taken with the utmost seriousness. No one who is unwilling to follow the Lord's procedure for restoration should superintend any process of restoration for another. Your discussion of the students' understanding and fitness on these subjects, therefore, is of critical importance, both to their own discipleship and the significant responsibility they will have to oversee such discipline in their own ministries.

6
Page 110
Student Questions and Response

Enabling the students to experiment with the concepts in these case studies will strength their ability to apply the Word in difficult situations. Any one who has ministered for any length of time in the inner city knows that one may encounter some of the most difficult situations imaginable, that is, from a moral standpoint. What is required of the developing leader is a sure and certain authority (i.e, the Word of God) and a credible strategy (the Lord's instruction in Matt. 18). Help the students to isolate as best they can the kinds of questions and issues they must in order to discern precisely what is the problem, and how they would best approach to resolve it, consistent with the clear teaching of Scripture.

7
Page 114
Case Studies

📖 **8**
*Page 117
Assignments*

By the end of the second class session, you ought to emphasize with the students the need for them to have done the spadework and thought out precisely how they intend on carrying out their Ministry Project. Also, by this time, you should have emphasized their selection of the passage they will study for their Exegetical Project. Both will be done with far better thought and excellence the earlier the students begin to think through them and decide what they want to do. Do not fail to emphasize their need to be decisive in choosing their work, for, as in all study, at the end of the course many things become due, and the students will begin to feel the pressure of getting a number of assignments in at the same time. Any way that you can remind them of the need for advanced planning will be wonderfully helpful for them, whether they realize it immediately or not.

Because of this, we advocate that you consider docking a modest amount of points for late papers, exams, and projects. Amazingly, most students will respond favorably, especially with the prospect of a modest penalty. This is not for their hurt; your enforcement of your rules will help them to learn to be efficient and on time as they continue in their studies.

Effective Counseling
Preparing, Caring, and Healing

MENTOR'S NOTES 4

📖 **1**
Page 121
Lesson Introduction

Welcome to the Mentor's Guide for Lesson 4, *Effective Counseling: Preparing, Caring, and Healing*. This lesson will concentrate upon the role of the Christian leader as both physician of the soul and shepherd of God's flock. These images are interrelated and connected, and your task will be to help the students think fluidly and scripturally with these notions in mind.

Please notice again in the objectives that these truths are clearly stated. As usual, your responsibility as Mentor is to emphasize these concepts throughout the lesson, especially during the discussions and interaction with the students. The more you can highlight the objectives throughout the class period, the better the chances are that they will understand and grasp the magnitude of these objectives.

📖 **2**
Page 122
Devotion

This devotion delves into the idea of shepherding and pastoring, based on the example of Christ. Shepherding at the time of Christ was a common occurrence, and so the analogy must have been immediately potent for all of his contemporaries. Listen to one commentator's understanding of the principles of this John 10 text.

> *The Middle Eastern sheepfold was very simple: a stone wall, perhaps ten feet high, surrounded it, and an opening served as the door. The shepherds in the village would drive their sheep into the fold at nightfall and leave the porter to stand guard. In the morning each shepherd would call his own sheep, which would recognize their shepherd's voice and come out of the fold. The porter (or one of the shepherds) would sleep at the opening of the fold and actually become "the door." Nothing could enter or leave the fold without passing over the shepherd. Christ points out that the true shepherd comes through the door (v. 1), calls his sheep by name, which recognize him (v. 3), and leads the sheep, which follow (vv. 4–5). False shepherds and strangers, who are thieves and robbers, try to get into the fold some subtle way, but the sheep will not recognize or follow them.*
>
> ~ W. W. Wiersbe. **Wiersbe's Expository Outlines on the New Testament** (John 10.1). Wheaton, IL: Victor Books, 1997.

In a real sense, the entire ministry of the bishop gets its cue from the ministry of Jesus Christ as the Chief Shepherd and Bishop of our Souls (cf. 1 Pet. 2.25 For you were straying like sheep, but have now returned to the Shepherd and Overseer of your souls; see also 1 Pet. 5.1-4). He is the one who knows his sheep, who leads them out, whom they follow, and who is the authentic head of the flock of God. All others who either function in formal pastoral roles, or who love the people of God in a pastoral way are in fact *undershepherds*, that is, there is truly only *one shepherd* and *one flock* (cf. John 10.16 And I have other sheep that are not of this fold. I must bring them also, and they will listen to my voice. So there will be one flock, one shepherd).

Notwithstanding Jesus' unique and singular role as the Shepherd of the people of God, he has through his Spirit appointed *undershepherds* to tend and guard his flock (cf. Acts 20.28 Pay careful attention to yourselves and to all the flock, in which the Holy Spirit has made you overseers, to care for the Church of God, which he obtained with his own blood). The New Testament outlines in a number of texts the centrality of the pastoral care of the people of God. Note this emphasis in the following verses:

> 1 Tim. 3.2 - Therefore an overseer must be above reproach, the husband of one wife, sober-minded, self-controlled, respectable, hospitable, able to teach.

> 1 Tim. 5.17 - Let the elders who rule well be considered worthy of double honor, especially those who labor in preaching and teaching.

> Titus 1.7 - For an overseer, as God's steward, must be above reproach. He must not be arrogant or quick-tempered or a drunkard or violent or greedy for gain.

> Heb. 13.17 - Obey your leaders and submit to them, for they are keeping watch over your souls, as those who will have to give an account. Let them do this with joy and not with groaning, for that would be of no advantage to you.

This entire lesson is on the importance of this ongoing ministry of guardianship, nurture, and feeding of the people of God by leaders who, like Christ, love them, lead them, and care for them.

Could there be any greater privilege?

📖 **3**
Page 137
Student Questions and Response

As in the previous lessons, these questions are designed to help you review the critical facts and principles brought out in the first video segment. Hopefully by now you have been able to sense the importance of this first attempt from the students to grasp the significance of the teaching.

📖 **4**
Page 138
Summary of Segment 2

The image of the shepherd as a form of leadership is well attested, both in terms of its relationship to God or gods (cf. Gen. 48.15; 49.24), and especially to the oversight of Yahweh over his people. Both Psalm 23 and Ezekiel 34 picture forth God as the leader guarding, tending, and caring for his people, his flock. Many other texts in the Psalms highlight this analogy (cf. 28.9; 74.1; 77.20; 78.52-53; 80.1; 95.7; 100.3; 121.3-8), as also do the Prophets (cf., Isa. 40.11; 49.9-10; Jer. 23.1-4; 31.10; 49.19-20; 50.17-19; Mic. 4.6-8; 7.14).

Often in Scripture, the analogy of shepherd is used in a negative way, for many of the political leaders and priests responsible for tending the people of the Lord neglected the herd, even feasted upon them(e.g., Jer. 10.21; 22.22; 23.1-4; 25.34-38; Ezek. 34.1-10; Zech. 10.3; 11.4-17). While this is prevalent, it is plain to see that this image is a critical image for a courageous, diligent, and vigilant leader, whether political or religious (e.g., Cyrus is called God's shepherd, Isa. 44.28). Notice God's description of David:

> Ps. 78.70-72 - He chose David his servant and took him from the sheepfolds; [71] from following the nursing ewes he brought him to shepherd Jacob his people, Israel his inheritance. [72] With upright heart he shepherded them and guided them with his skillful hand.

The promise is given by the Lord that he would eventually provide his people with shepherds who would properly care for his people (Jer. 3.15; 23.4). Ultimately, God would provide a shepherd for his people, the Messiah would not only be from the line of David, but would also die and suffer on behalf of them (Ezek. 34.23; 37.22, 24; Zech. 13.7 cf. 12.10).

This deep rootedness in the Hebrew thought makes the choice of this image as a dominant image of Christian leadership all the more important and instructive. Not only is Yahweh a shepherd, and his righteous agents called shepherd, but Messiah himself would also be a shepherd of God's flock. Now, we who represent the interests of Christ, attain the same high rank and privilege to care for and guard God's people, through the Holy Spirit (Acts 20.28).

Congratulations! You have facilitated the entire module of learning, discussion, and prayer. However, don't be too anxious to move on! Your work as an instructor and grader begins in earnest now.

5
Page 159
Assignments

By now, all students should have given you their commitments and possibilities regarding their ministry projects, exegetical projects, and any other assignment data you need to determine the student's overall grade. Again, your discretion regarding late work can easily determine whether you dock students some of the possible points, which may result in letter grade changes. You may elect as instructor to give students an "Incomplete" on their transcript until their assignments are completed, graded, and recorded. Whichever option you adopt, you must ensure that your standards are fair and equally applied across the board with all your students.

Remember, of course, that our courses are not primarily about giving the students a great grade or score, but rather ensuring that they learn the principles and truths that will enrich their lives and ministries. The spiritual nourishment and training these courses provide are the true payoff. Nevertheless, we honor those students who have worked hard and sacrificed their time and effort to do well by acknowledging their good effort in their grade reports. We want in every way to encourage students to strive for excellence, and grading can be an integral part of that encouragement.

Make certain that the students know how the course will "close;" inform them about when the papers, reports, and exams will be graded and returned, and when you hope to have their grades tallied and communicated. Thank the students for their good effort, and encourage them to continue in their learning in Christ's school of discipleship.

www.ingramcontent.com/pod-product-compliance
Lightning Source LLC
Chambersburg PA
CBHW080731300426
44114CB00019B/2548